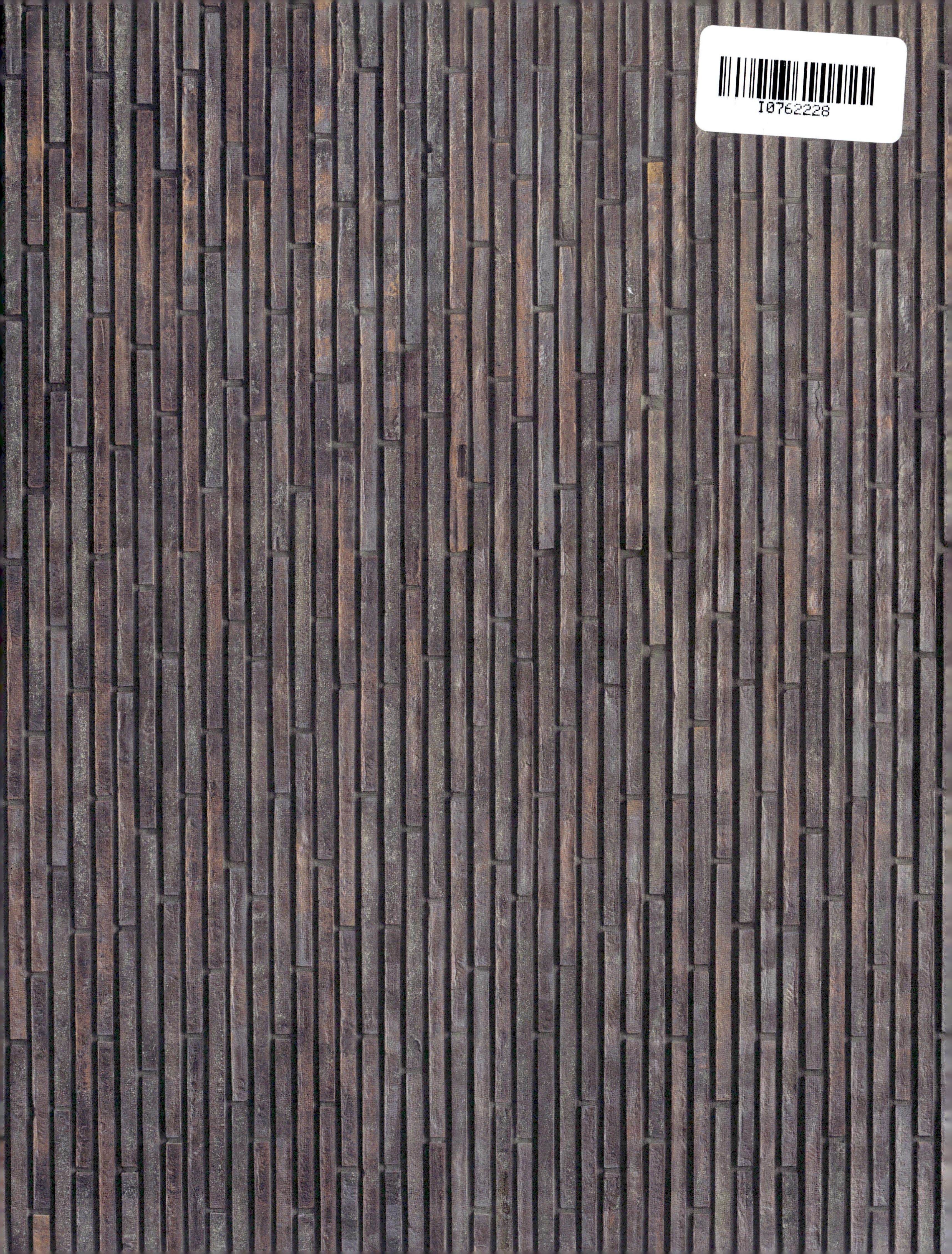

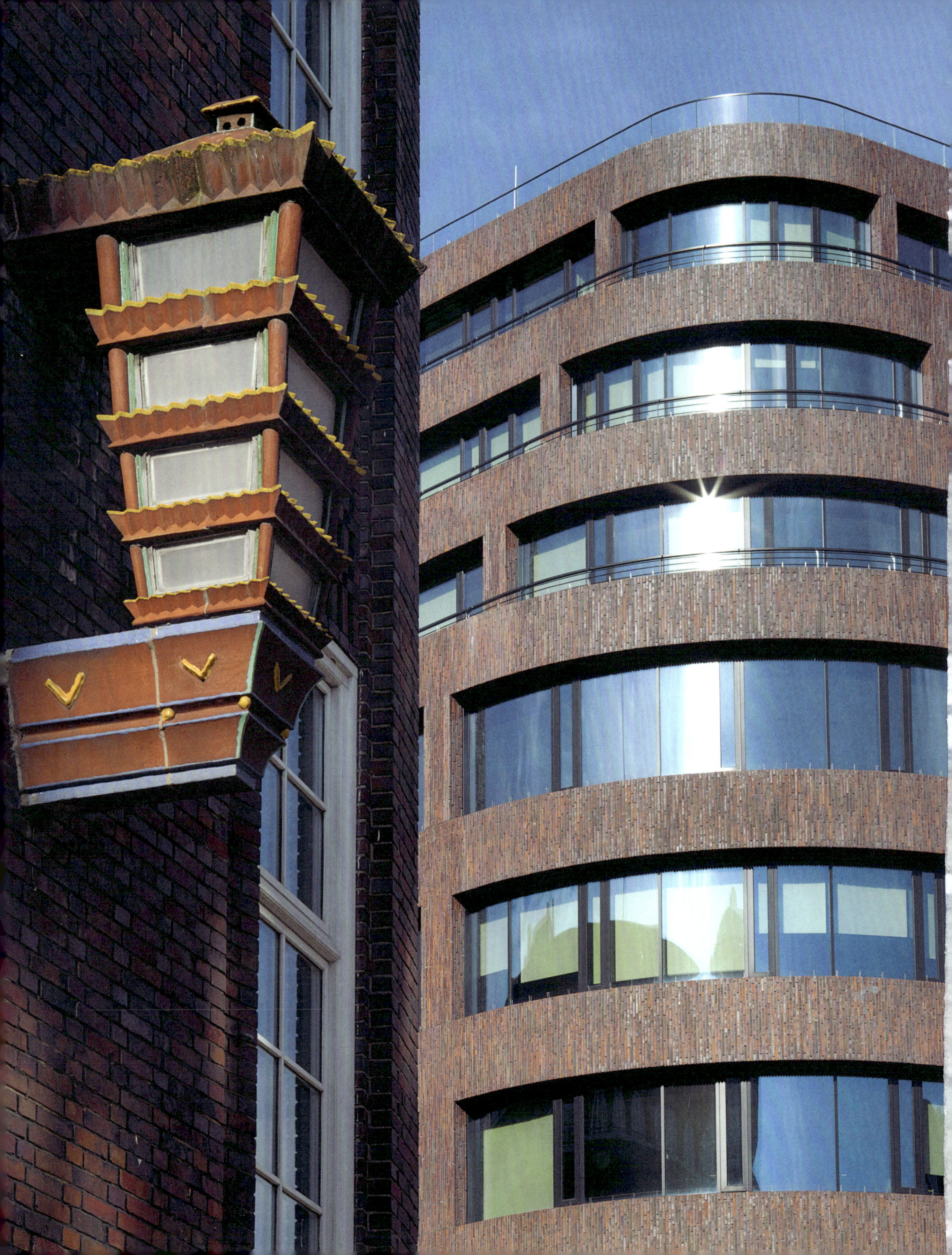

DEUTSCHLANDHAUS

Photography meets Architecture

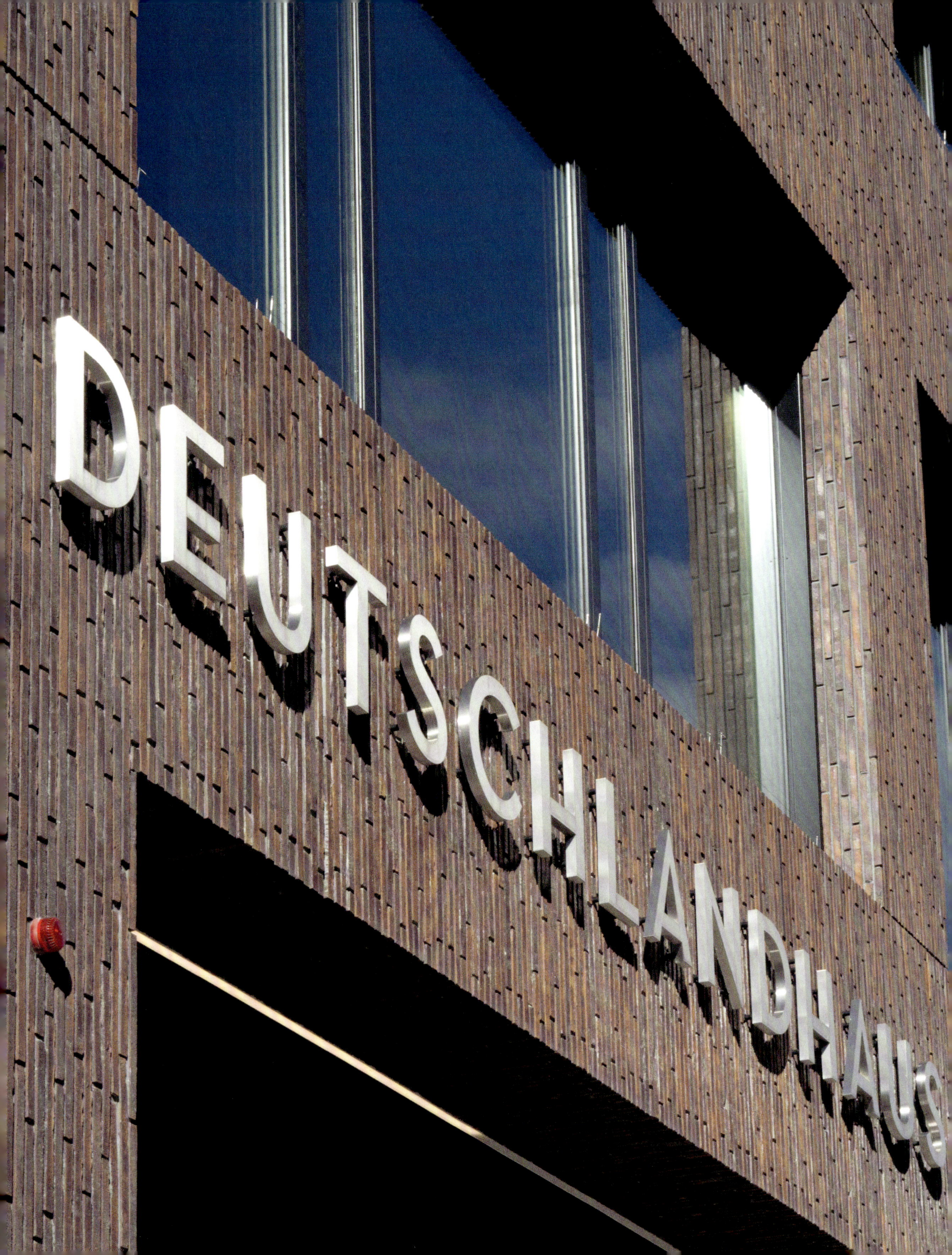
DEUTSCHLANDHAUS

DEUTSCHLANDHAUS

Photography meets Architecture

KLAUS FRAHM 2024 – FRITZ BLOCK 1930

Editor / Essays **Roland Jaeger**

HIRMER

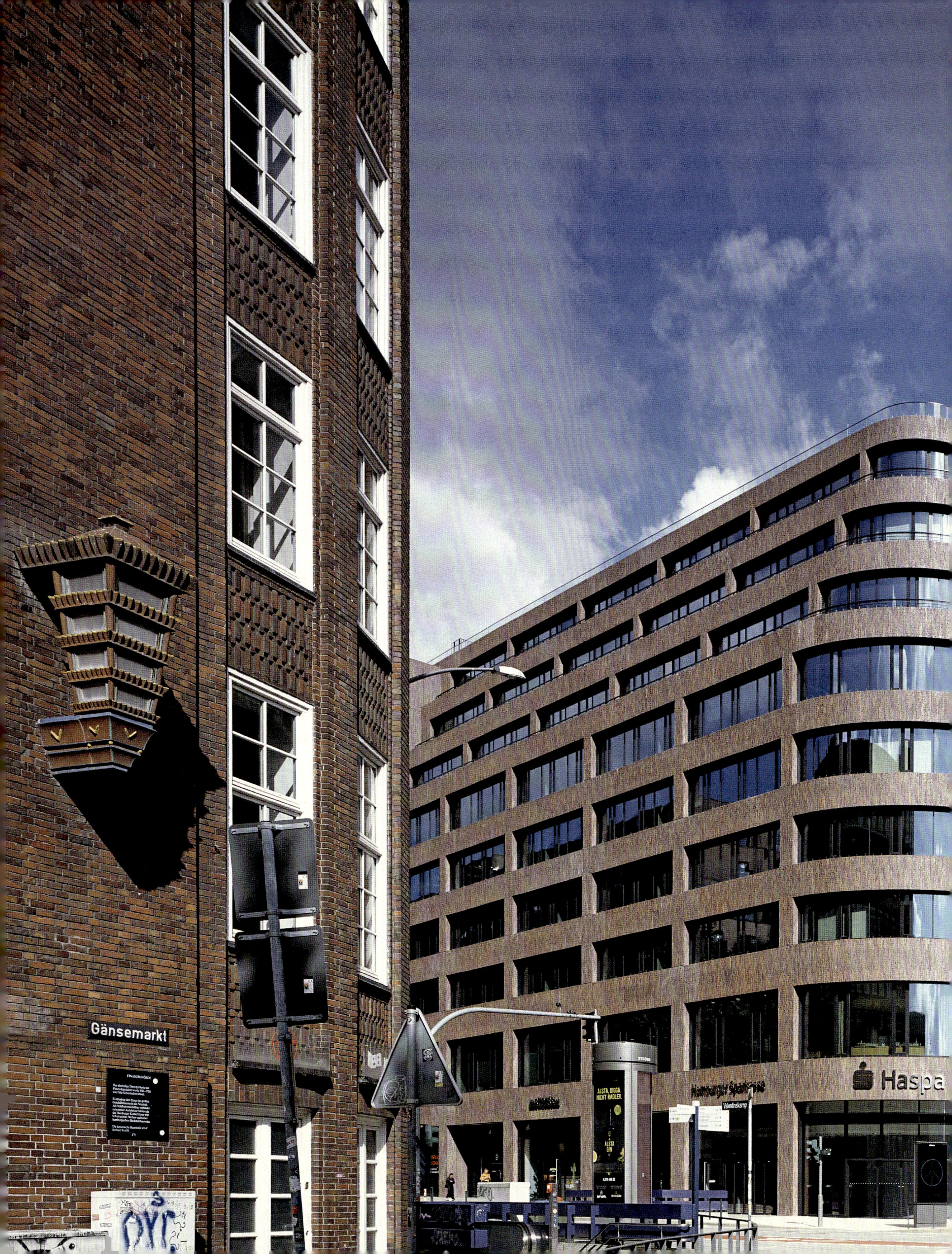
Gänsemarkt
Hamburger Sparkasse
Haspa
Valentinskamp

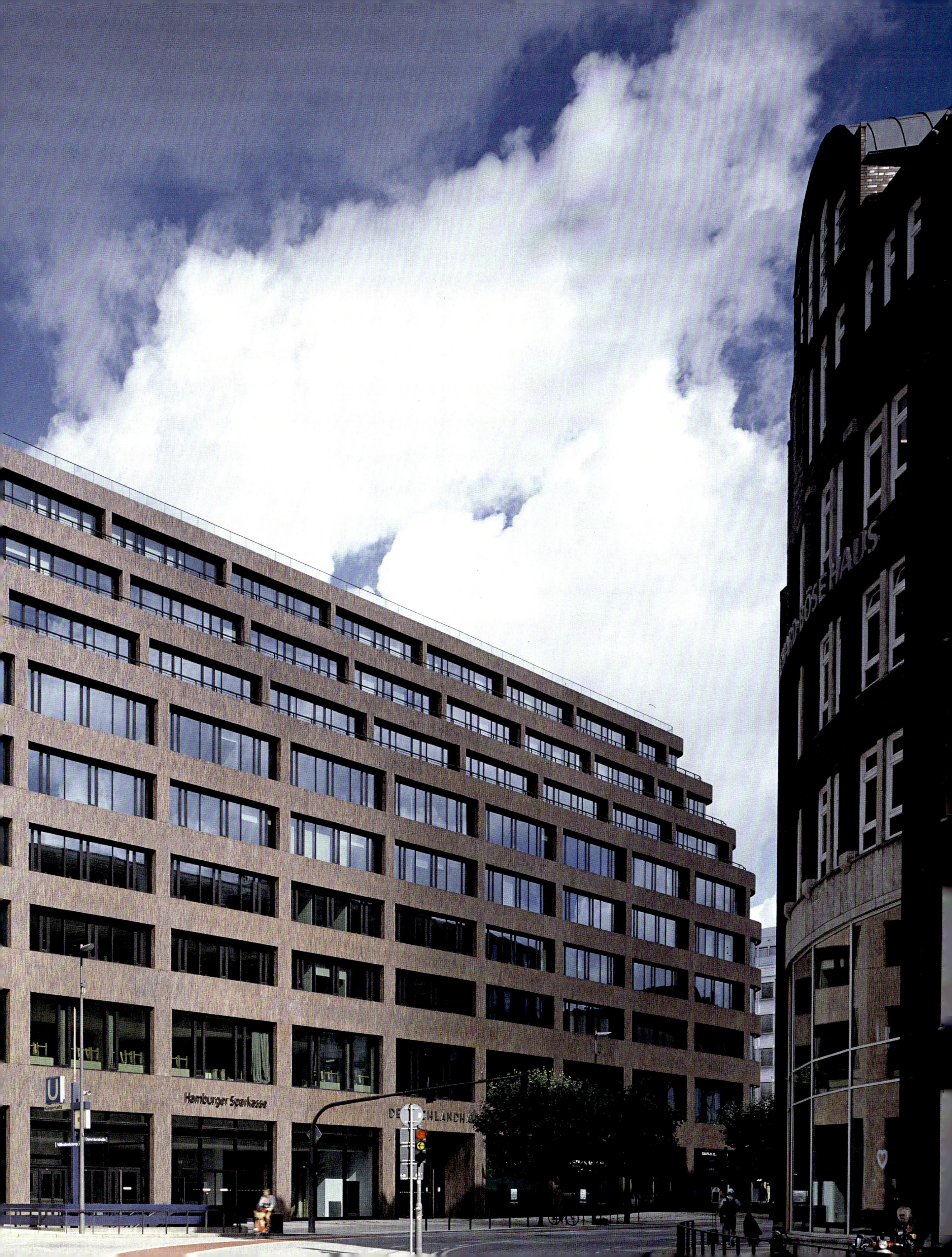
Hamburger Sparkasse

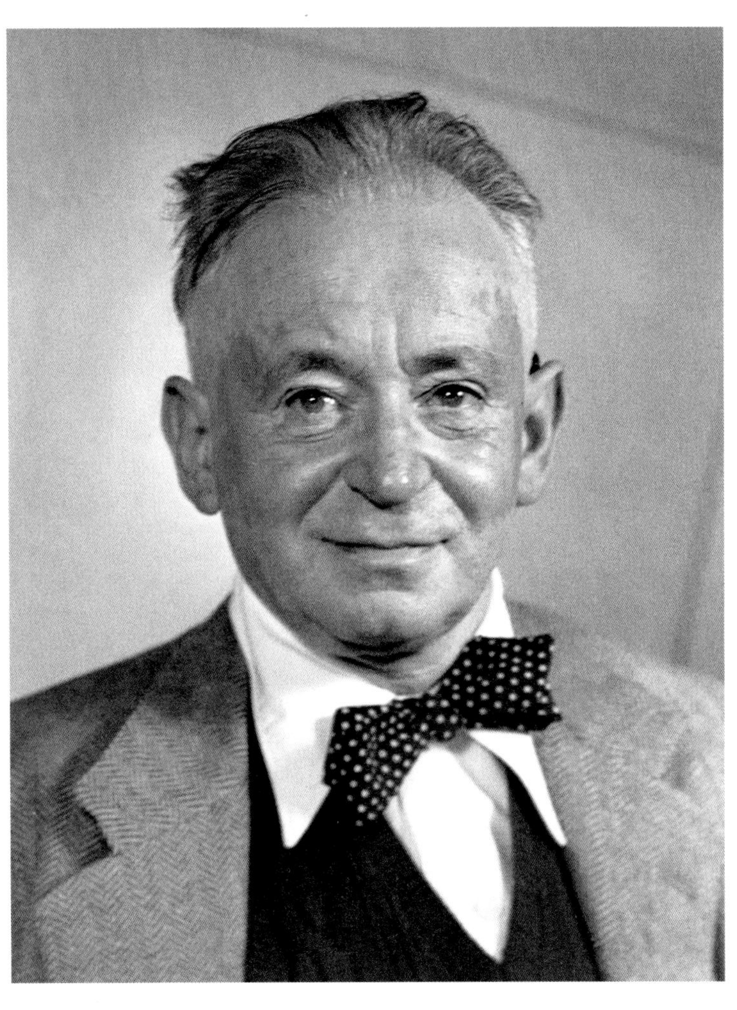

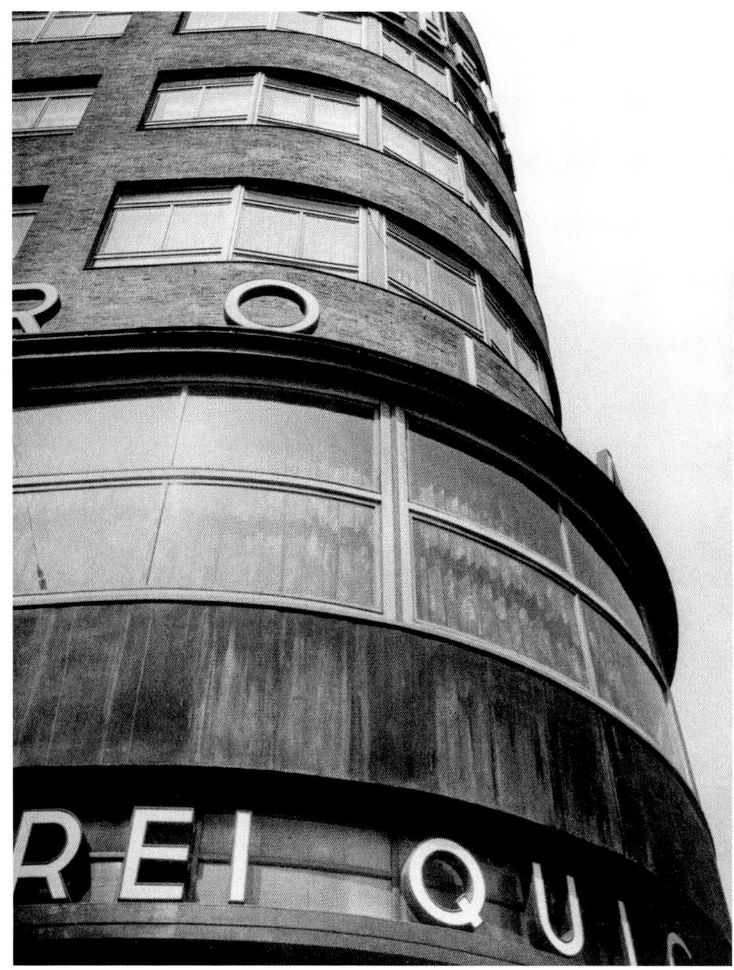
RO
REI QUI

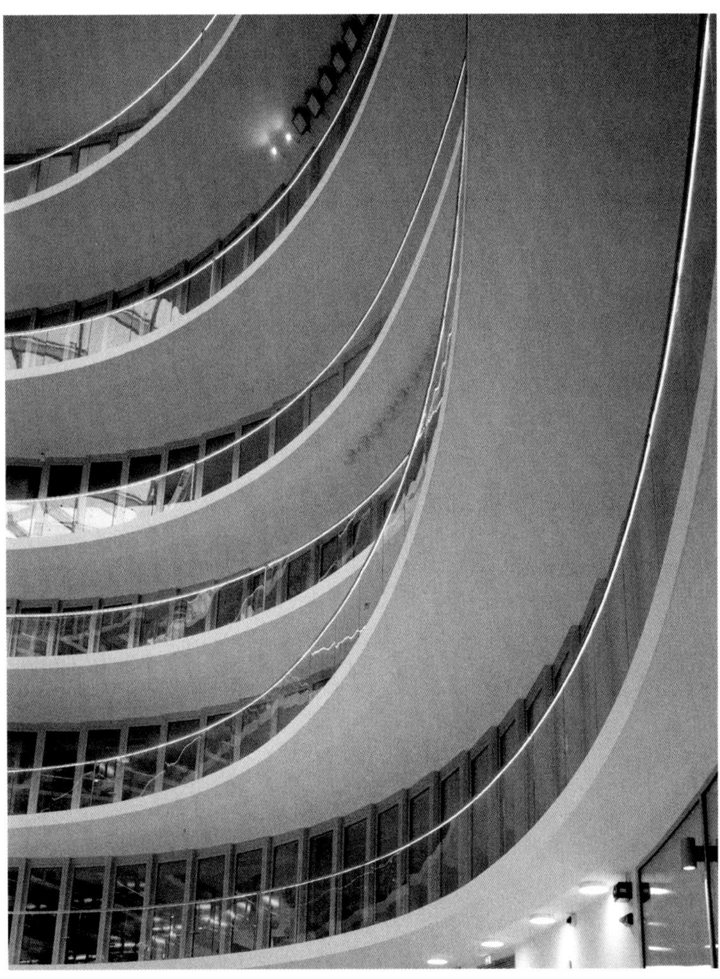

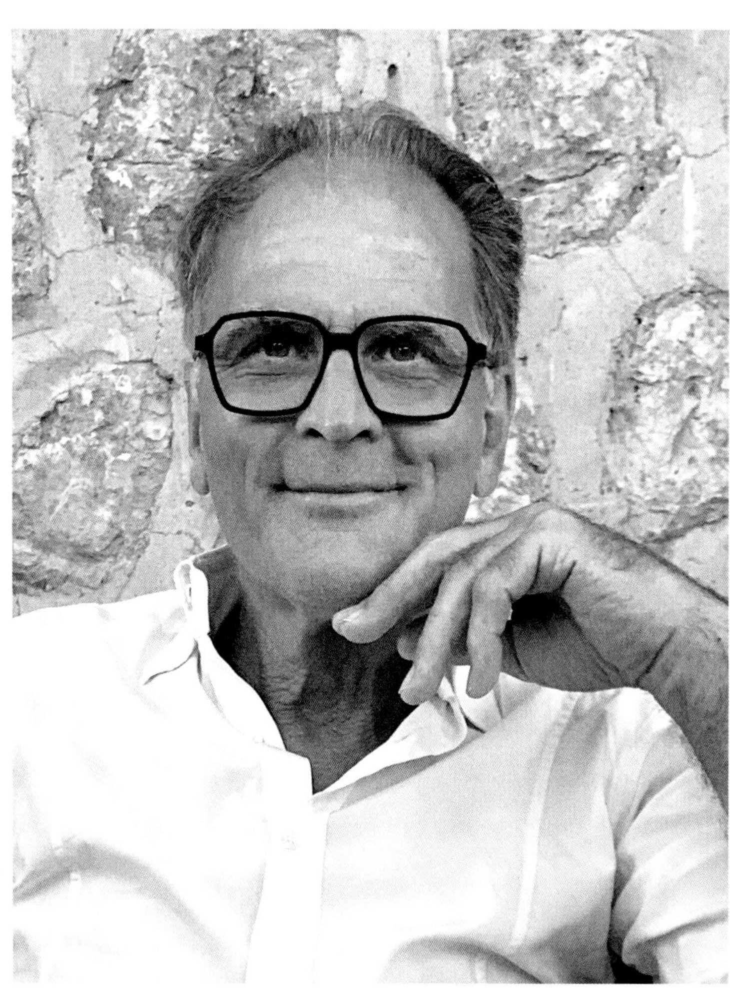

ARCHITECTURE AND PHOTOGRAPHY

Since the invention of photography in the mid-nineteenth century, architecture and photography have had a close relationship with one another. As buildings are immobile, perception of them is largely disseminated through photographs. These may be for documentary, information, publication, and many other purposes. Sometimes architects have reached for the camera to photograph their own buildings. But most architectural photographs are taken by specialized architectural photographers, who have thus established a genre of their own. To the extent that photography has developed into an independent artform, however, architecture has also become a subject of photographic interpretation and artistic expression. Some buildings are particularly suitable for this because of their history, location, form, and significance. One such building was and is the *Deutschlandhaus*, a mixed-use office building in central Hamburg, Germany.

The original *Deutschlandhaus* was built in 1928/29 from a design by the Hamburg architects Fritz Block and Ernst Hochfeld. It was the city's first commercial building in the international modernist style. It also integrated the *Ufa-Palast*, then the largest cinema in Europe. The auditorium was destroyed in the Second World War and never rebuilt, but after war damage was cleared the building continued to be used commercially. A total renovation that considerably altered its structure was carried out around 1980. Because it had been neglected to put a preservation order on the *Deutschlandhaus*, a real-estate investor and developer was able to have it demolished it in 2019.

Until 2024 a new building, again named *Deutschlandhaus*, was constructed on the same site from a design by the Hamburg office Hadi Teherani Architects, with Christian Bergmann as partner-in-charge. It is oriented to its predecessor in cubage, façade material, and façade structure, but at the same time develops a formal language of its own. This particularly applies to its impressive interior atrium. So the new *Deutschlandhaus* is not a reconstruction or replica but the contemporary interpretation and further development of a monument of modern architecture in keeping with today's requirements and design principles.

As well as having their place in the history of architecture, the original *Deutschlandhaus* and its successor have also been the subject matter of photography. In 1930 the architect Fritz Block took photographs of the building he had designed, while in 2024 the new *Deutschlandhaus* was photographed by Klaus Frahm, who regularly portrays Hamburg's new buildings for the city's architects and for architectural publications. But in this case it was not a commercial commission but an artistic project providing the necessary latitude for a detailed and analytical examination of the architectural intention and visual impact of the new construction, in black and white and in color. The present publication brings together these dialogues between architecture and photography, confronting two architectural positions and two photographic points of view with one another.

The initiative for the book came from Manfred Heiting, the German-American photography expert, collector, author, and patron. Heiting had acquired the photographic archive of Fritz Block from the architect's heirs, and donated it to the Deutsche Fotothek in Dresden (black-and-white vintage prints) and the Getty Research Institute in Los Angeles (color slides) in order to make it available to scholarship. He knew and appreciated the Hamburg-based architecture photographer Klaus Frahm, one of the leading representatives of his profession in Germany, from an earlier collaboration. It was this constellation that gave rise to Heiting's idea of commissioning Frahm with a photographic project on the newly built *Deutschlandhaus* and juxtaposing the result with the images of the original made by the architect Block. Manfred Heiting has additionally purchased documentary material on the building, and intends to transfer its ownership, along with the vintage prints by Fritz Block and the modern prints by Klaus Frahm, to the Department of Photographs of the J. P. Getty Museum in Los Angeles. The *Deutschlandhaus* Hamburg will thereby gain attention as a notable example of the relationship between architecture and photography.

Architecture photography can provide various kinds of perceptual and expressive access. Necessarily only looking at a portion of reality, and excluding distracting aspects (such as surroundings, people, sound, and sometimes even color), it enables a more focused view and leads to a better recognition of design features—not least when images are compiled in the format of a photobook. But it must also be said that architecture photography can't replace a historical and critical examination of the actual buildings. For it tends to aestheticize and isolate architecture, especially as it usually shows newly built structures without the people who use them and without the urban-planning context. A proper understanding of architecture, however, requires a knowledge of the circumstances in which it is applied. For this reason the history of both the old and the new *Deutschlandhaus* will be outlined at the end of this book. Readers will therefore be able to form their own view of this building in the combination of images and information.

FRITZ BLOCK
Deutschlandhaus 1930

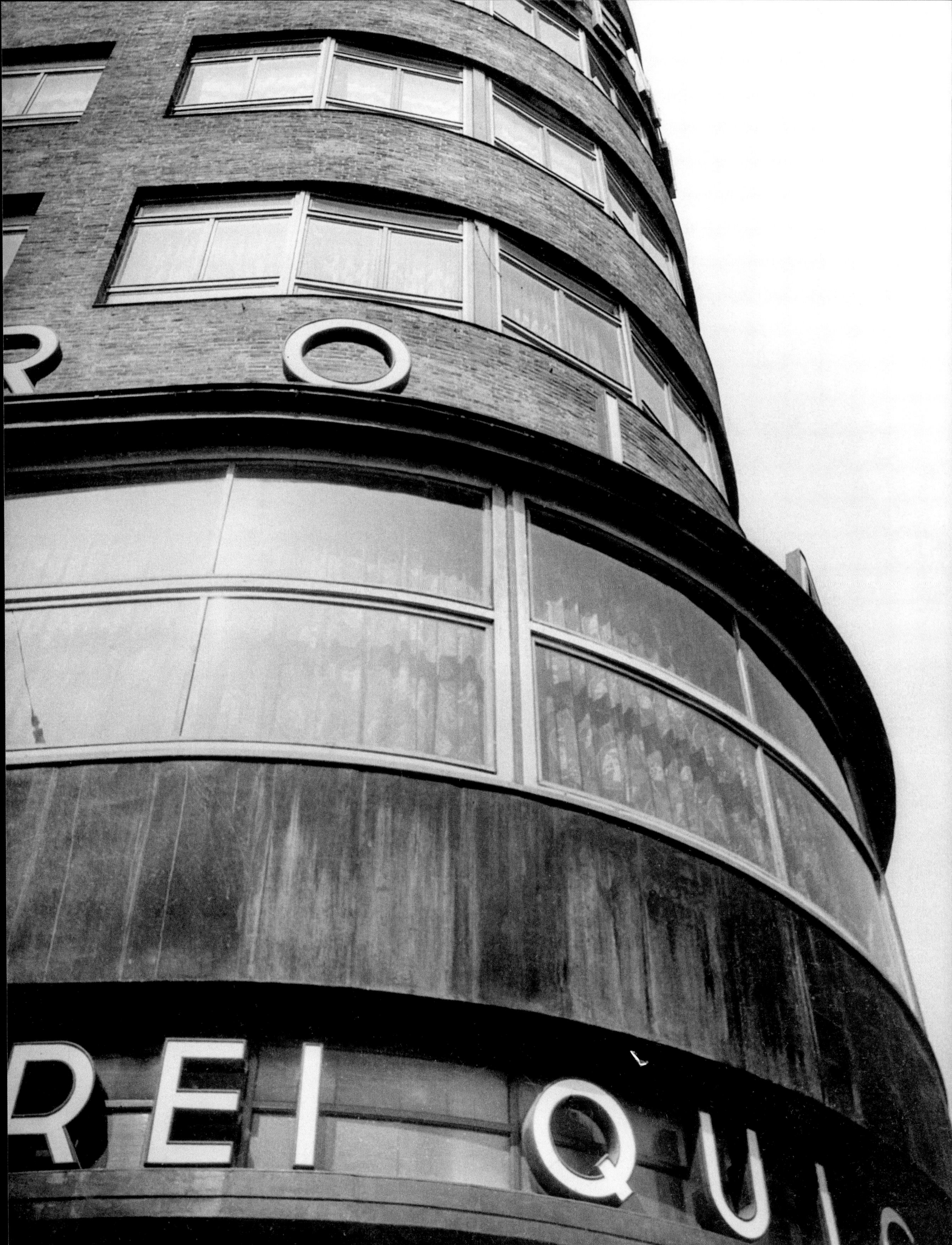
R O
REI QUI

Fritz Block (1889–1955) came from a Jewish merchant family in Warburg (Westphalia). He completed his training as an architect at the technical university in Dresden in 1913. Because of a hearing impairment he first served as a paramedic and was then deployed in a civilian building authority during the First World War, and was therefore still able to gain a PhD. In 1921 he opened the architectural office Dr. Block & Hochfeld in Hamburg with a friend from university, Ernst Hochfeld (1890–1985). The office initially designed modern funerary monuments for the Jewish cemetery. These were followed by several residential and commercial buildings. From 1926 onward Dr. Block & Hochfeld contributed to in the most important building project of the 1920s, the provision of housing developments. Typically for the time, they made the transition to objectivity and functionality—with cubic structures, flat roofs, and rational floor plans. In the late 1920s they were among the leading Hamburg representatives of the modern movement in architecture known as *Neues Bauen* (New Building). Block also promoted this new architecture in articles and lectures.

In 1927 Dr. Block & Hochfeld received their most important commission, for an office building with an integrated big cinema—the *Deutschlandhaus*, built in 1928/29 on the Gänsemarkt, a busy square in the center of Hamburg. The architects had previously had their buildings photographed by specialist professionals, but Block took the project of the *Deutschlandhaus* as an opportunity to teach himself photography. He bought a medium-format camera, with which he recorded the building's various stages of construction. In accordance with contemporary interest in technical forms and structures, he primarily documented structural details, particularly the steel-frame construction.

Block also took photographs showing various views of the finished building, which is edged by the streets named Valentinskamp, Dammtorstraße, and Drehbahn. The selection reproduced here follows a tour beginning at the cinema wing of the *Ufa-Palast* on Valentinskamp, where Block also looked into the elegant entrance hall with its ticket booths and light-filled foyer. He didn't photograph the auditorium, though, because its fittings had not been designed by Dr. Block & Hochfeld. His subsequent images exemplify the two main characteristics of the *Neue Fotografie* (New Photography) of the 1920s. On the one hand Block documented the clearly structured and dynamically rounded structure of the *Deutschlandhaus* in the straight style of *Neue Sachlichtkeit* (New Objectivity); on the other he experimented, in the spirit of *Neues Sehen* (New Vision), with a view from above from the tower of the Finance Authority Building opposite, unusual perspectives along the façades, low-angle views of the striking rounded corners, and a plummeting view down the stairwell. Block also published his photographs of the *Deutschlandhaus* in architectural magazines.

In the meantime he exchanged his unwieldy medium-format camera for a 35 mm Leica, and photography now became a form of artistic expression for him alongside architecture, although not in the area of architectural photography. Block was more interested in contemporarily typical subject matter such as port technology and ships, natural objects, the workplace, and the circus, about which he also published photo stories in newspaper supplements and magazines. But he particularly took photographs on his numerous European travels, so that urban and travel photography became his specialty. His richest photographic harvest was the result of a journey of several weeks through the United States in 1931. It is safe to say that hardly any other German architect of his time took as many photographs as Fritz Block.

The *Deutschlandhaus* in Hamburg remained the main work of Dr. Block & Hochfeld, as soon after its completion the world economic crisis constrained the office's activities. More severe were the effects of the seizure of power by the National Socialists in 1933, for as a Jew Block could no longer work as a self-employed architect, nor could he publish his photographs. Under the threat of persecution, Fritz Block and Ernst Hochfeld eventually emigrated in November 1938 to Los Angeles, where their careers went in different directions, however. Block never returned to architecture, making photography his regular occupation. He turned to the new color photography, and engaged in the professional production of thematic color-slide series for schools and universities nationwide. These series were also distributed by the Museum of Modern Art in New York, and two of them showed Californian 1940s and early 1950s modernist buildings in color for the first time.

Fritz Block never saw his *Deutschlandhaus* again, the starting point of his second career as a photographer—he died in Los Angeles in 1955. Regarding the technical quality of his photographs of the building, it must be remembered that the architect was a complete newcomer to photography. And the surviving vintage prints have a turbulent history because of his exile. Alongside other contemporary photographs, Block's images nevertheless provide a particularly authentic reminder of the original *Deutschlandhaus*.

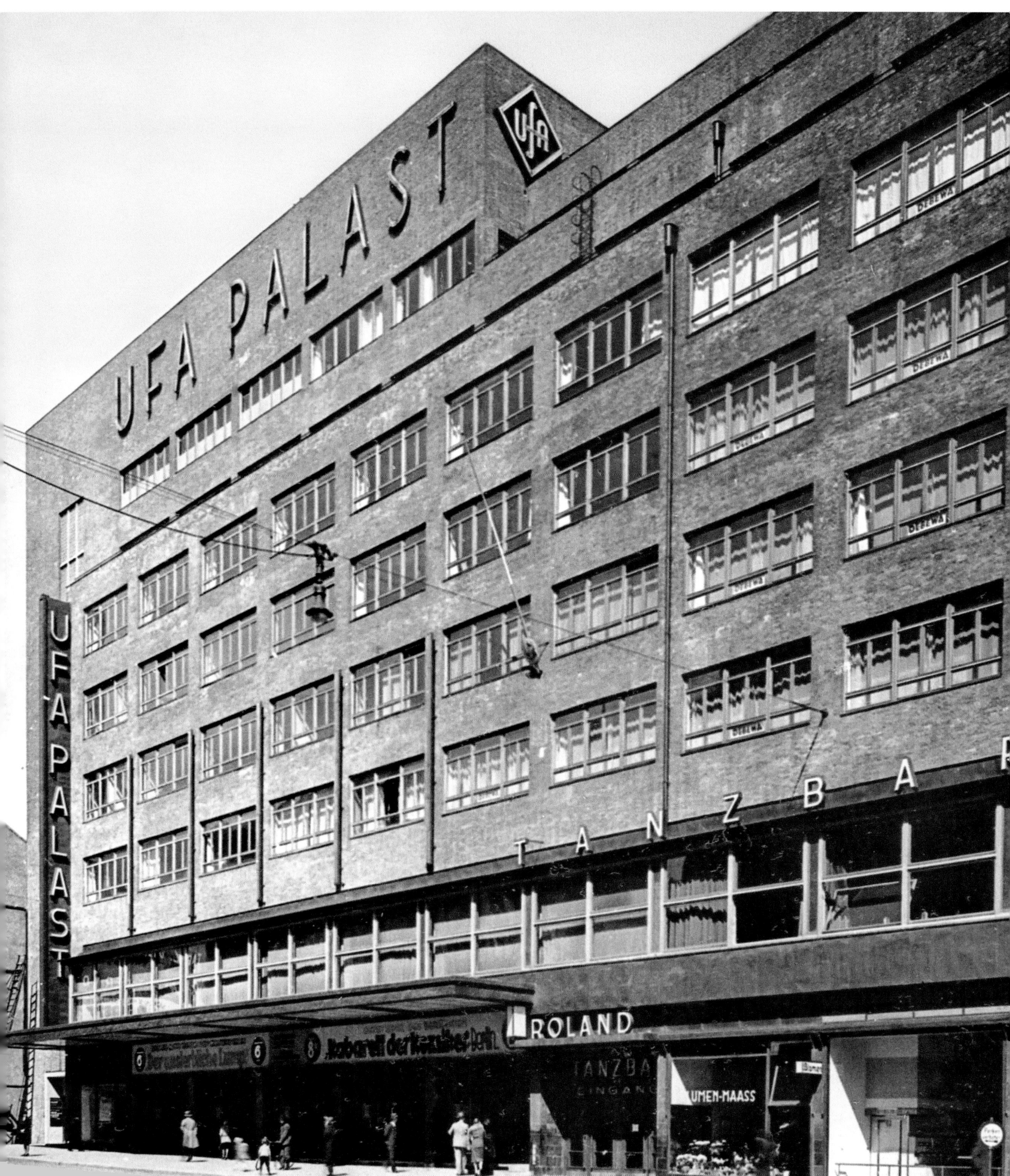
UFA PALAST
UFA
UFA PALAST
ROLAND

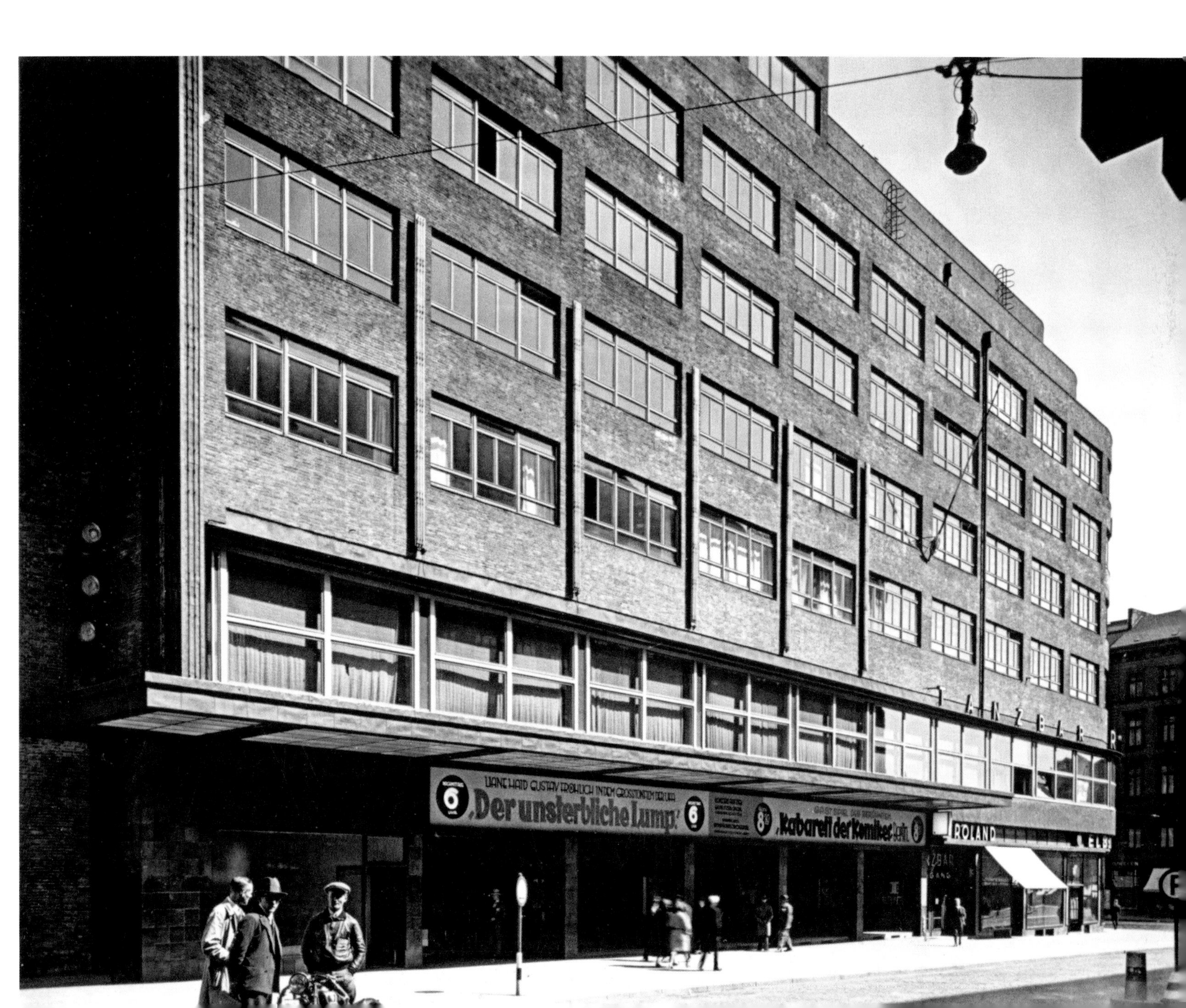

LIANE HAID GUSTAV FRÖHLICH IN DEM GROSSTONFILM DER UFA
„Der unsterbliche Lump"
„Kabarett der Komiker" Berlin
ROLAND

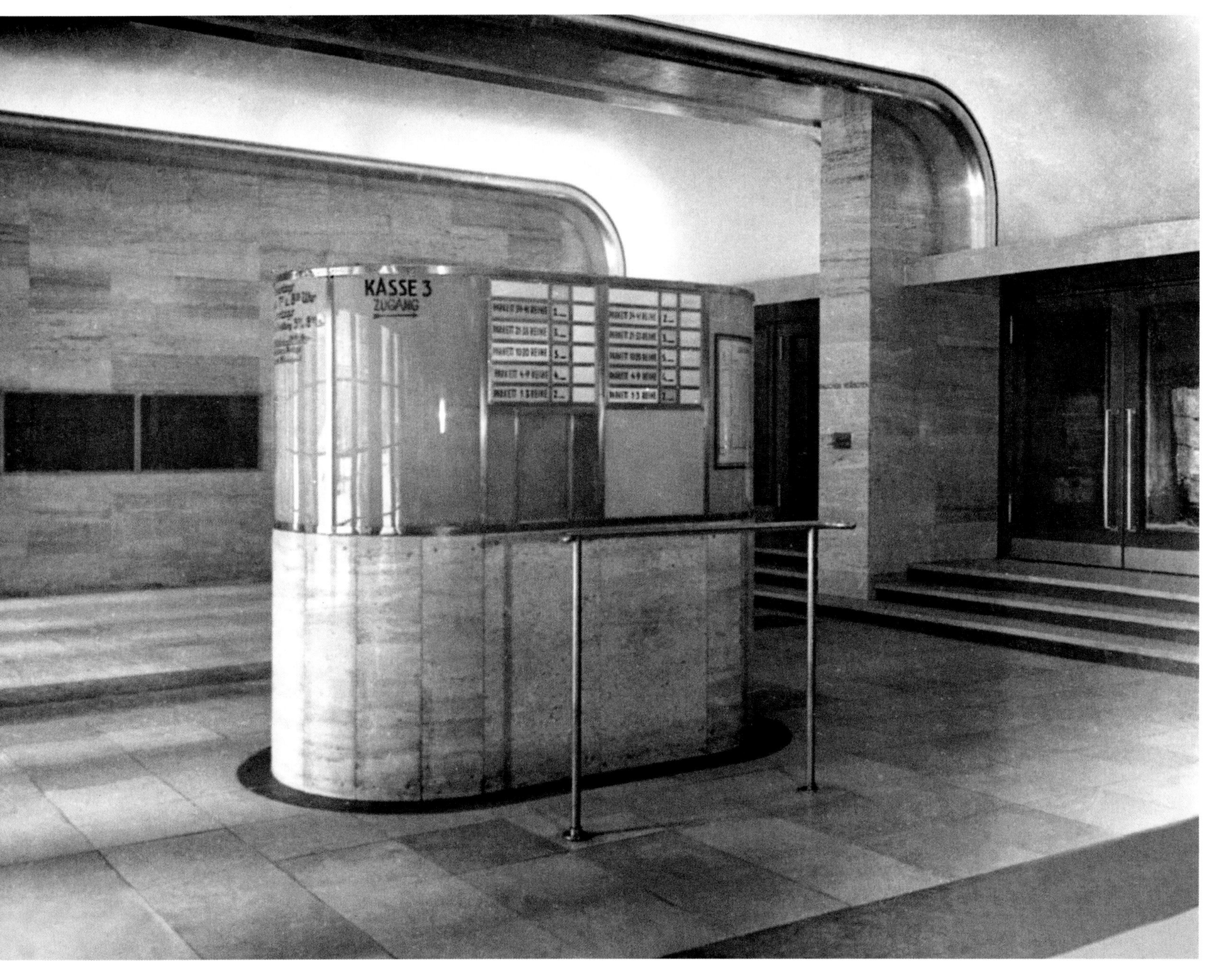
KASSE 3
ZUGANG

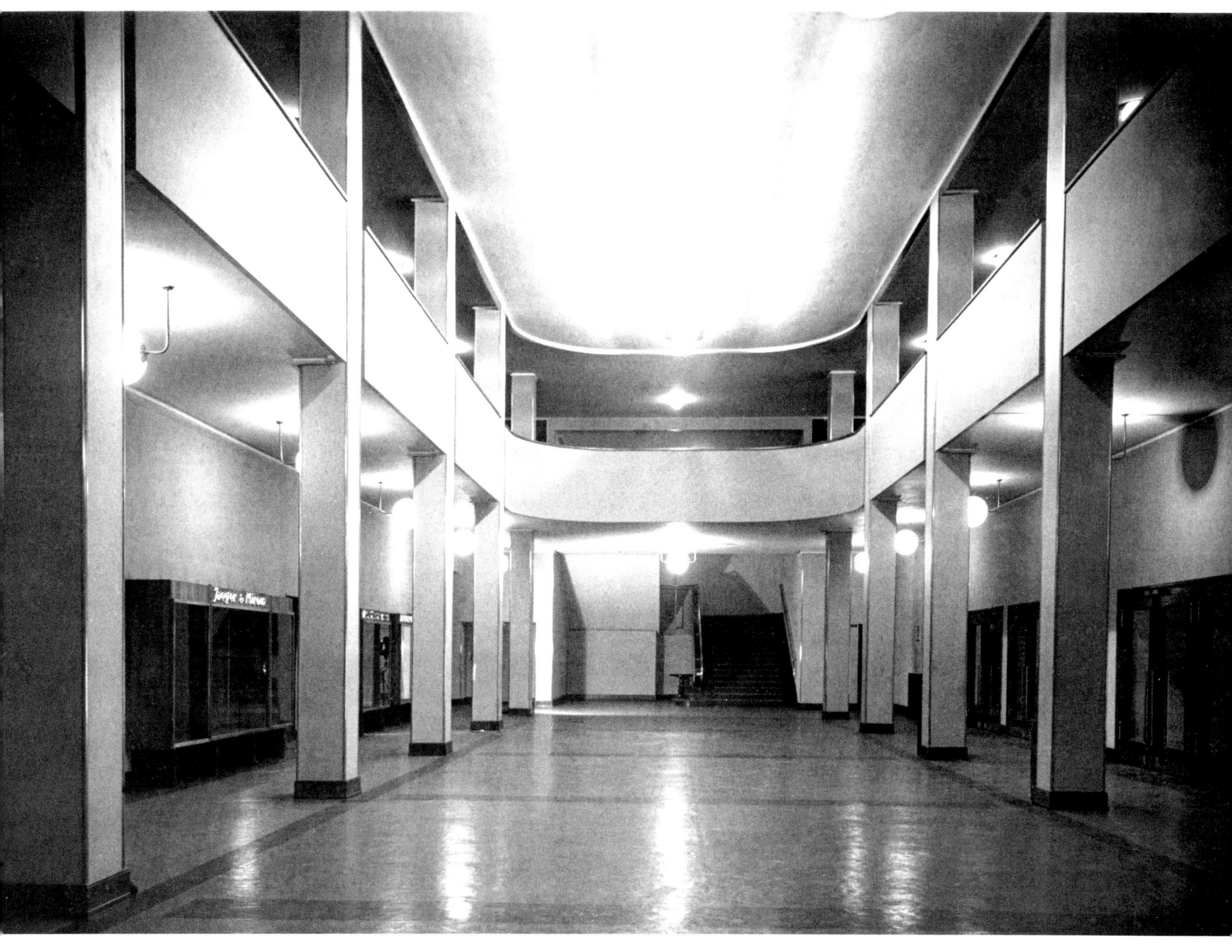

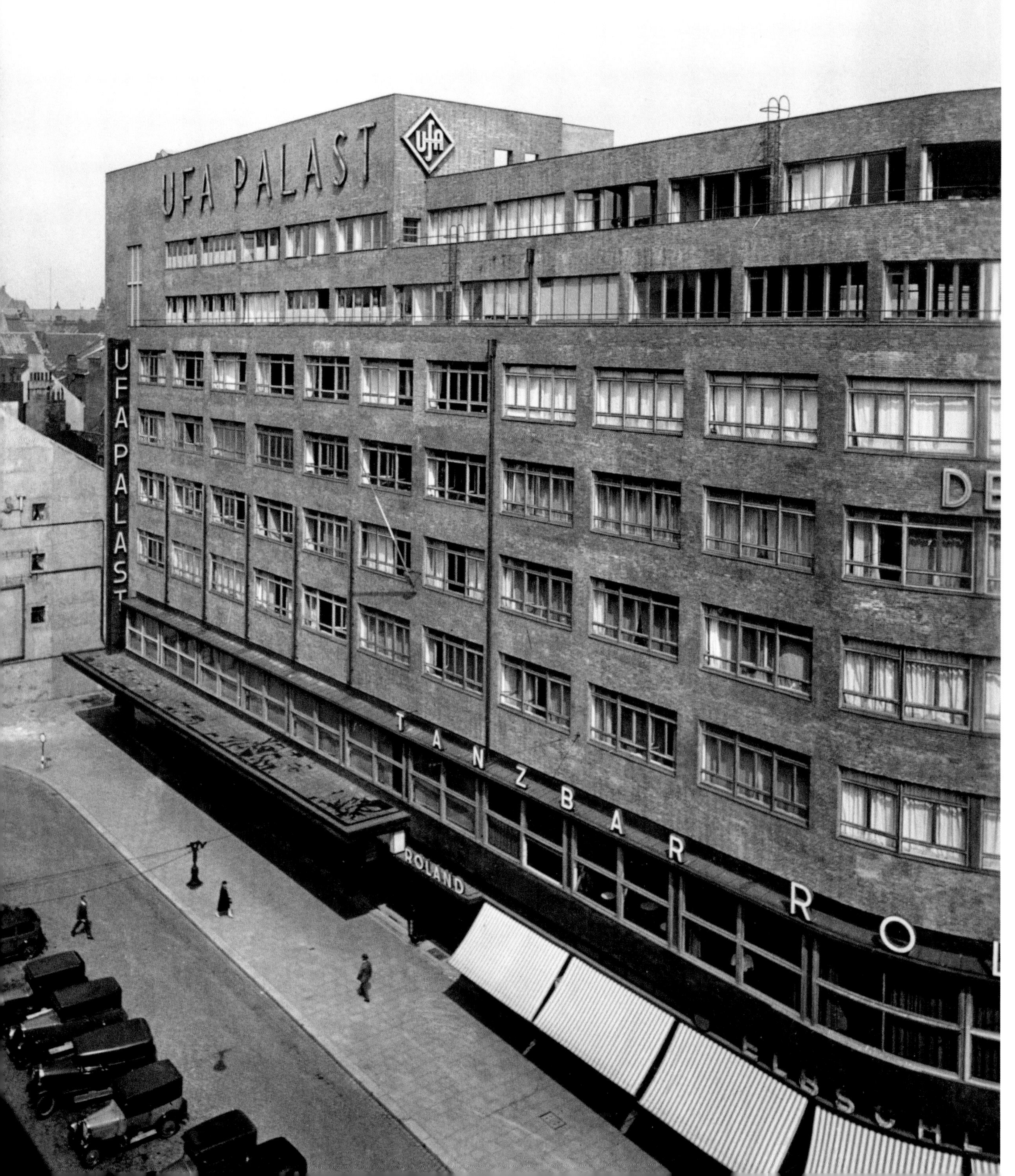
UFA PALAST
UFA
UFA PALAST
TANZBAR
ROLAND

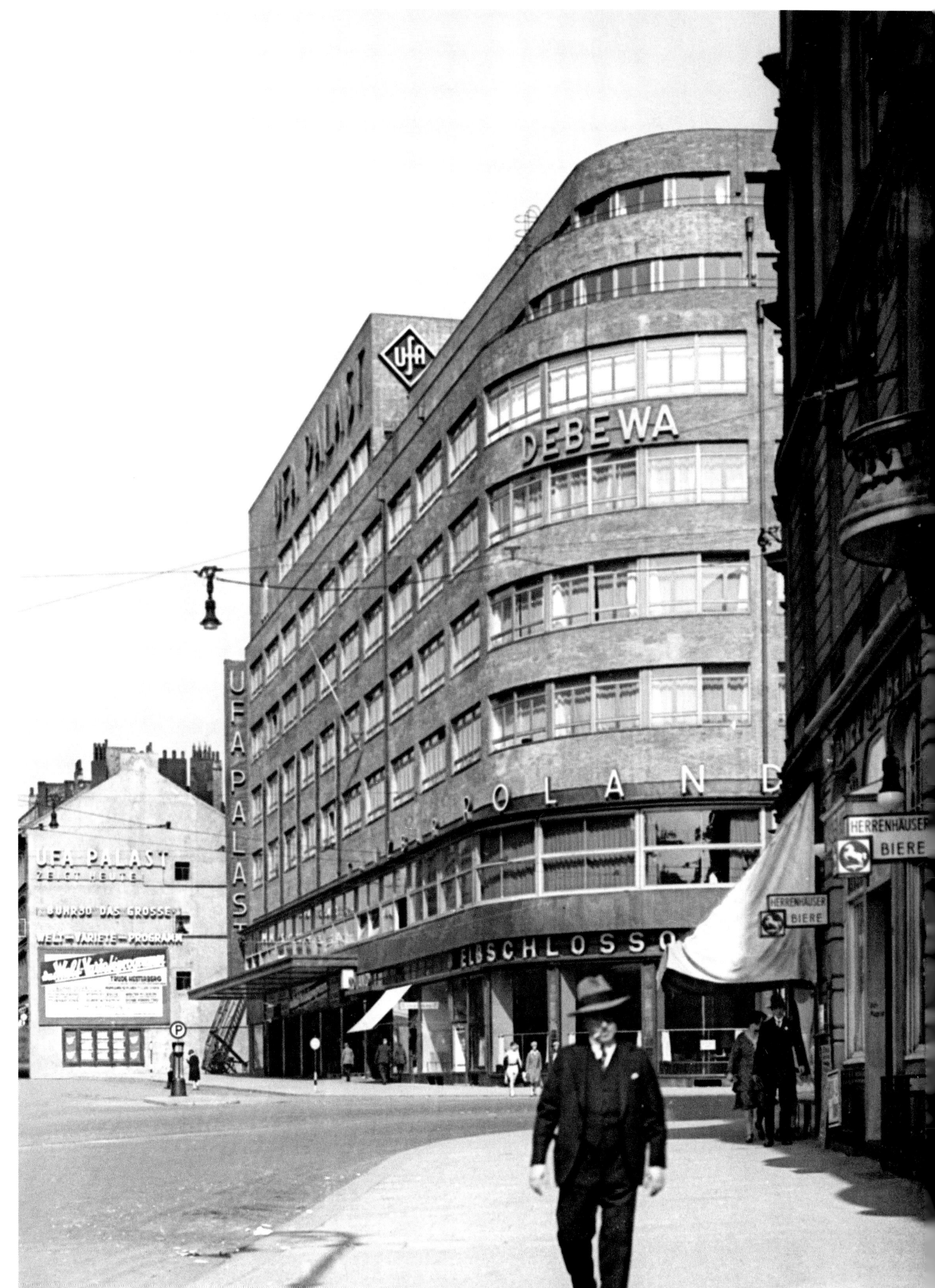
UFA
DEBEWA
UFAPALAST
ROLAND
ELBSCHLOSS
UFA PALAST
WELT-VARIETE-PROGRAMM
HERRENHÄUSER BIERE
HERRENHÄUSER BIERE

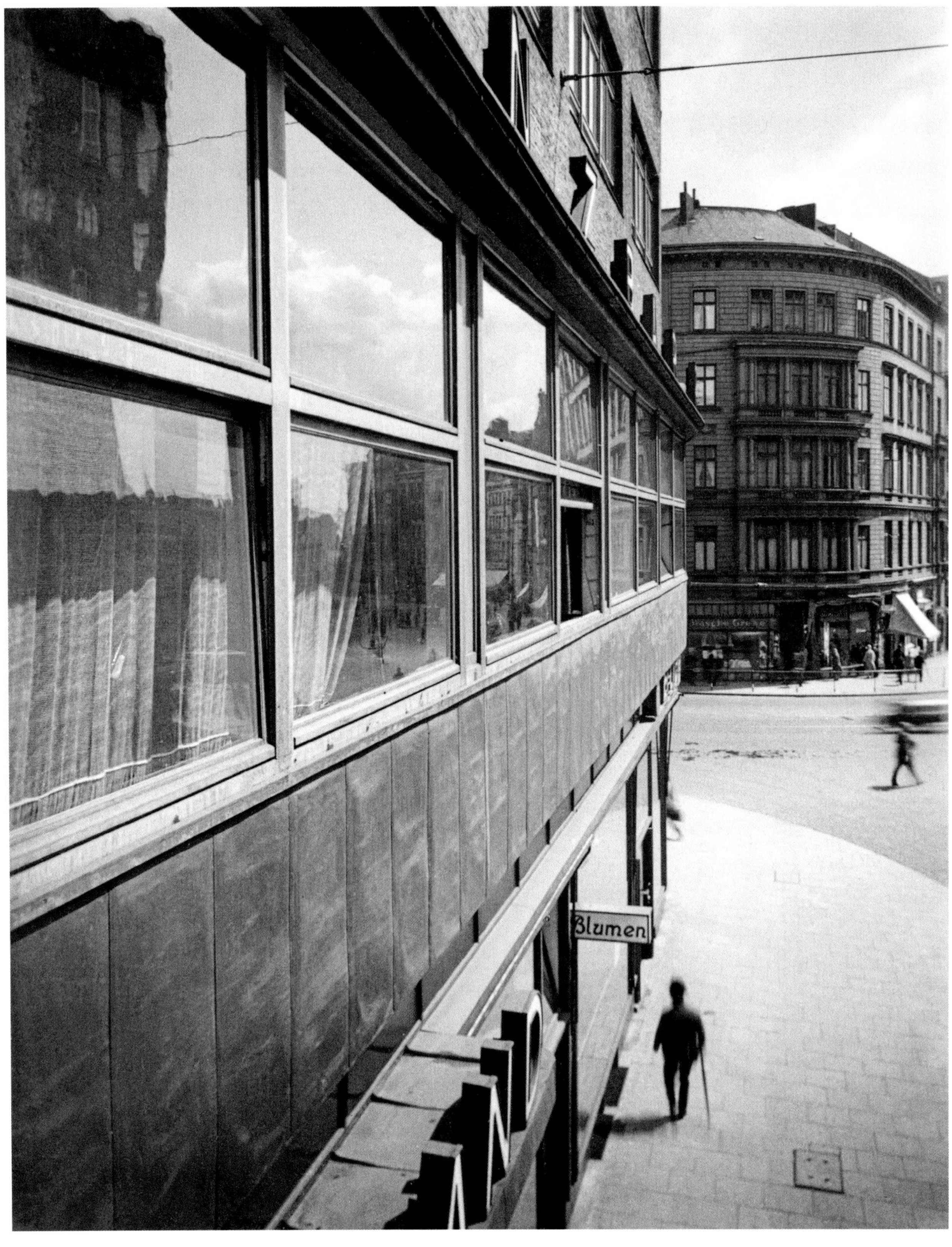
Blumen

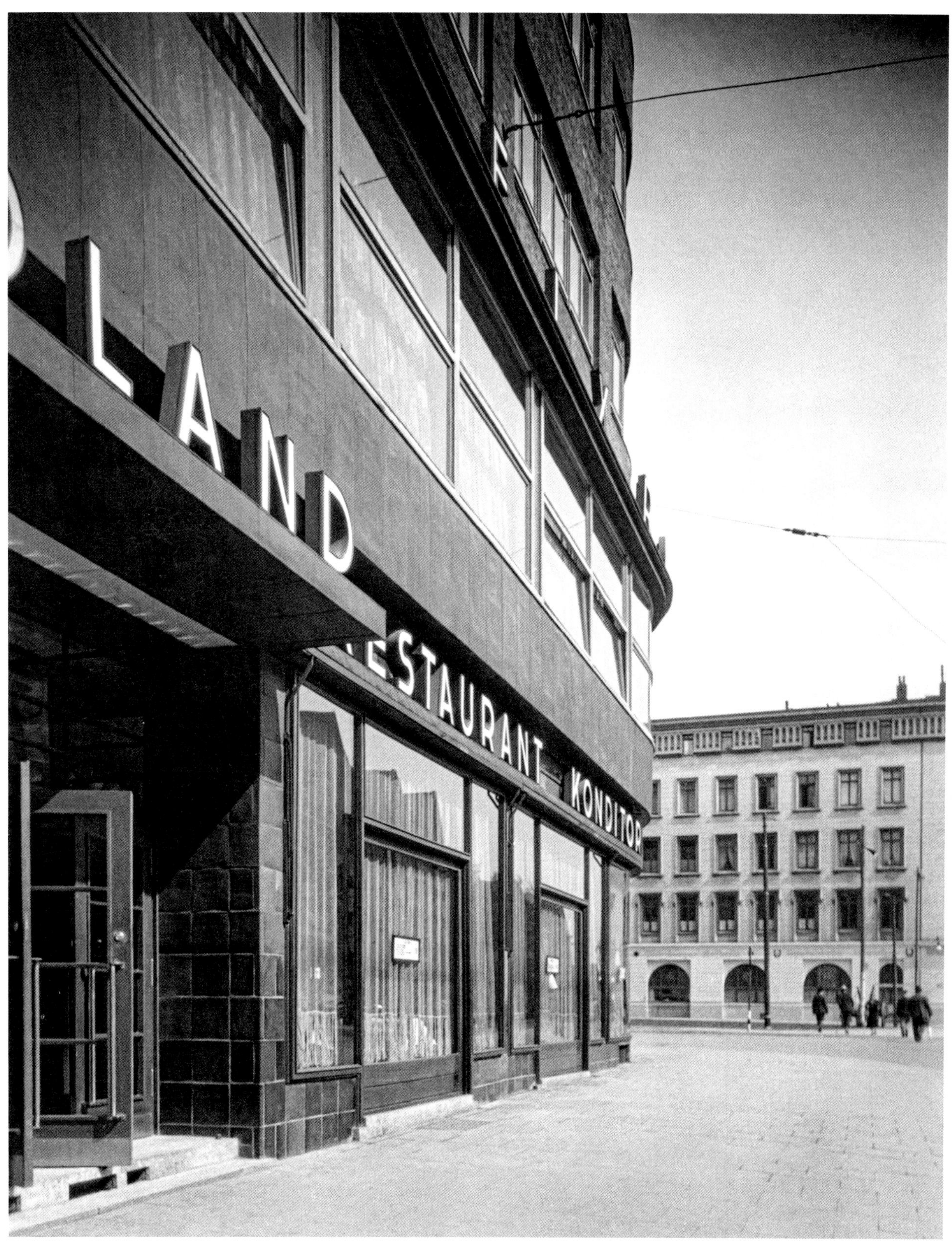
LAND
ESTAURANT KONDITOR

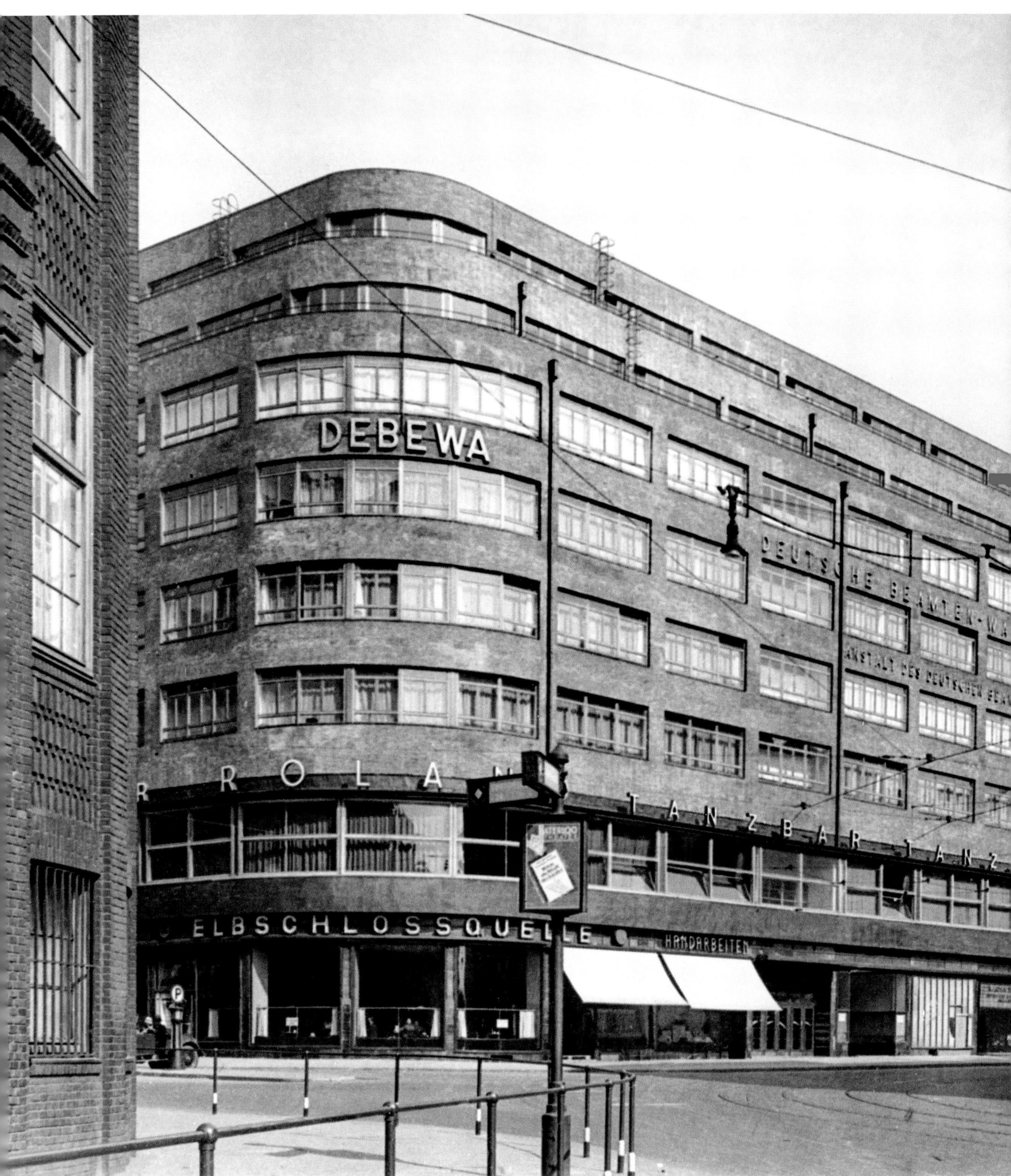
DEBEWA
DEUTSCHE
TANZBAR
ELBSCHLOSSQUELLE
HANDARBEITEN

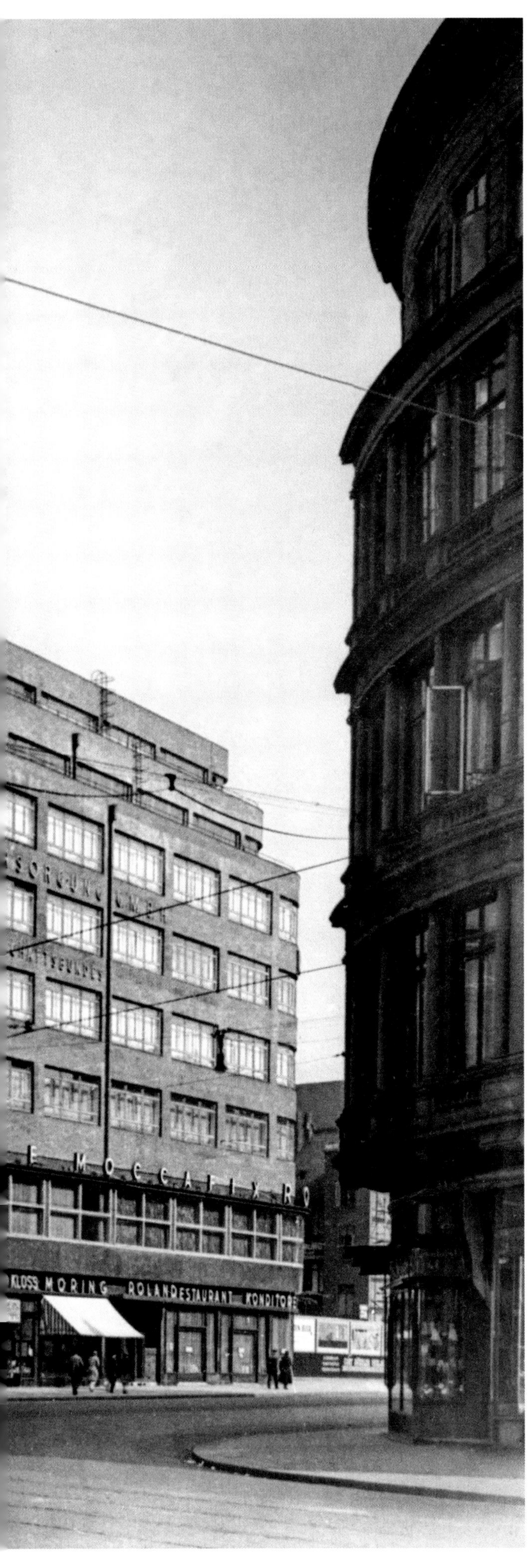
E MOCCAFIX RO
KLOSS MORING ROLANDESTAURANT KONDITOR

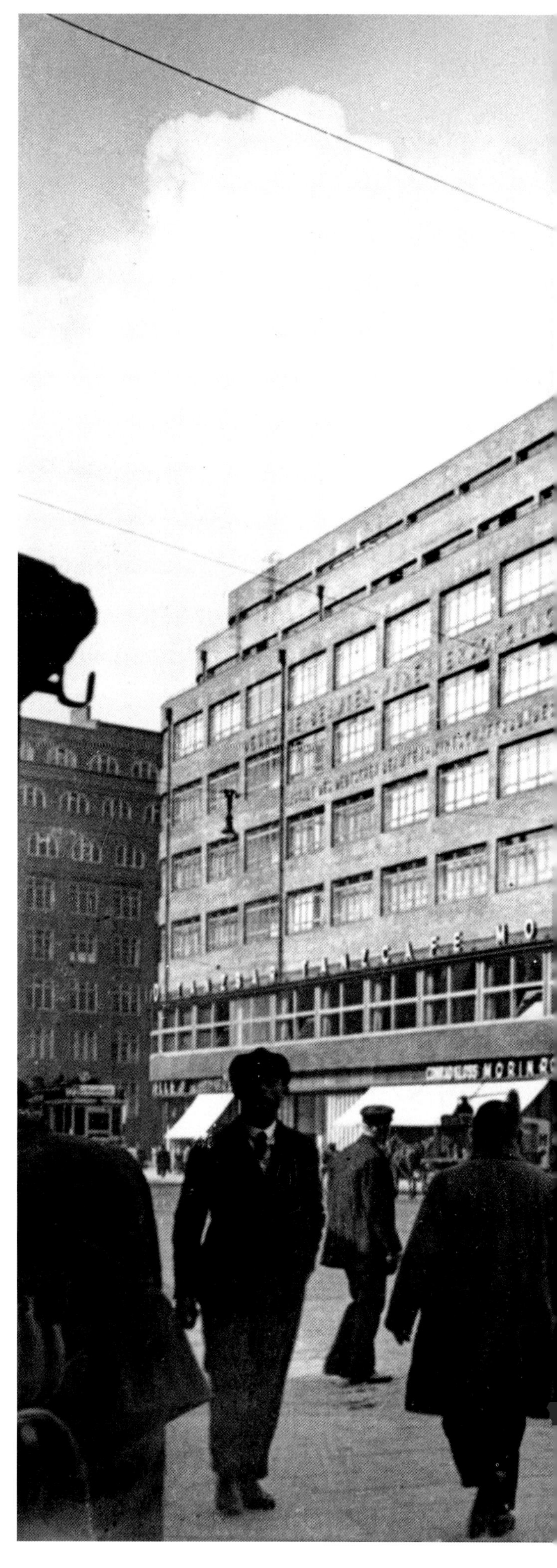

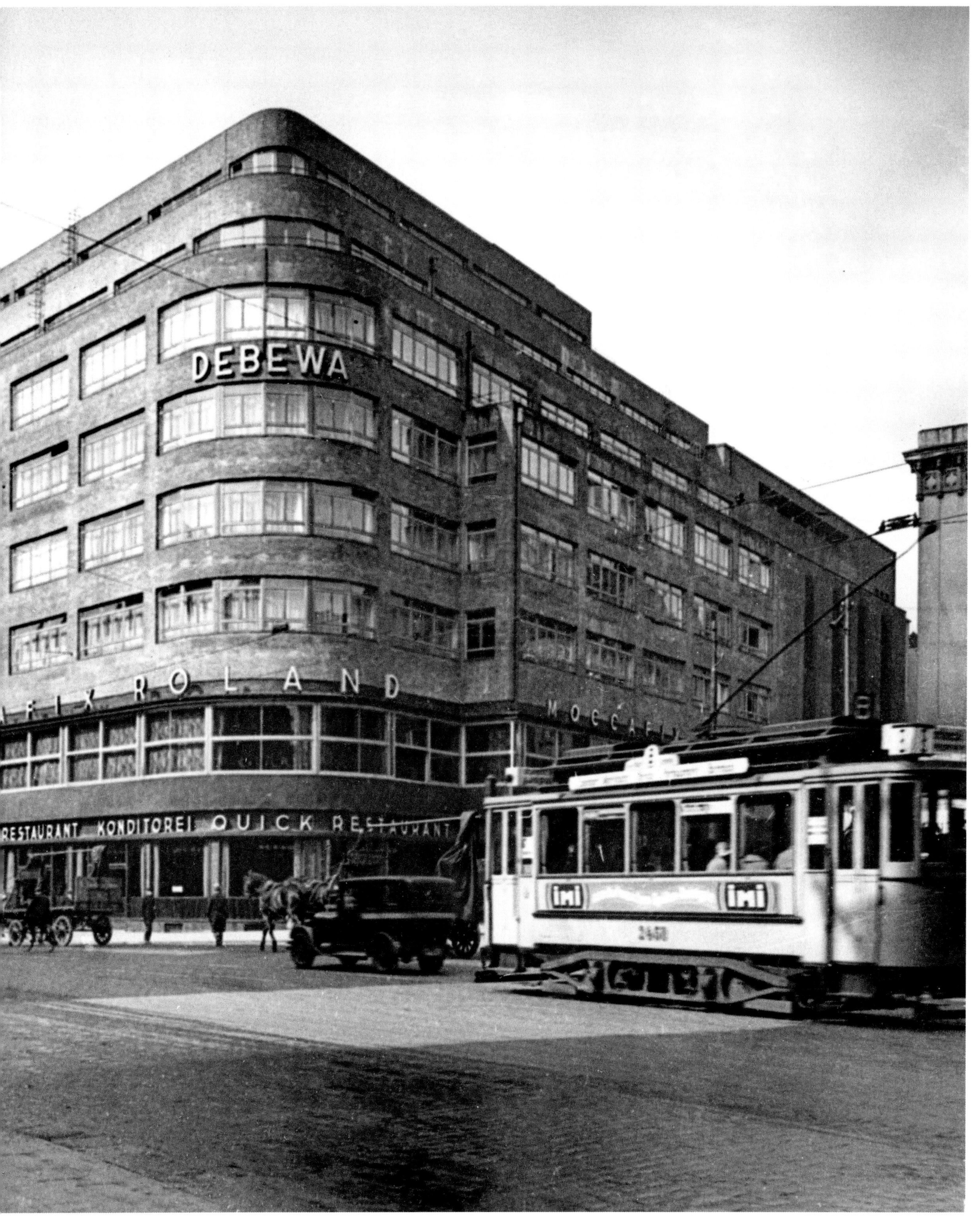
DEBEWA
ROLAND
RESTAURANT KONDITOREI QUICK RESTAURANT
imi
imi

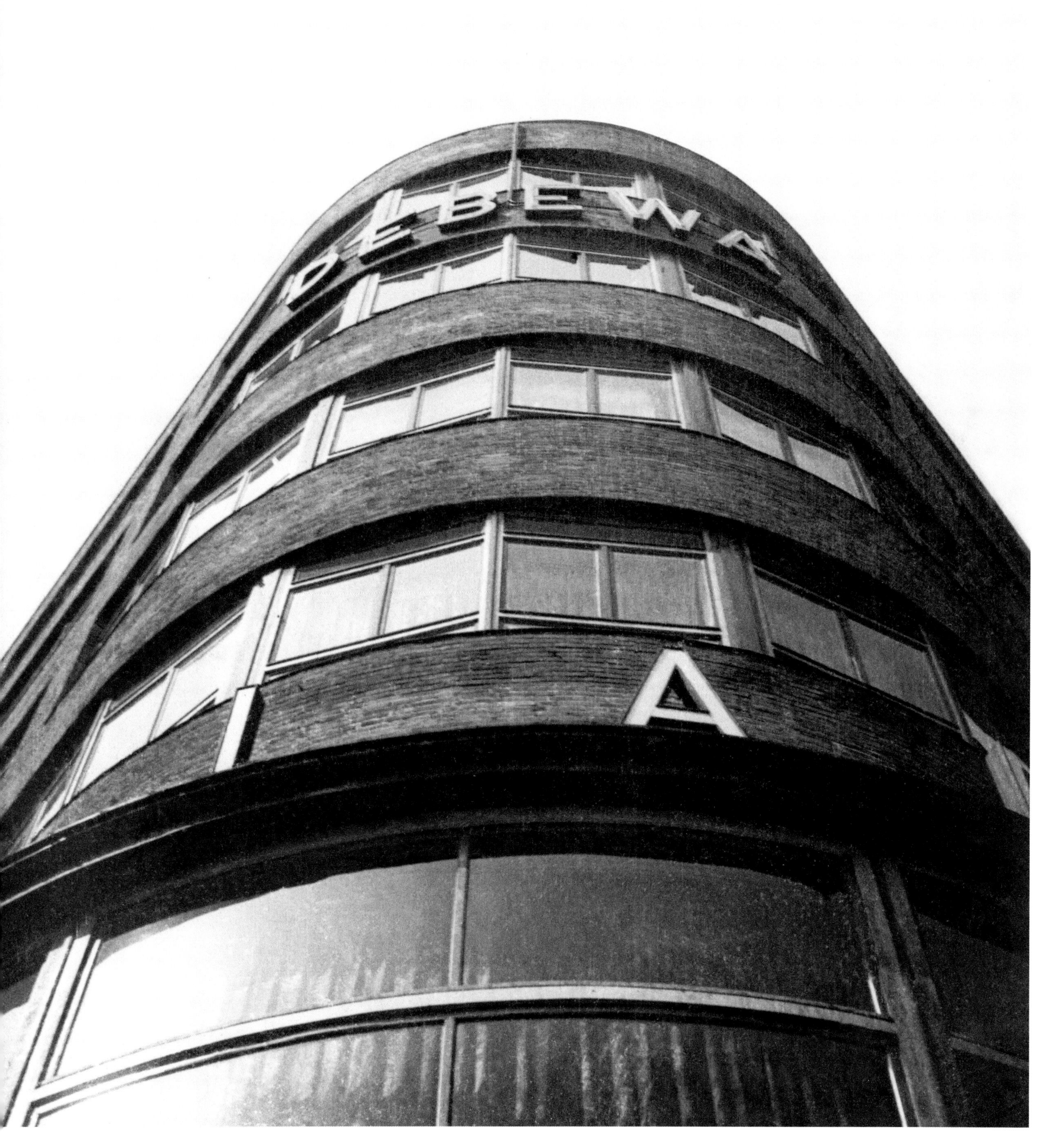
DEBEWA
A

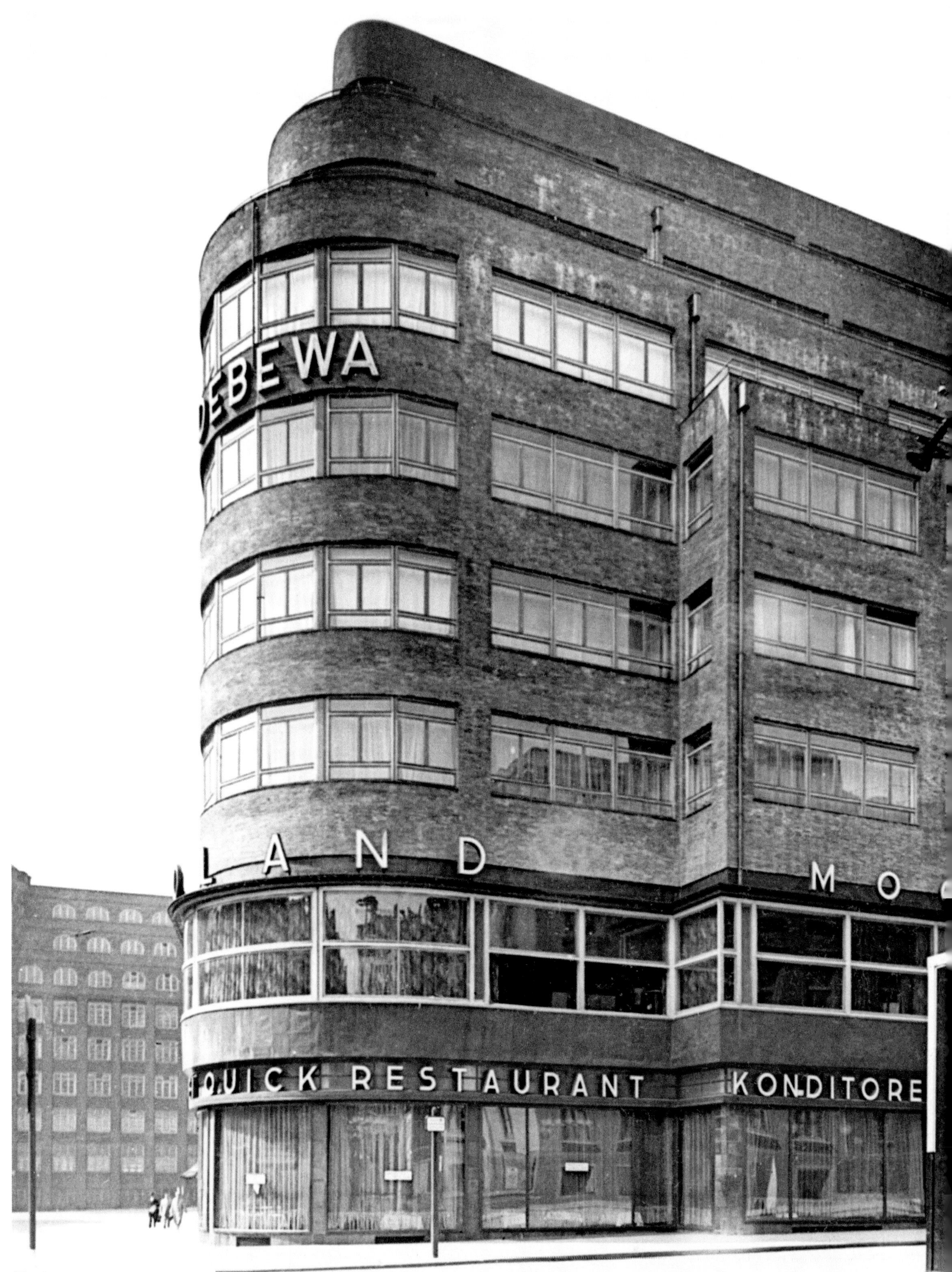
DEBEWA
LAND
MO
QUICK RESTAURANT
KONDITORE

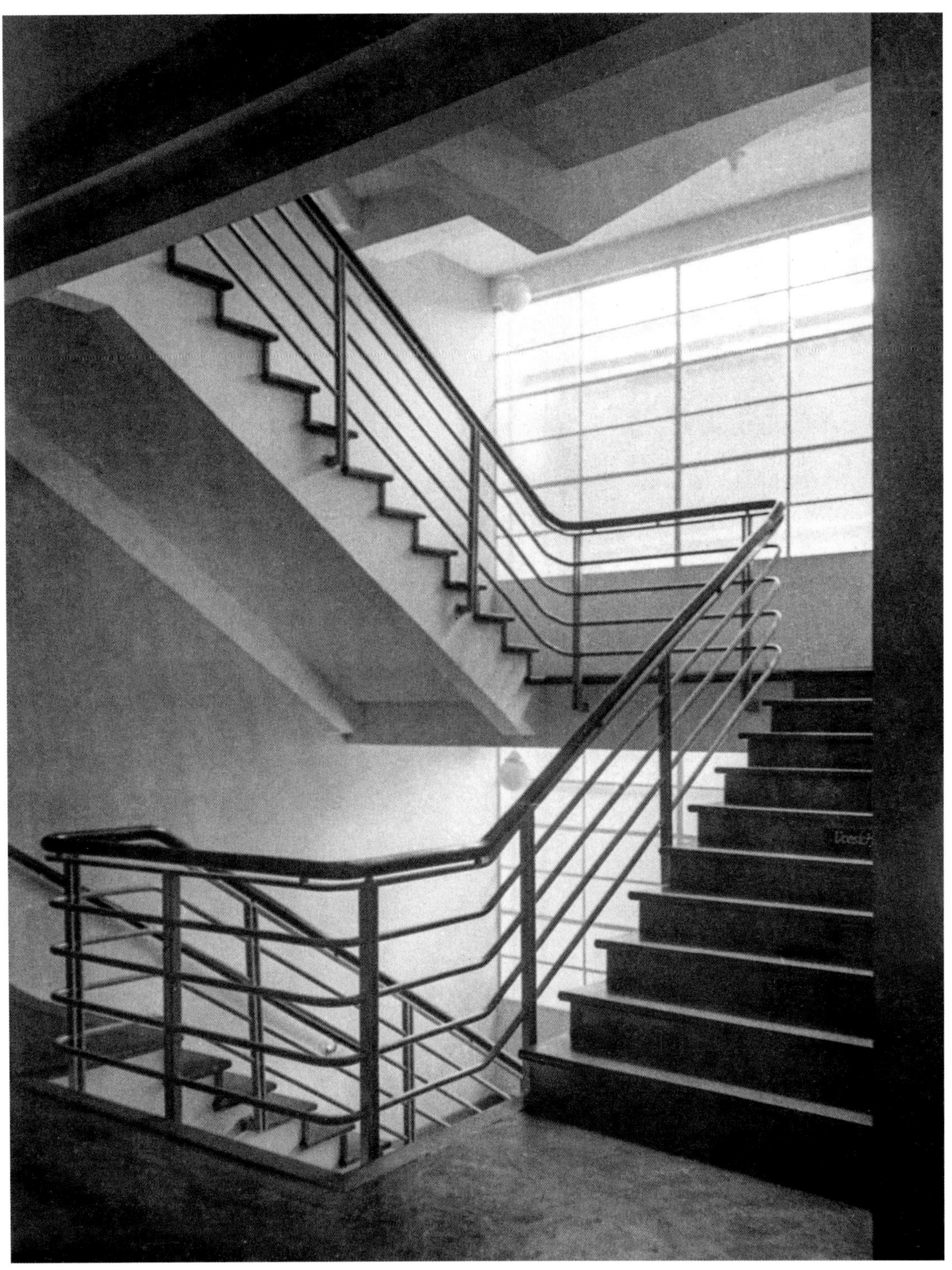

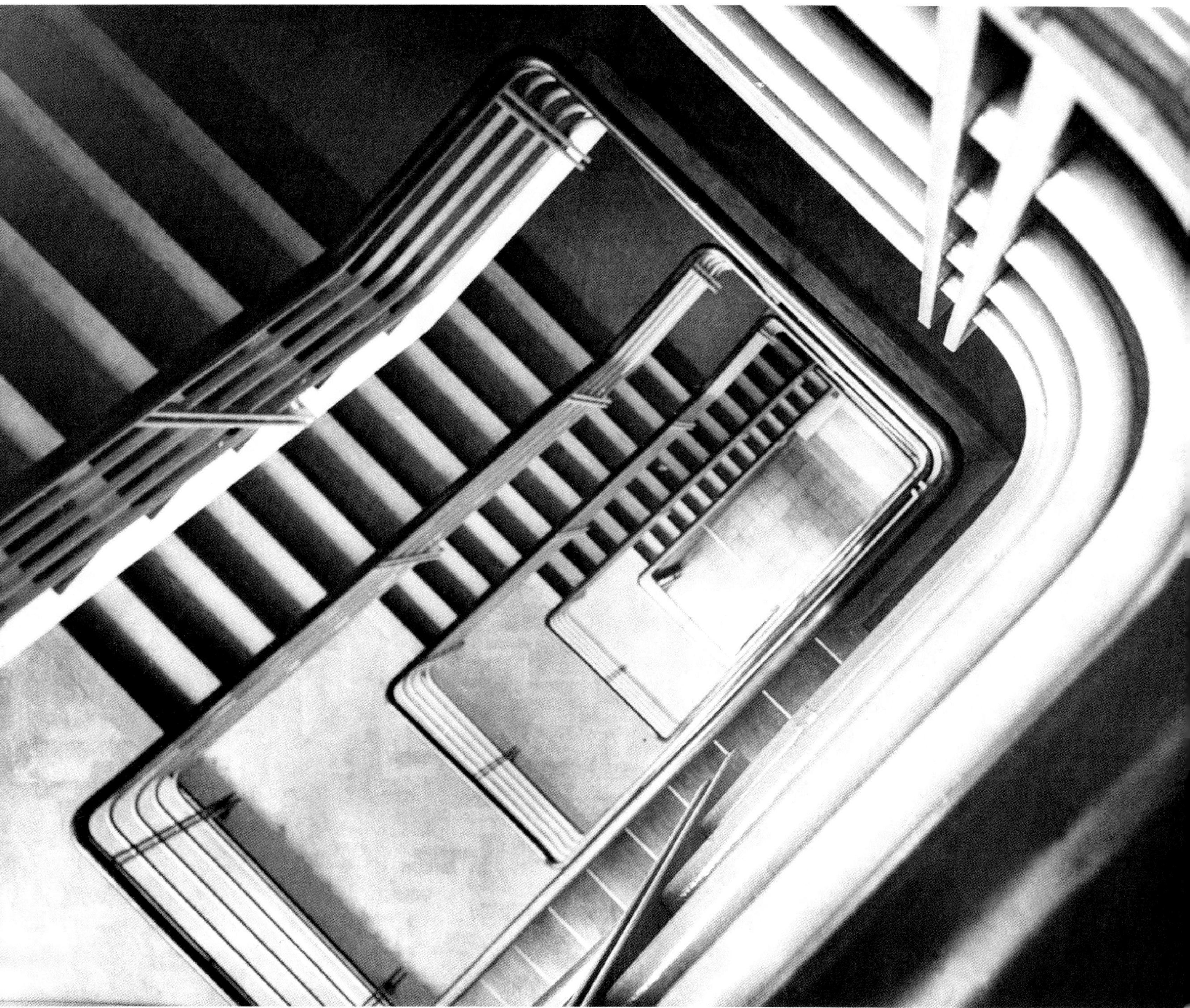

KLAUS FRAHM

Deutschlandhaus 2024

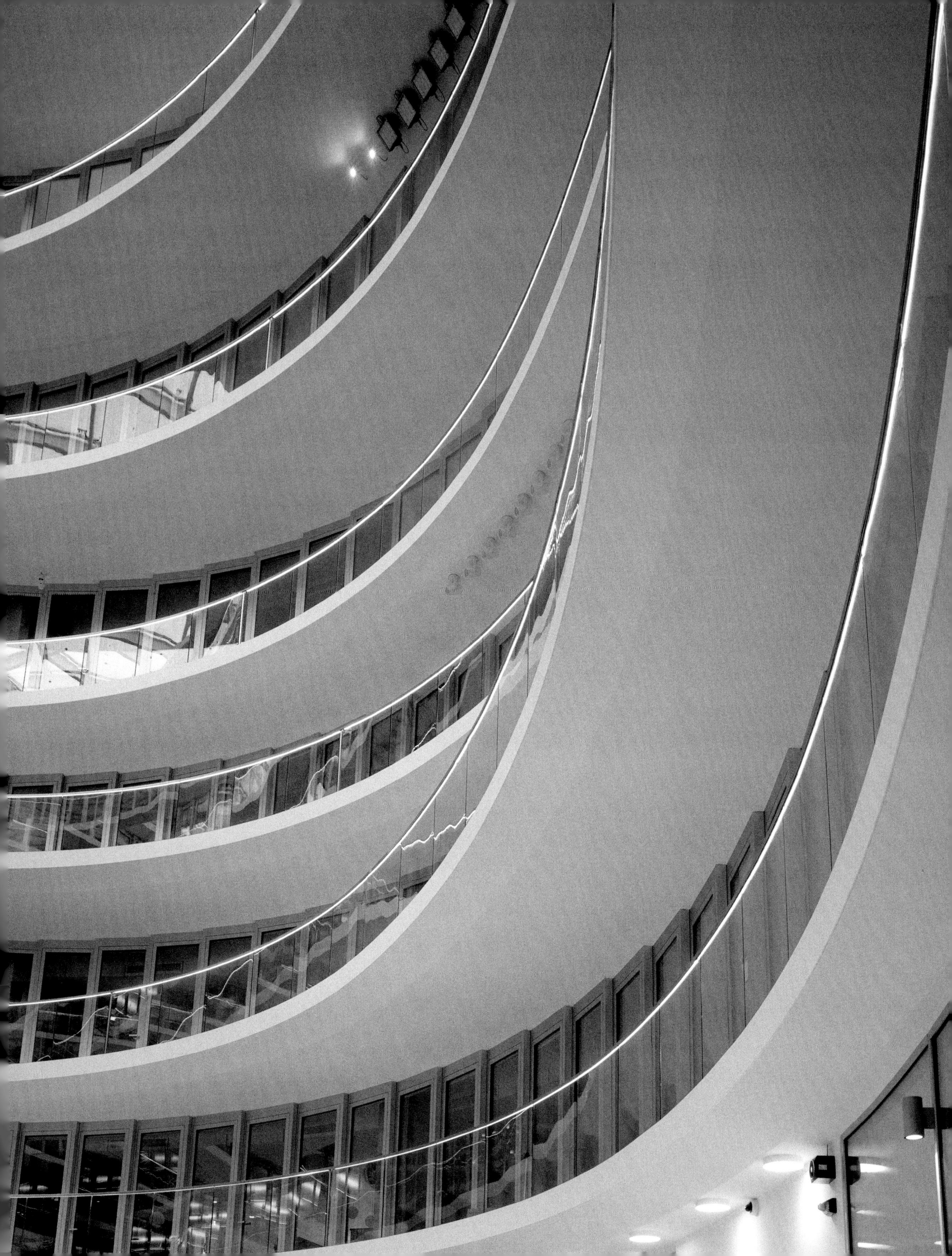

Klaus Frahm (*1953), based in Börnsen near Hamburg, is one of Germany's leading architecture photographers. His work is found in important national and international collections and museums, and has been exhibited frequently. Frahm has been the recipient of various awards, including that of the Art Directors Club, the Graphis Photo Award, and the European Architecture Photography Award. He is a member of the German Photographic Society (DGPh).

Self-taught as a photographer, Frahm worked as a photojournalist after university before going freelance in 1980, photographing architecture and landscape, and publishing photobooks in collaboration with various authors since then. His photographs of the new *Deutschlandhaus*, which were taken in the early summer to autumn of 2024, stand in the long tradition of his interest in the city of Hamburg and its architecture. Frahm's photobooks on this subject range from *Bahnhofswelt. Bahnen und Bahnhöfe in Hamburg* [Station World. Railways and Stations in Hamburg] (1983) to *Hamburg-Panorama* (2006) to *HafenCity Hamburg, Baustelle / Construction Site* (2009). His books *Hamburgs Backstein* [Hamburg's Brick] (1986) and *Das Chilehaus in Hamburg. Architektur und Vision* (1999) are devoted to Hamburg's architecture from the 1920s.

But Frahm's continual preoccupation has been current building activity in the city. He has collaborated with renowned architects such as Meinhard von Gerkan and Volkwin Marg (gmp), and with Hadi Teherani, the architect of the new *Deutschlandhaus*. Frahm's photographs of new buildings have regularly appeared in the yearbook *Architecture in Hamburg* and in architectural and photographic journals.

Frahm has also illustrated photobooks about *Potsdam. Palaces and Gardens of the Hohenzollern* (1996) and *Prussia. Art and Architecture* (1999). He has photographed celebrated modernist buildings, including Walter Gropius's *Fagus Factory* and *Bauhaus Building*, Giuseppe Terragni's *Casa del Fascio*, Ludwig Mies van der Rohe's *Barcelona Pavilion* and his *National Gallery* in Berlin, Daniel Liebeskind's *Jewish Museum* in Berlin, James Stirling's *Braun Factory* in Melsungen and his *Staatsgalerie Stuttgart*, and Richard Meier's *Chiesa del Giubileo* in Rome, to name only a few. The monographs on the architects *Giuseppe Terragni* and *Carlo Scarpa* (both 1999) are based on his photographs. Frahm has also extensively documented Peter Eisenman's *Memorial to the Murdered Jews of Europe* (2005) in Berlin.

Klaus Frahm's architectural photography is characterized by a clear and precise visual language that gives equal expression to the tectonic and artistic intentions of the architect. He has a particularly keen eye for sections and details, for structures and materials. This also applies to his fine-art work on self-selected subject matter, which is primarily and deliberately carried out in black and white. His project on the new *Deutschlandhaus* oscillates between these creative poles of architectural documentation and fine art, as it was not undertaken for advertising purposes but as an analytical and artistic engagement with architecture in a combination of black-and-white studies and color photographs. Frahm restricted himself to authentic views and viewing positions, and the photographs were taken with a 4 x 5 in. large format camera and a digital Leica.

Photographers of architecture often have only a narrow timeframe between the removal of building-site rubble and the occupiers moving in. With the *Deutschlandhaus* Frahm chose a relatively late construction phase as his starting point. The scaffolding still standing in the atrium and the already planted palms offered him an attractive contrast between technical structures and natural forms. Later the focus was on the dialogue between the palms and the fan-like glazed curvature of the white interior façade of the atrium and its vaulting skylight.

Frahm's exterior photographs of the building, also in black and white and color, are arranged in this book according to the sequence of the streets Valentinskamp, Dammtorstraße, and Drehbahn. The images reveal both the cohesiveness of the building and the plasticity of its façade, with its low-set windows and staggered stories. The interplay of stone and glass, rounded and angular forms, and the coloration of the brick is conveyed in numerous detailed views. The photographic project was concluded with night views of the building.

In its stringency, and by selecting and focusing, Frahm's work offers an interpretation that is also a self-sufficient statement in its own right. His photographs of the new *Deutschlandhaus* exemplify what technically skilled and artistically inspired architectural photography is specifically able to do—especially as opposed to AI-generated or animated renderings from architectural offices, which conjure up a building as complete and lively even before its foundation stone has been laid.

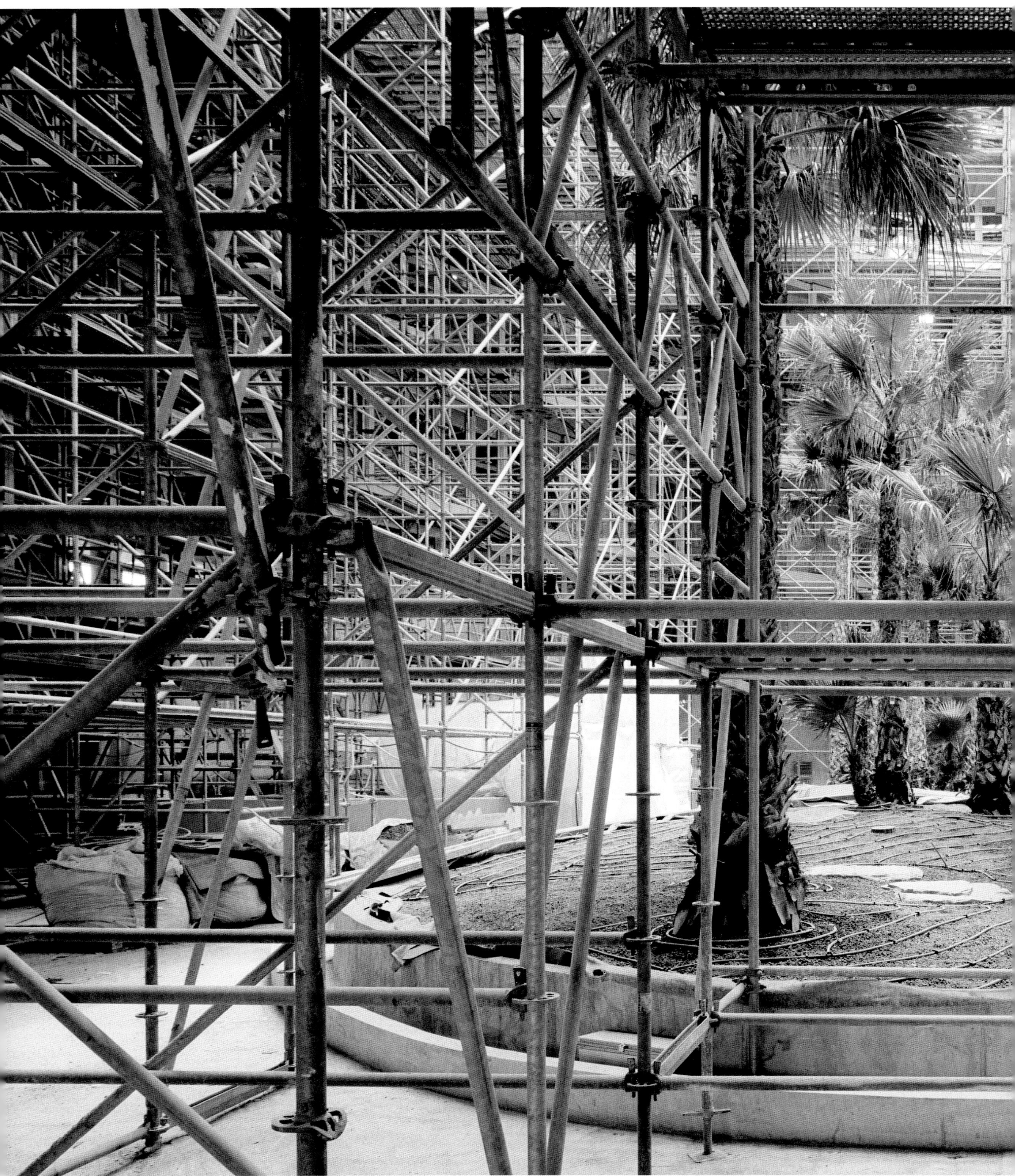

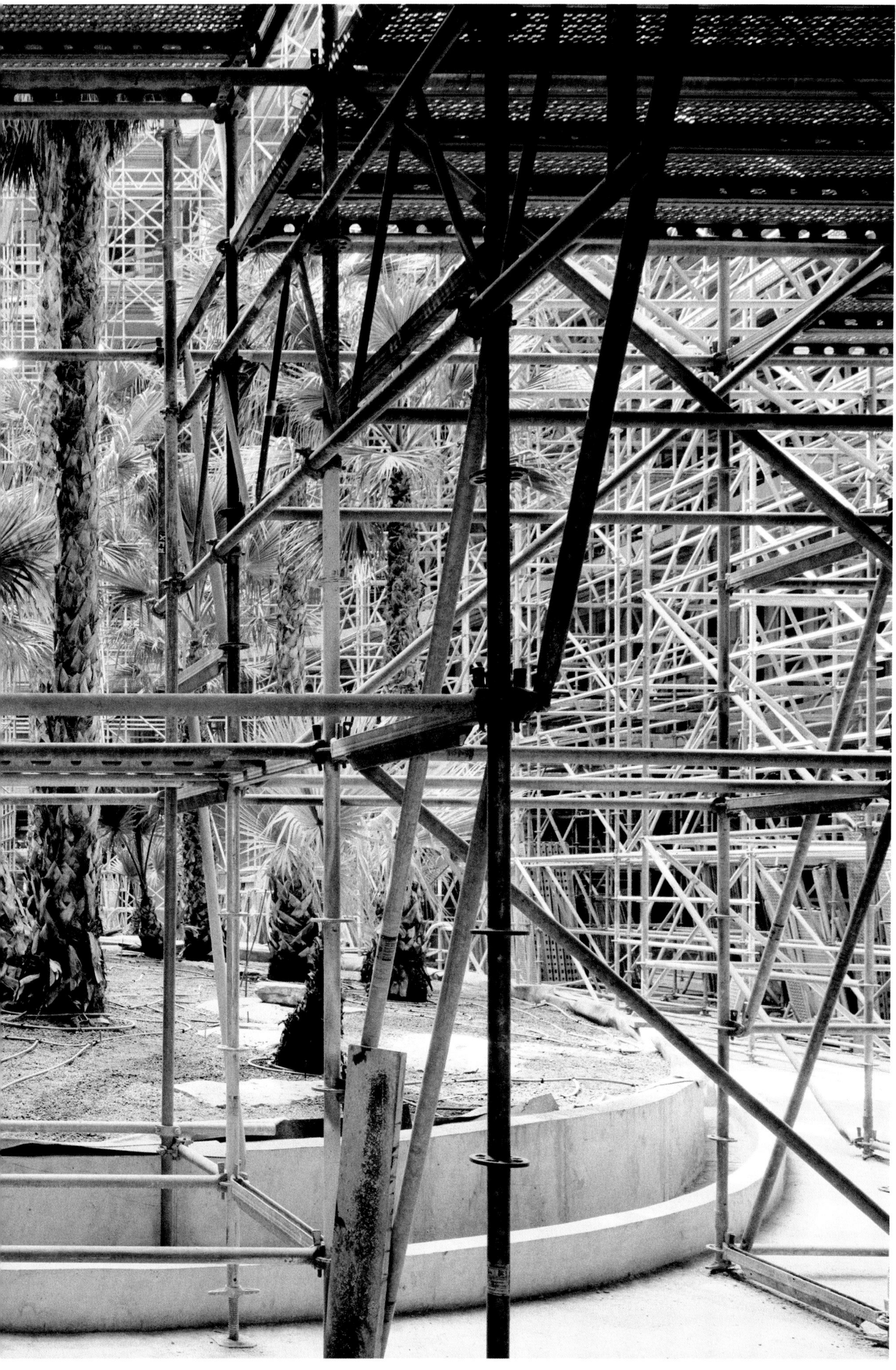

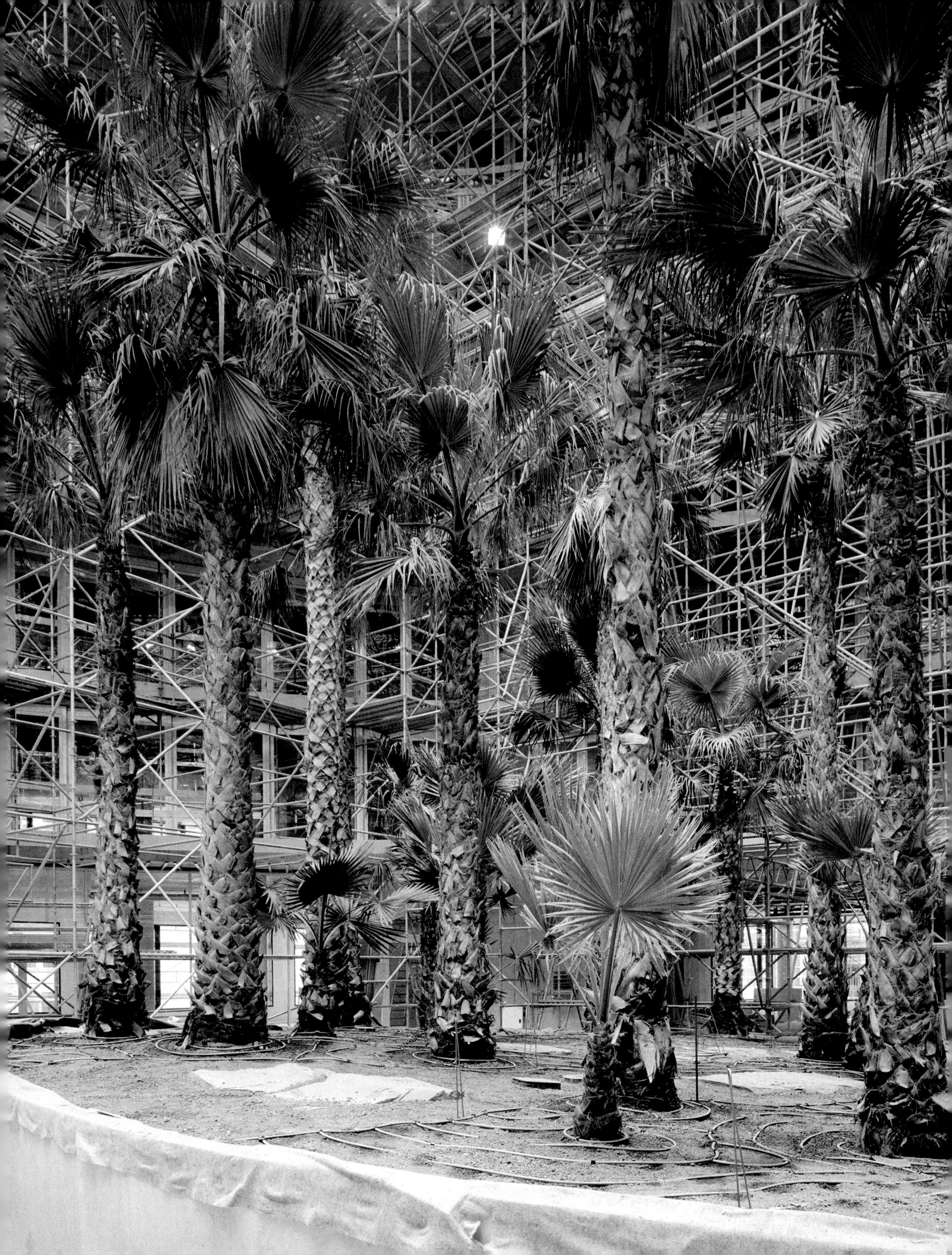

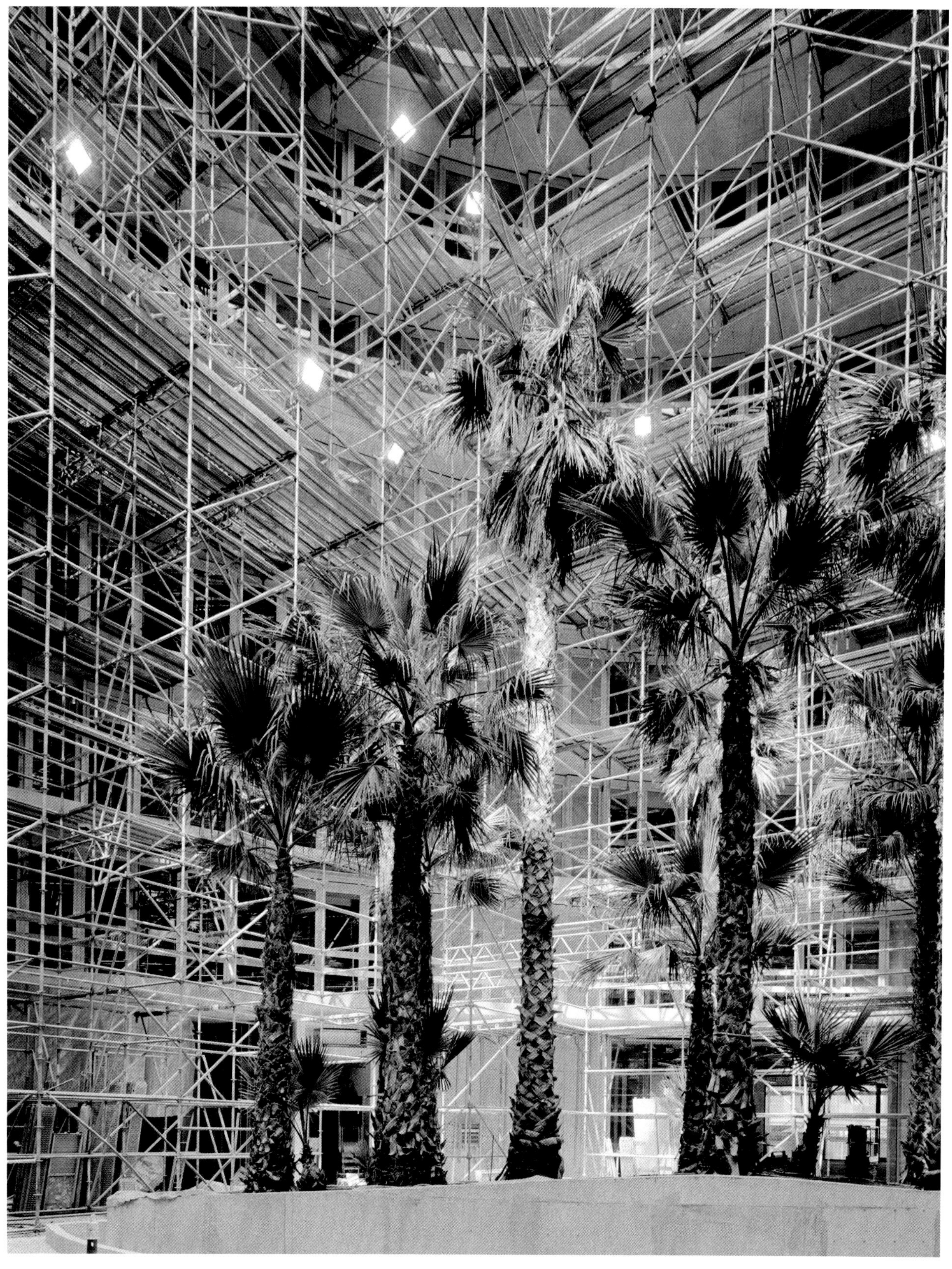

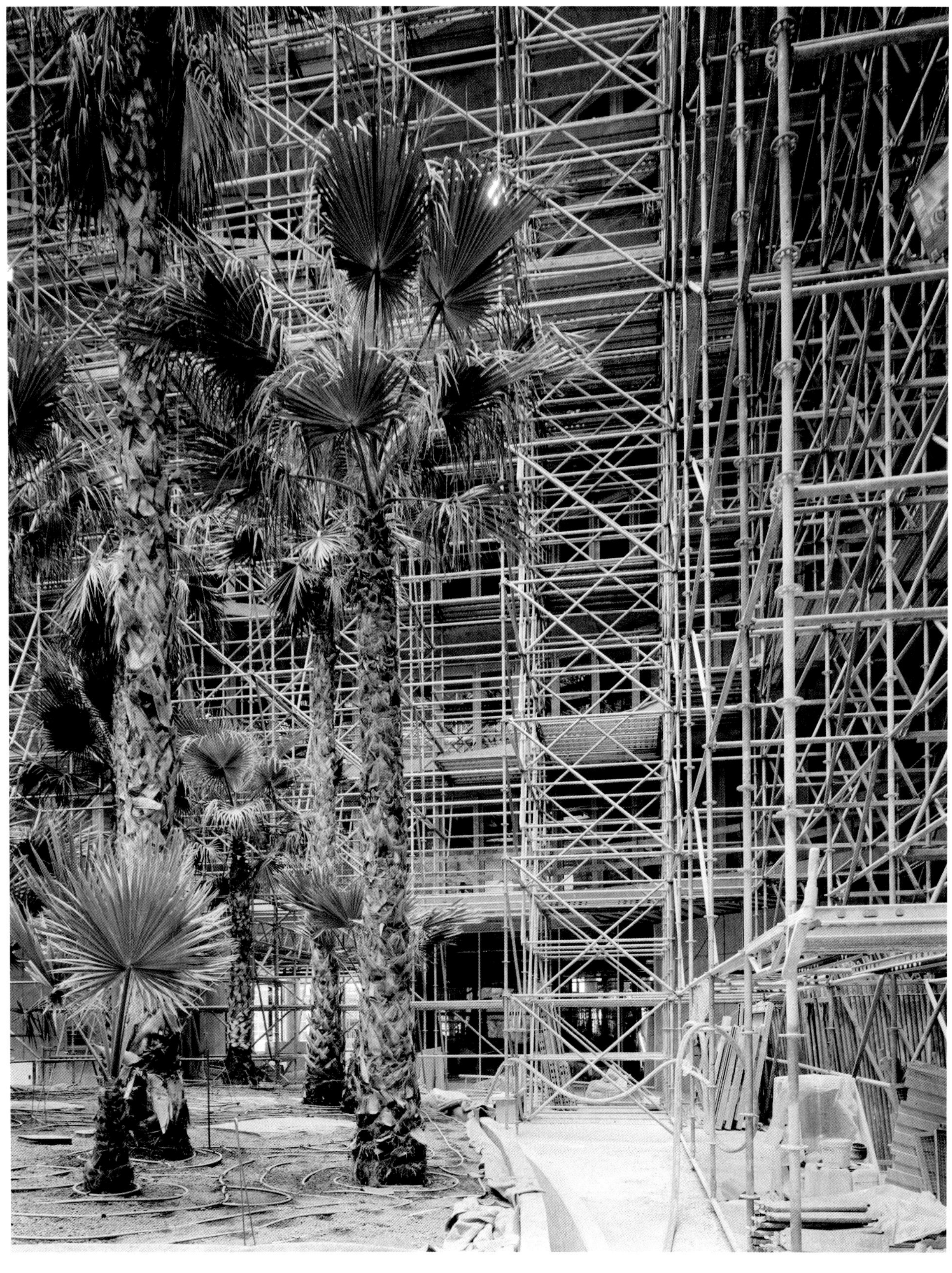

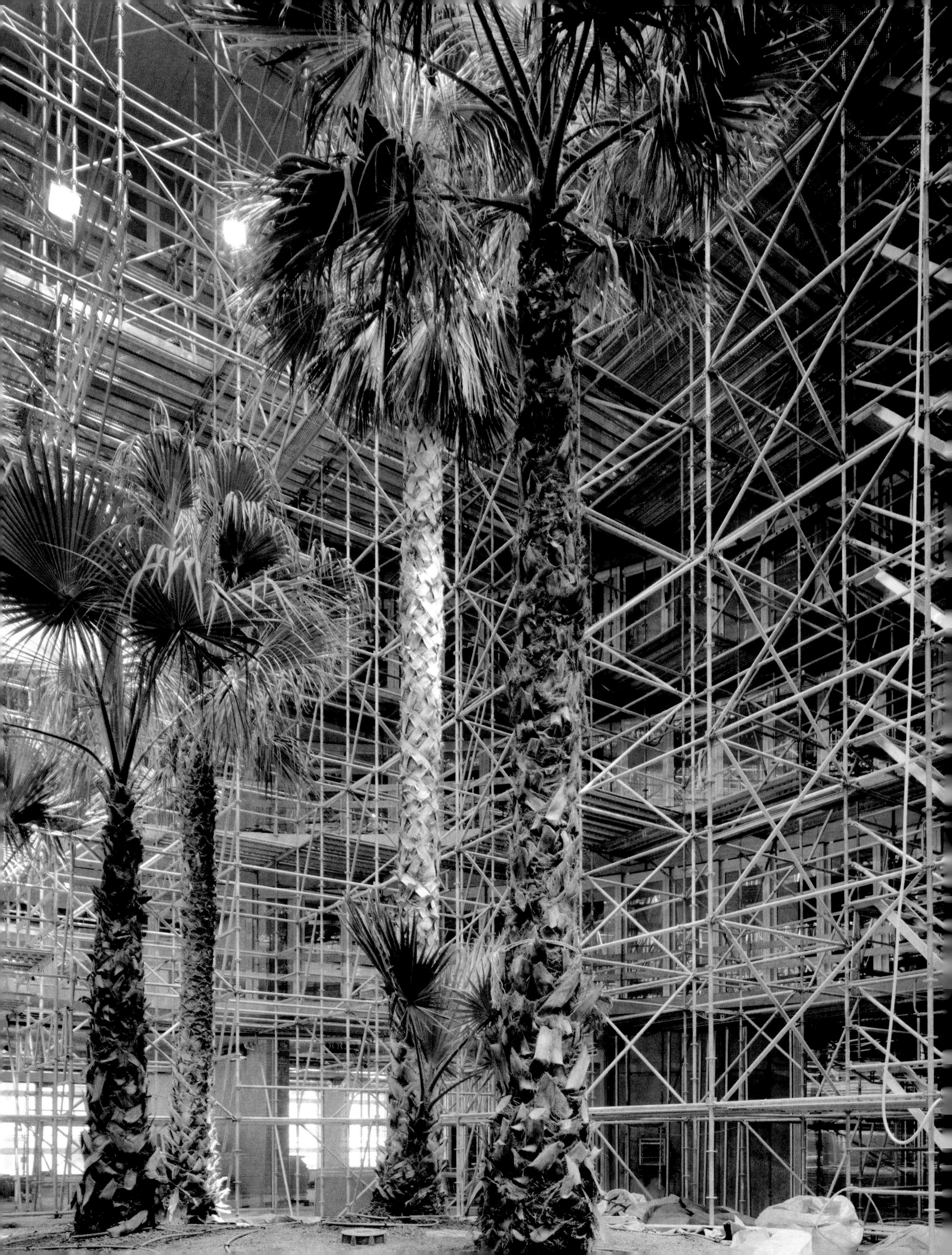

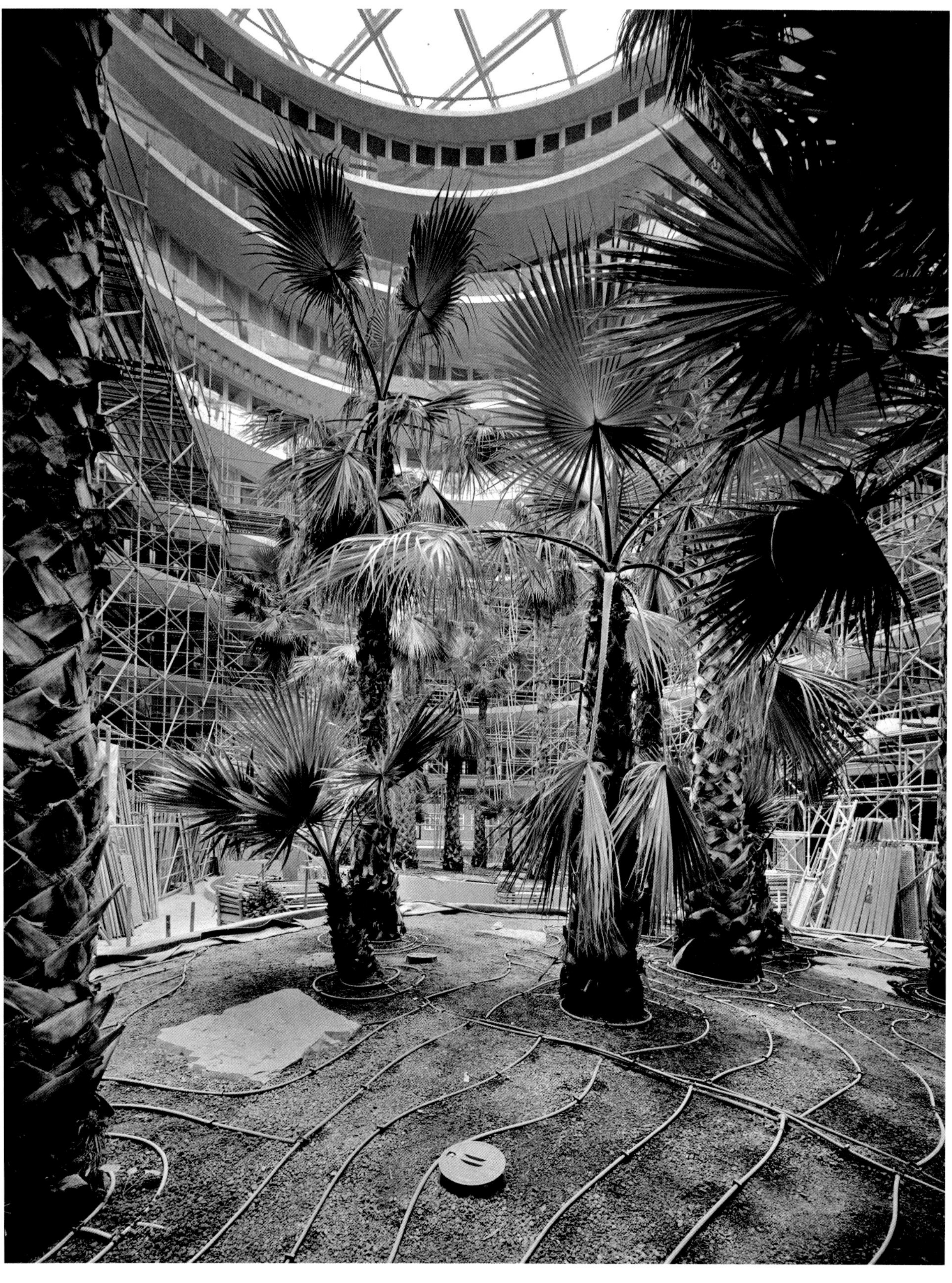

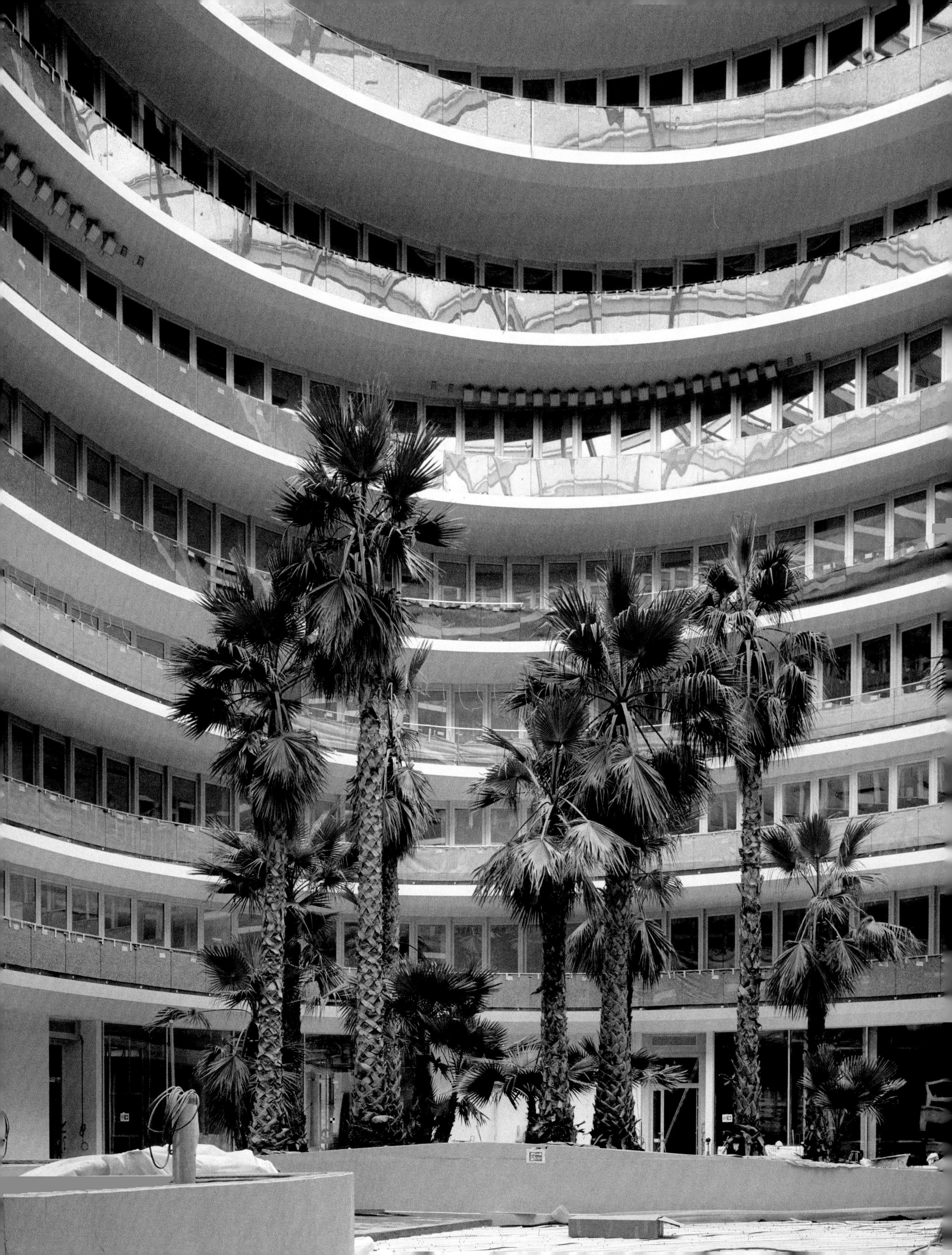

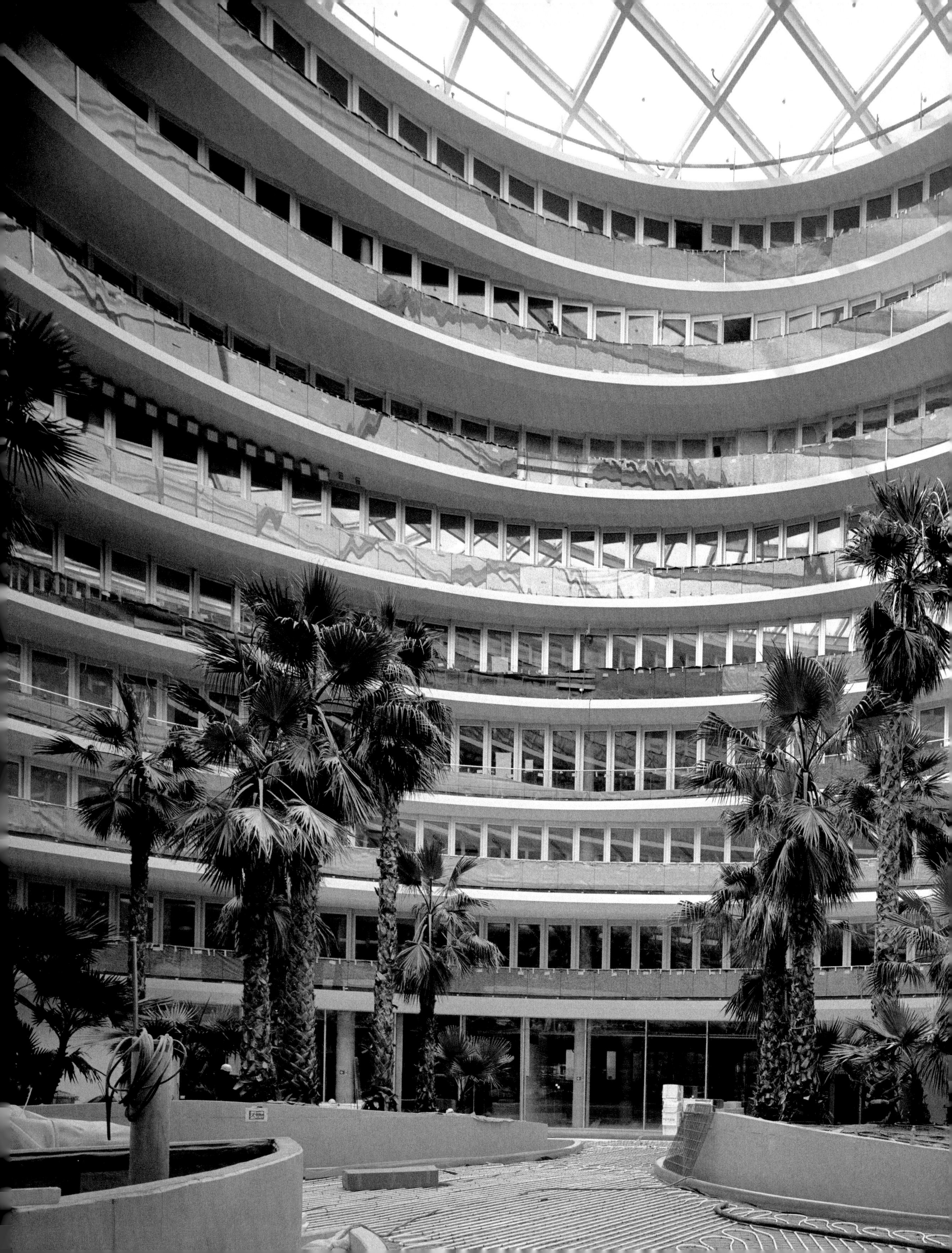

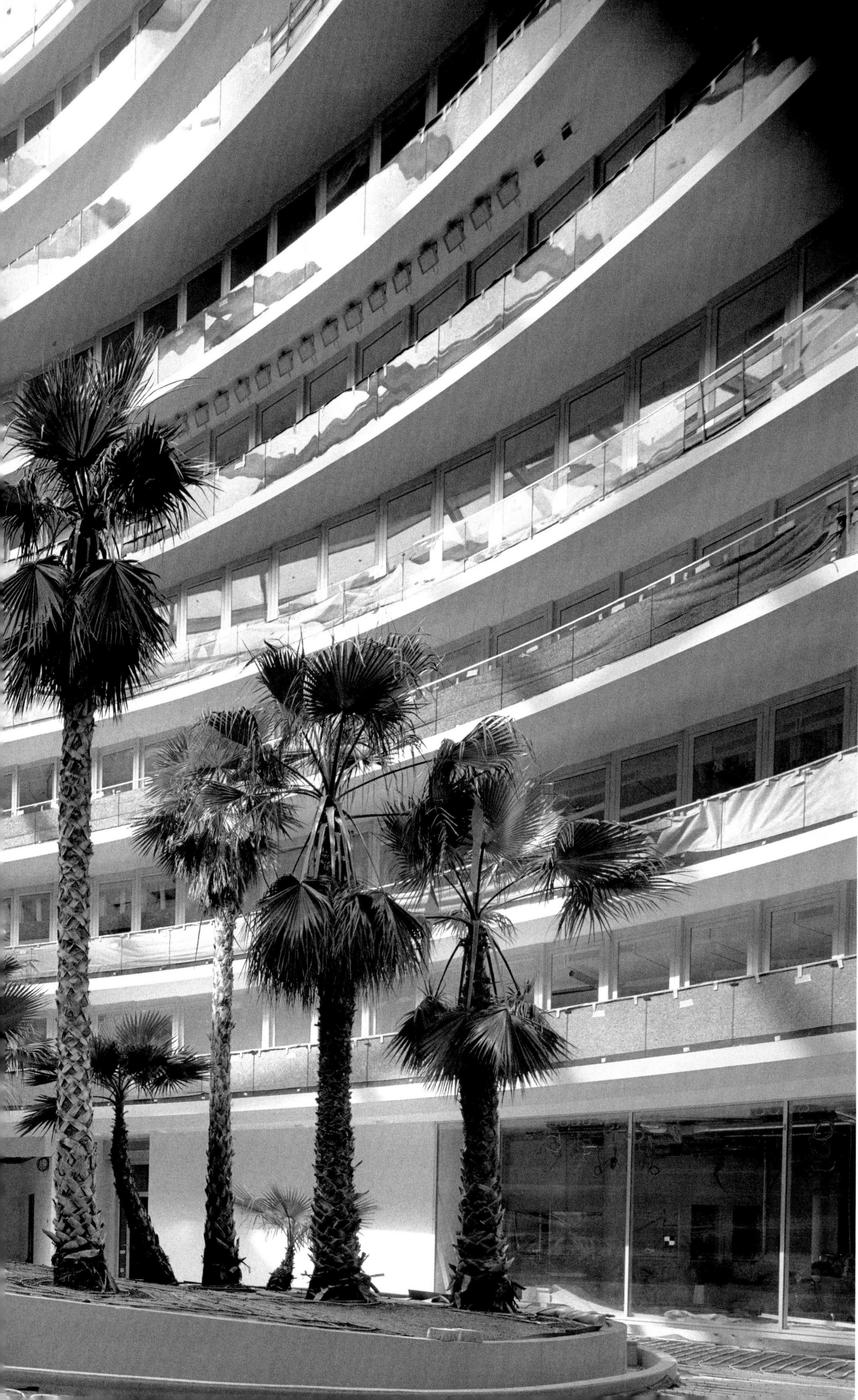

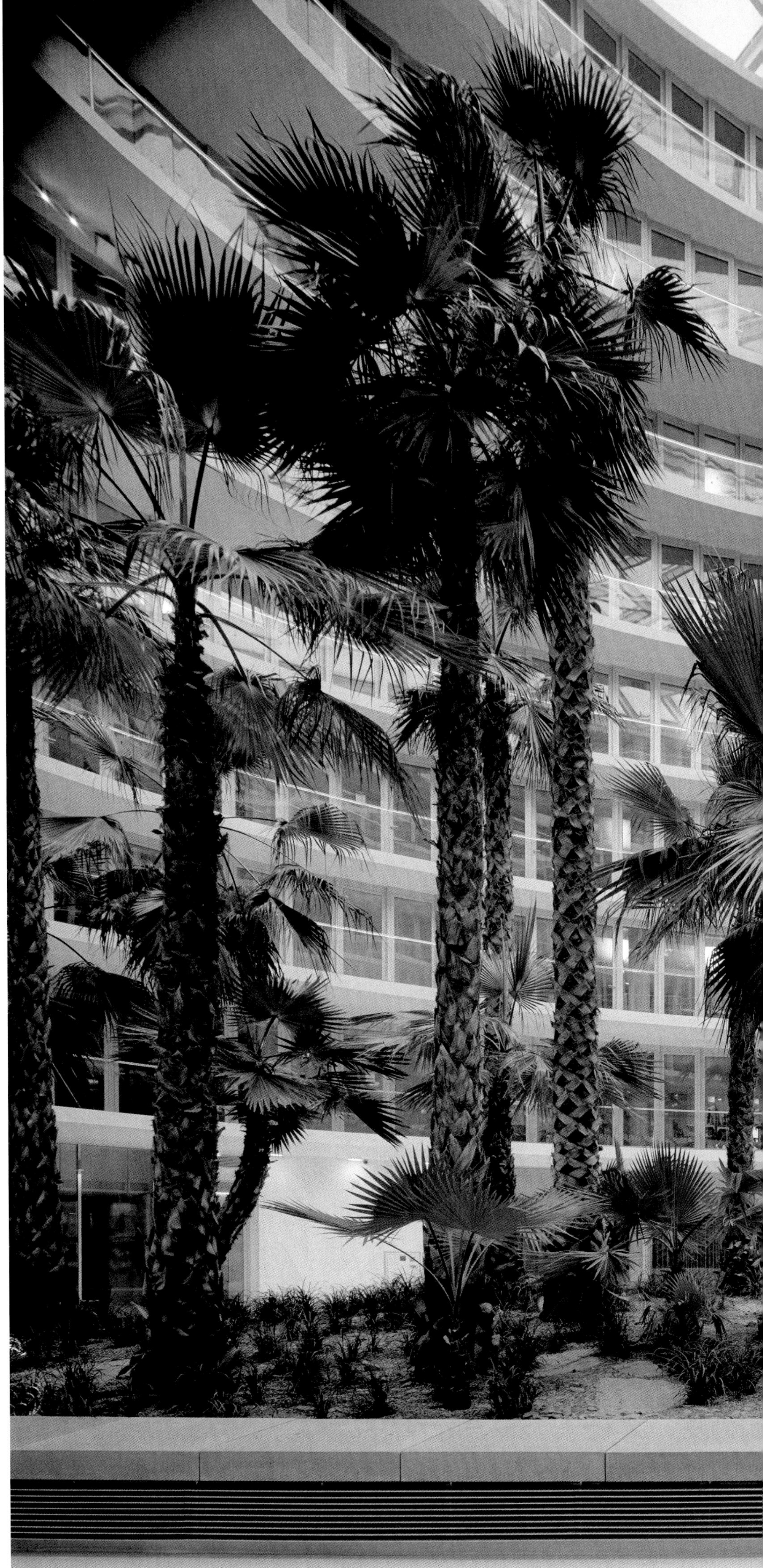

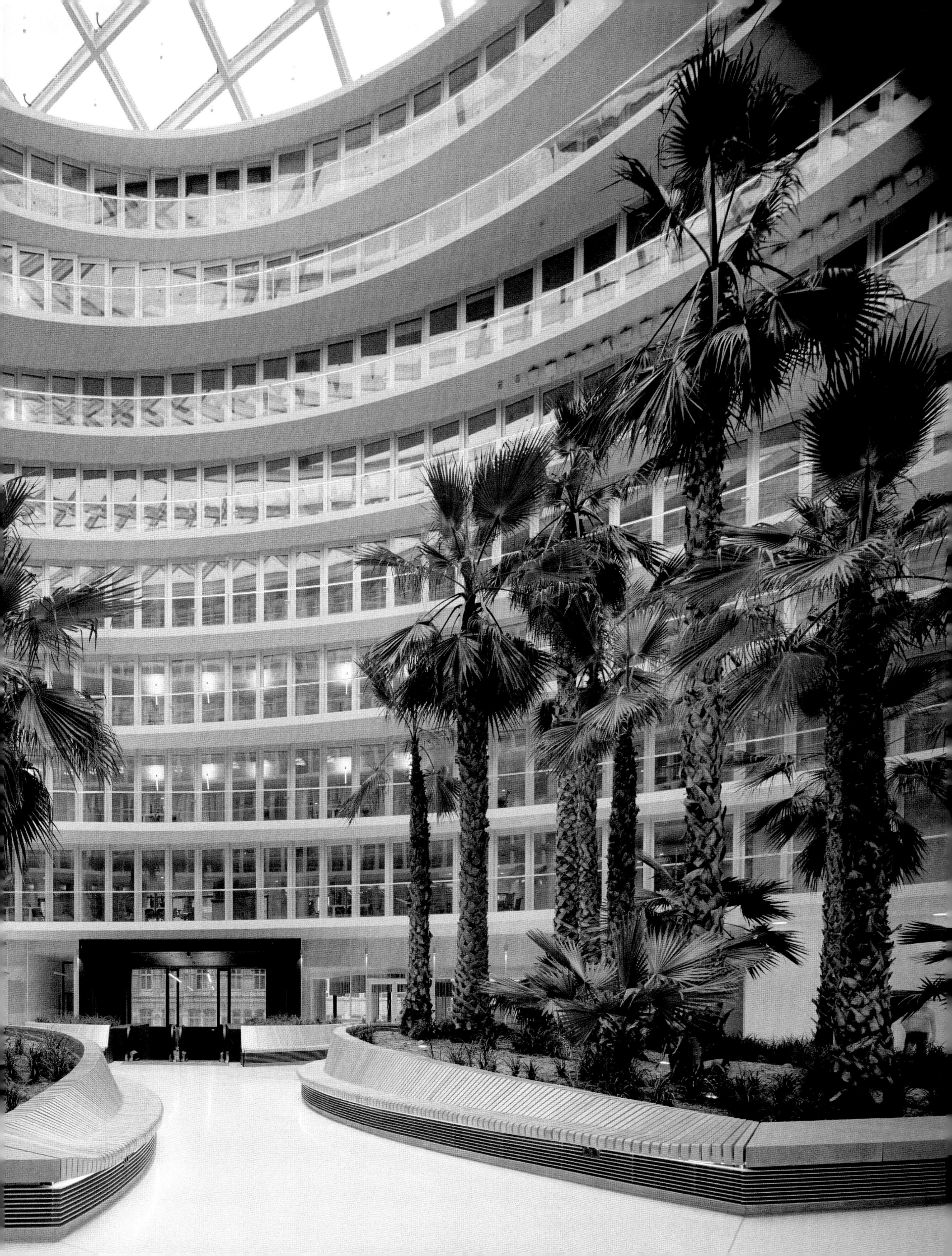

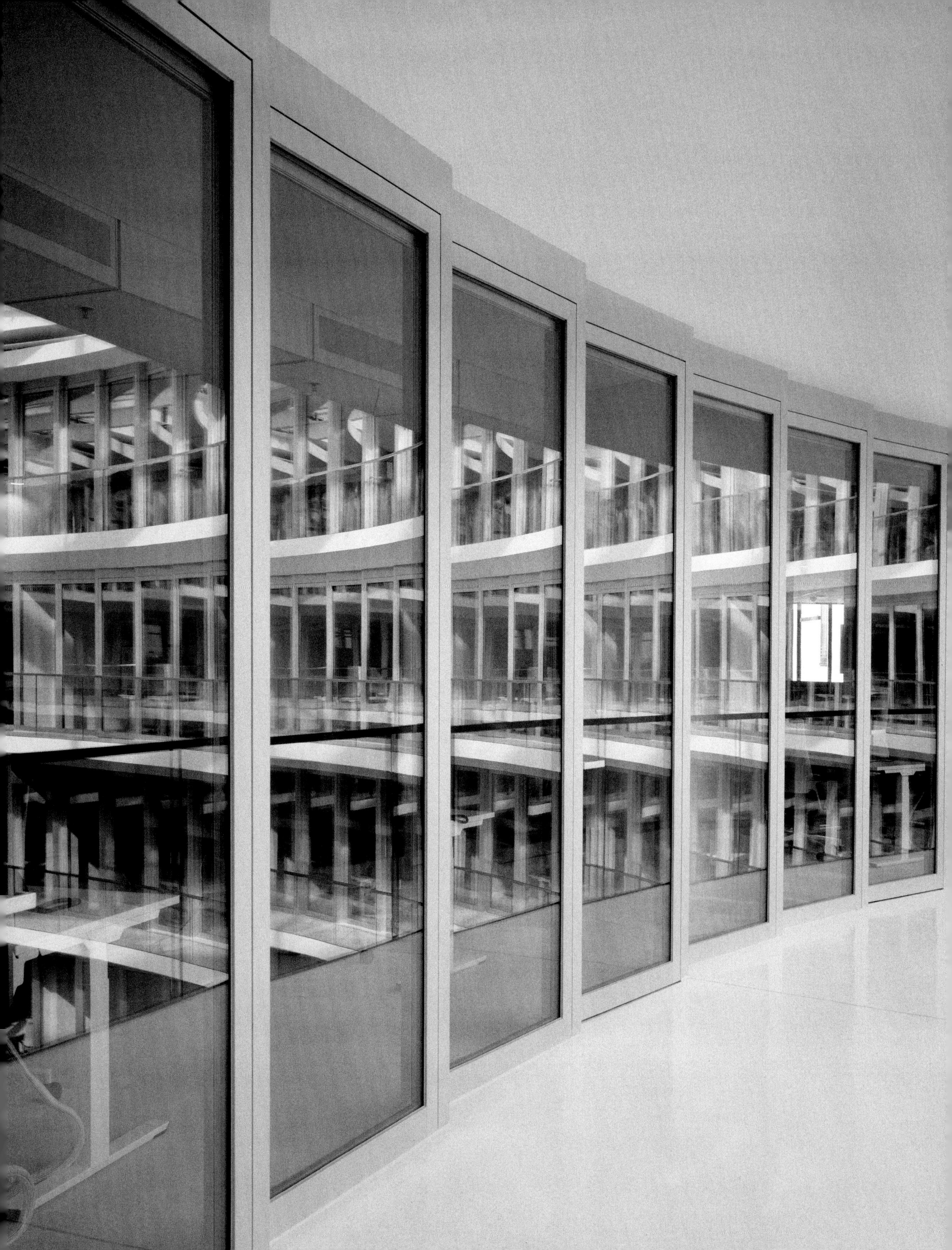

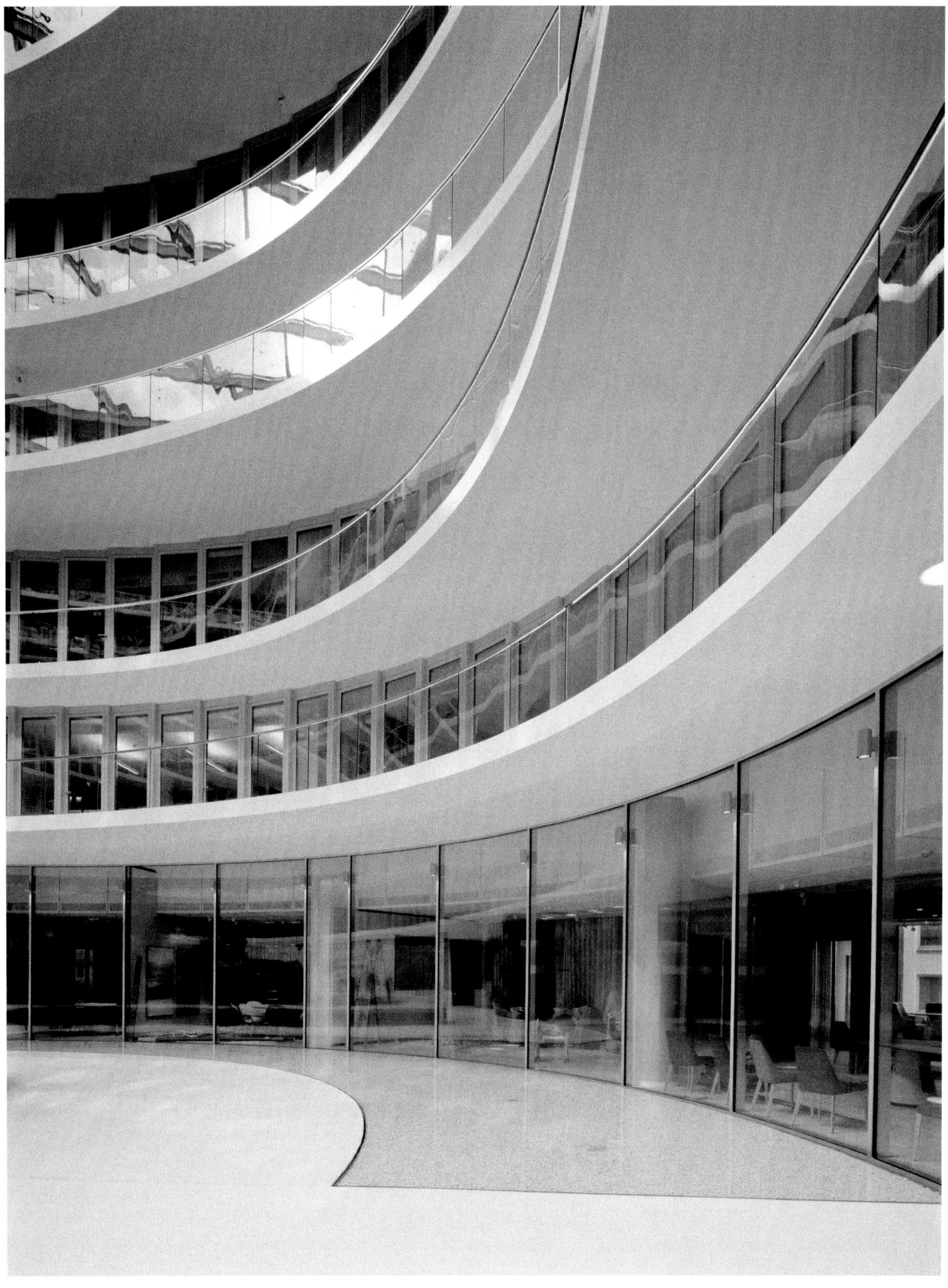

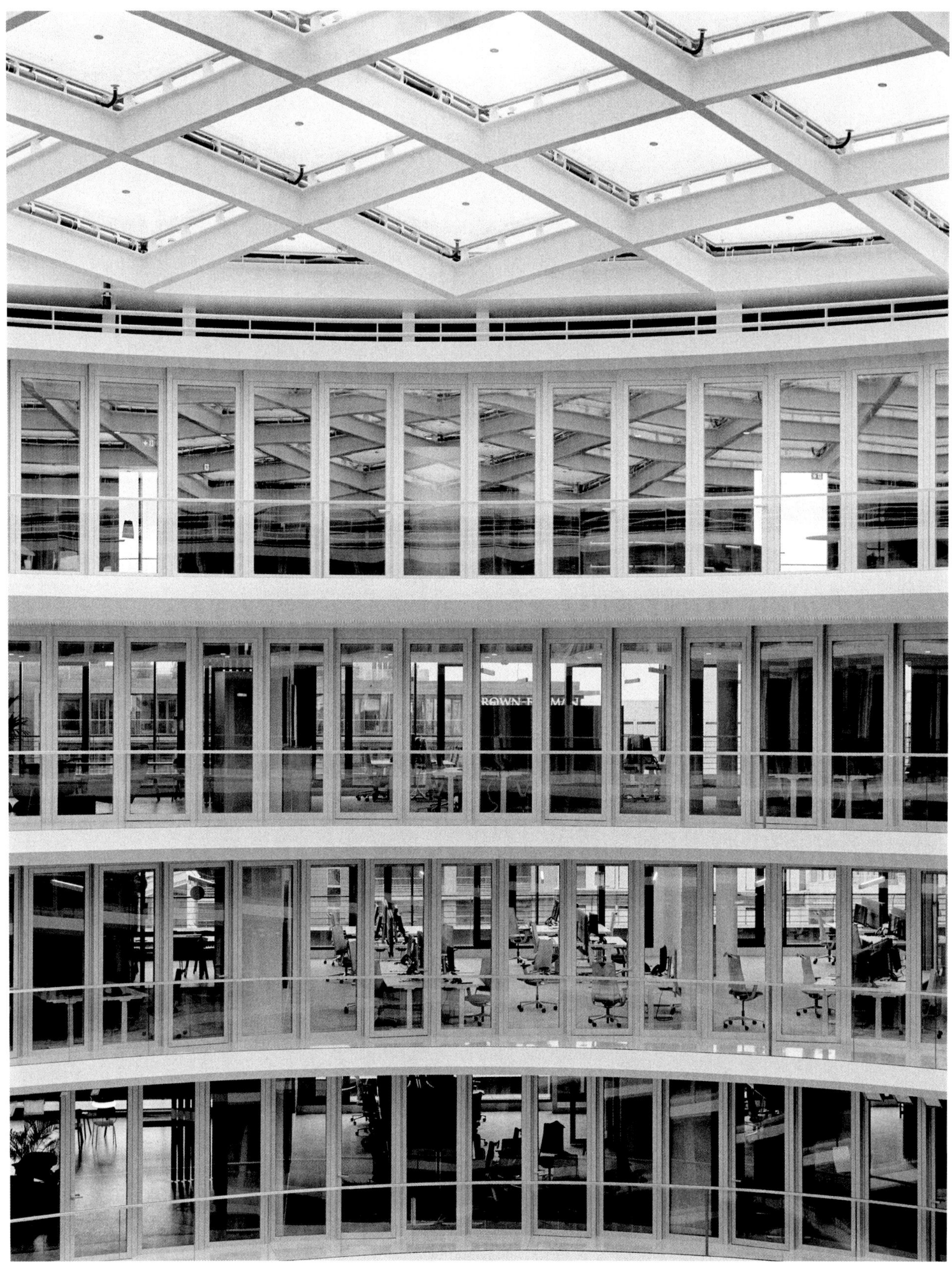

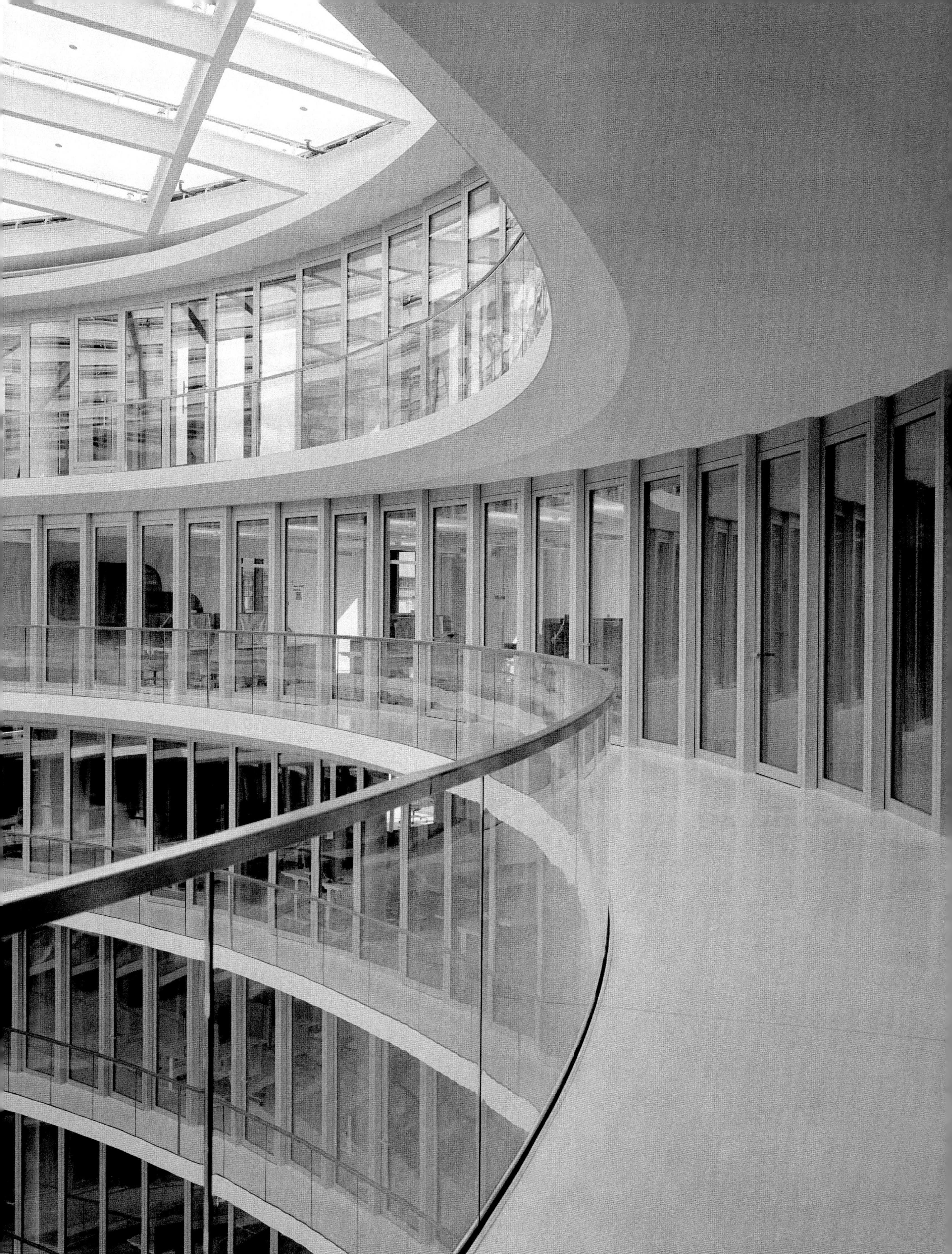

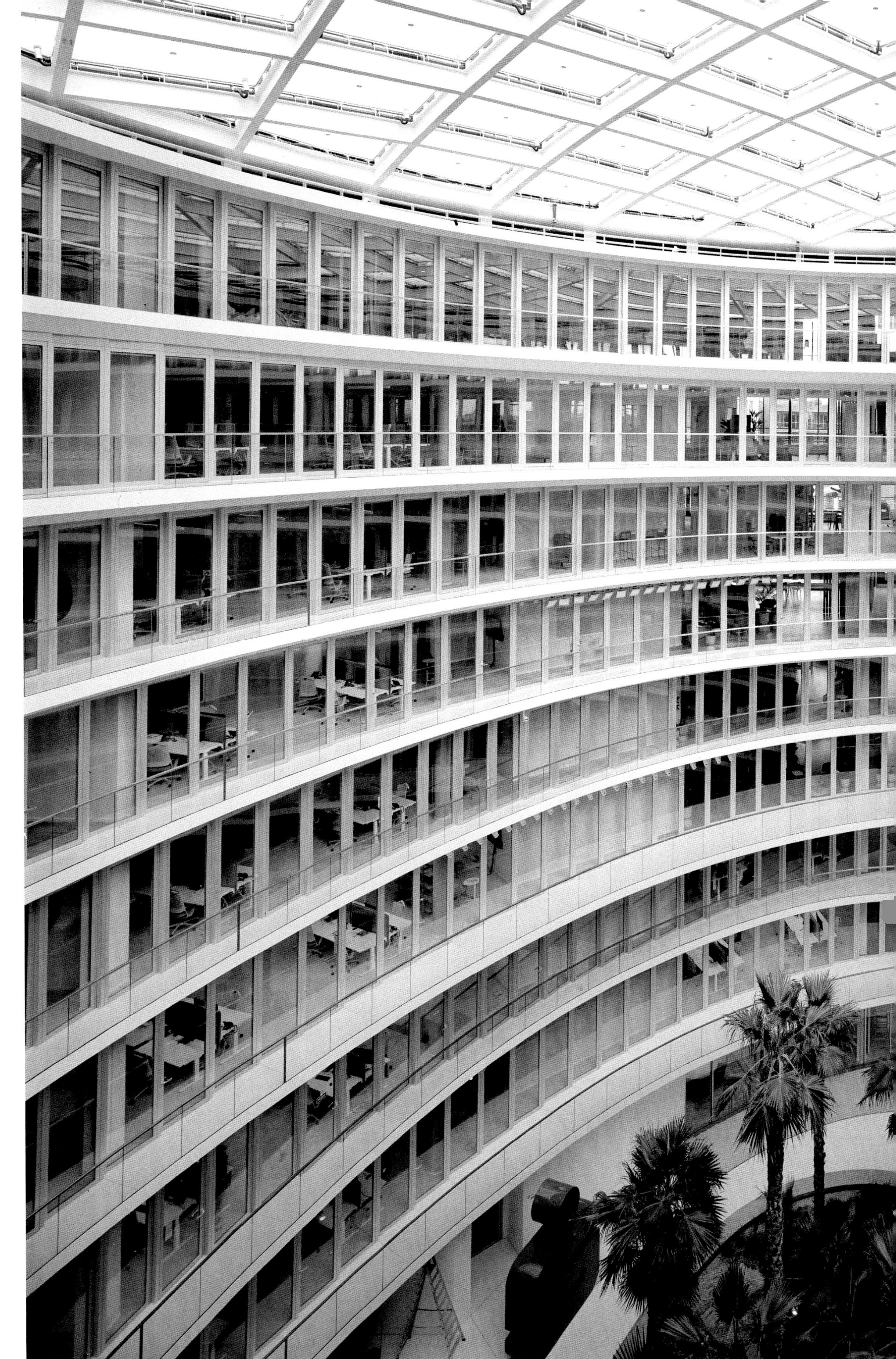

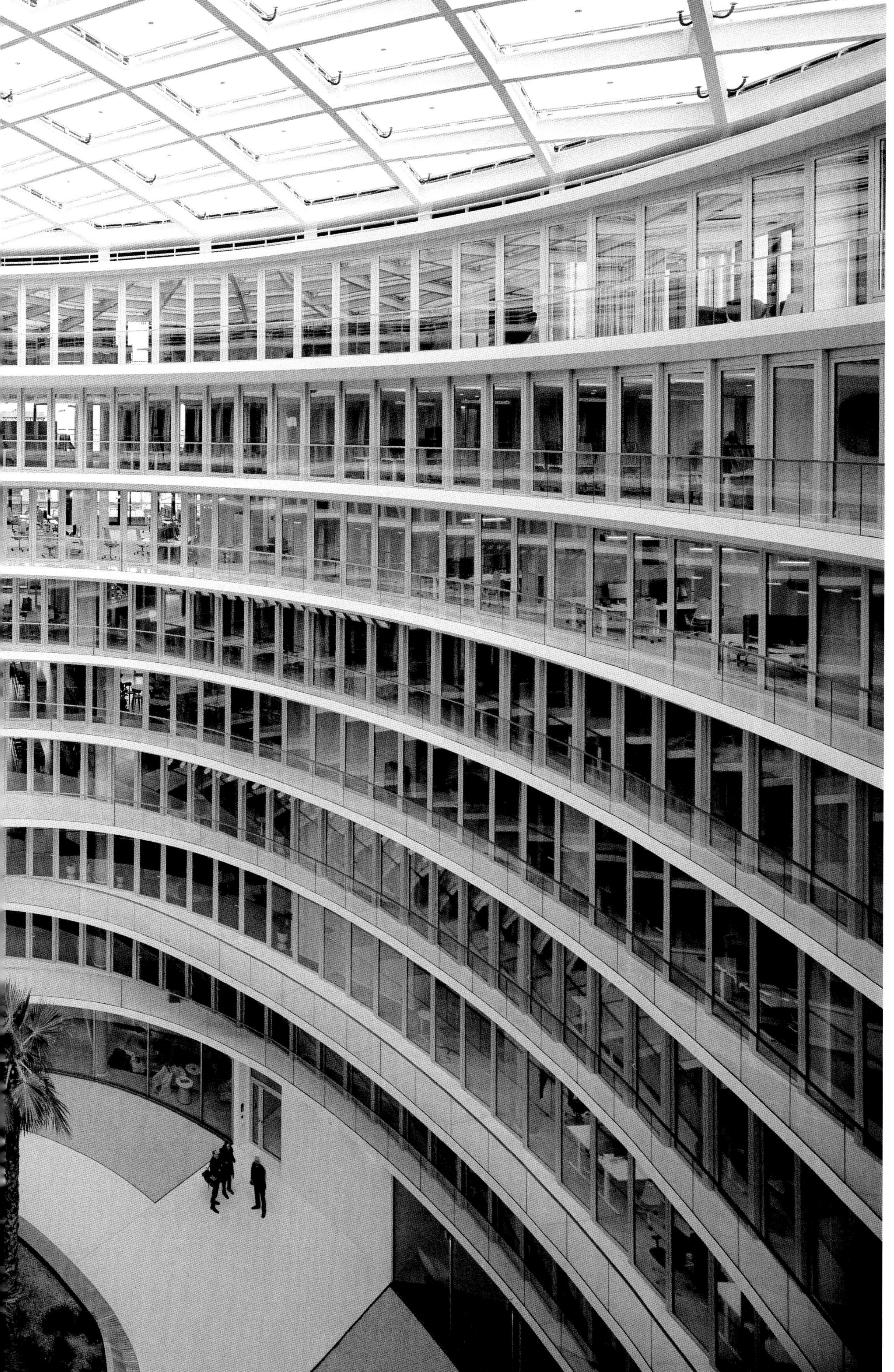

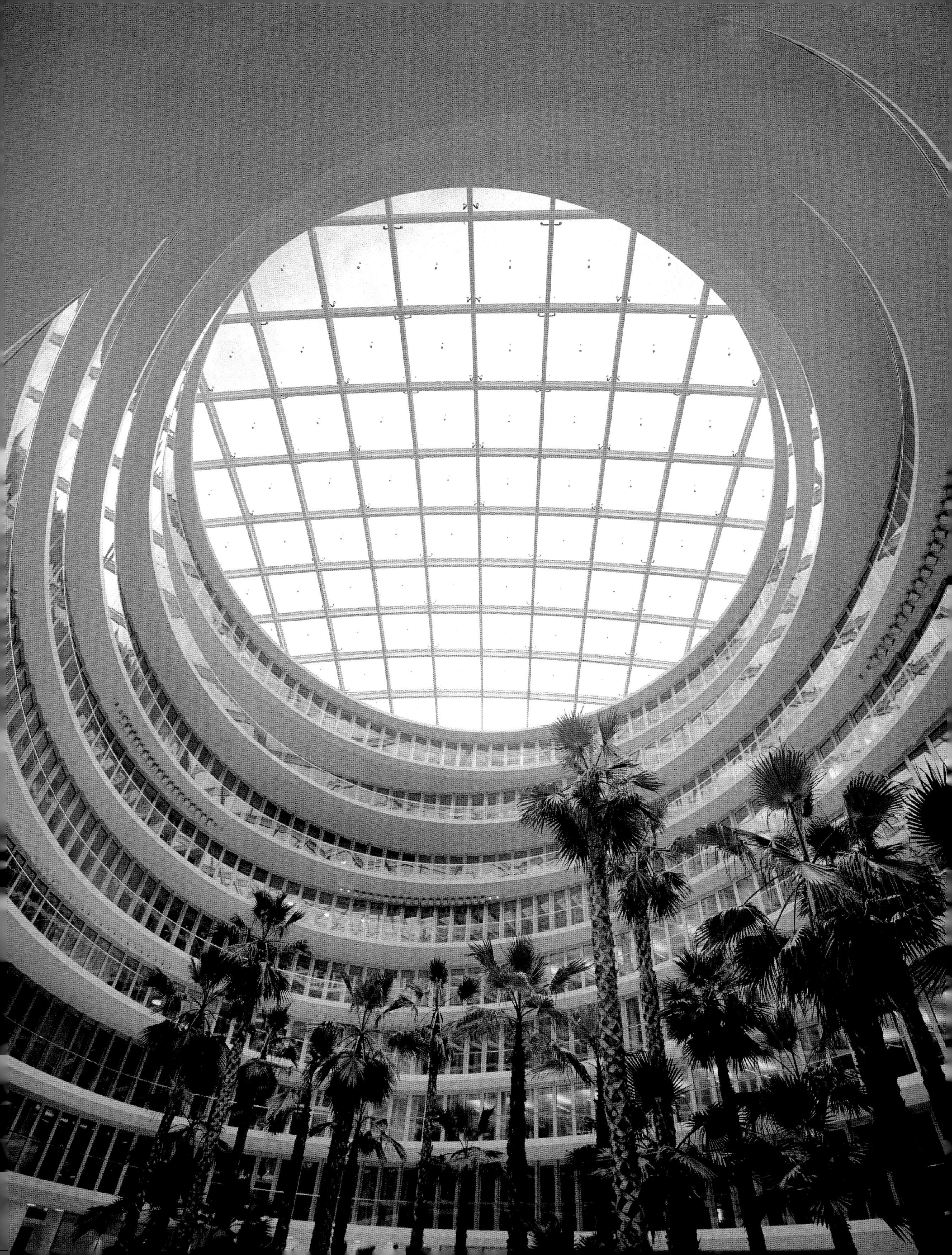

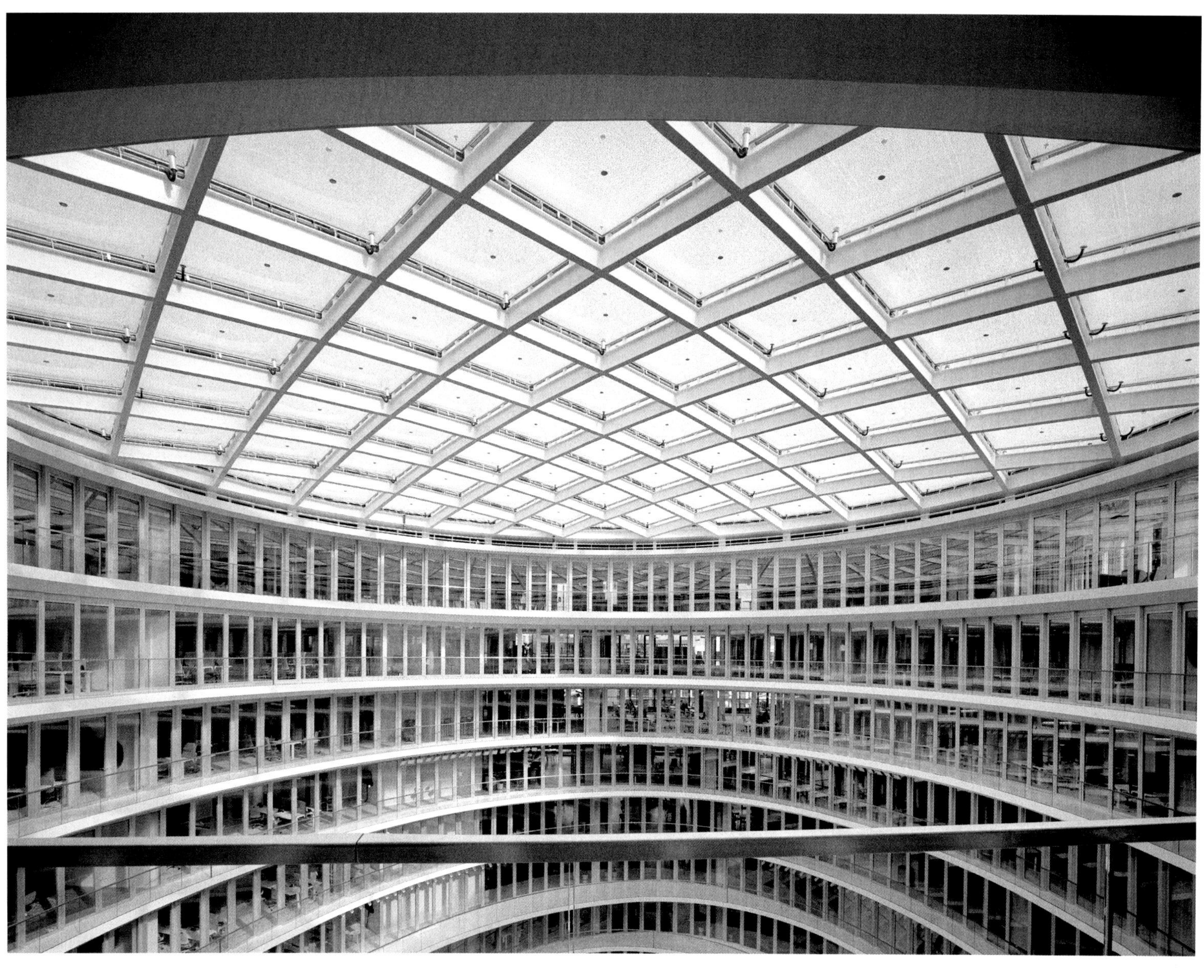

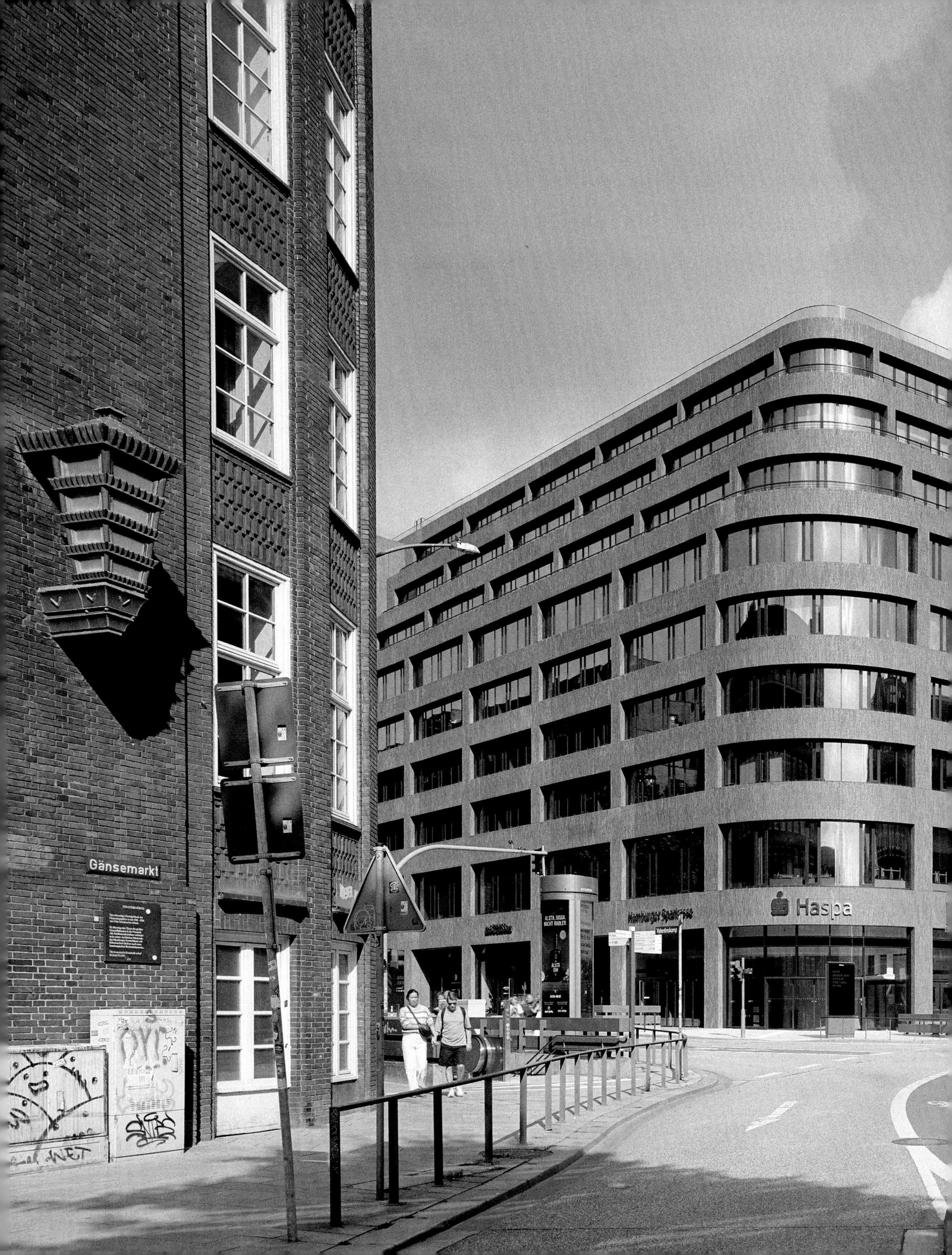
Gänsemarkt
ALSTA, DIGGA.
NICHT RADLER.
ALSTA
GIN
Hamburger Sparkasse
Valentinskamp
Haspa

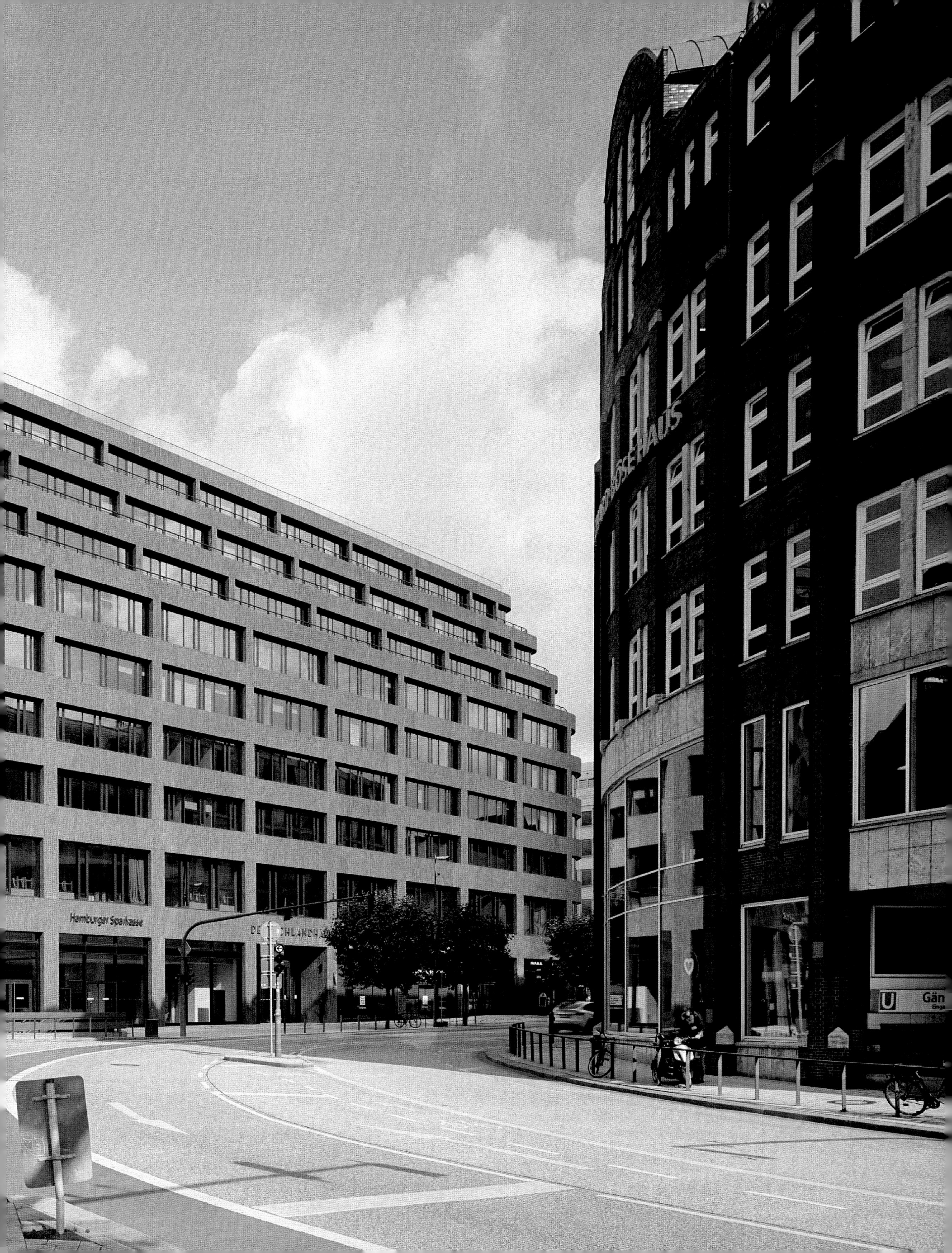
Hamburger Sparkasse

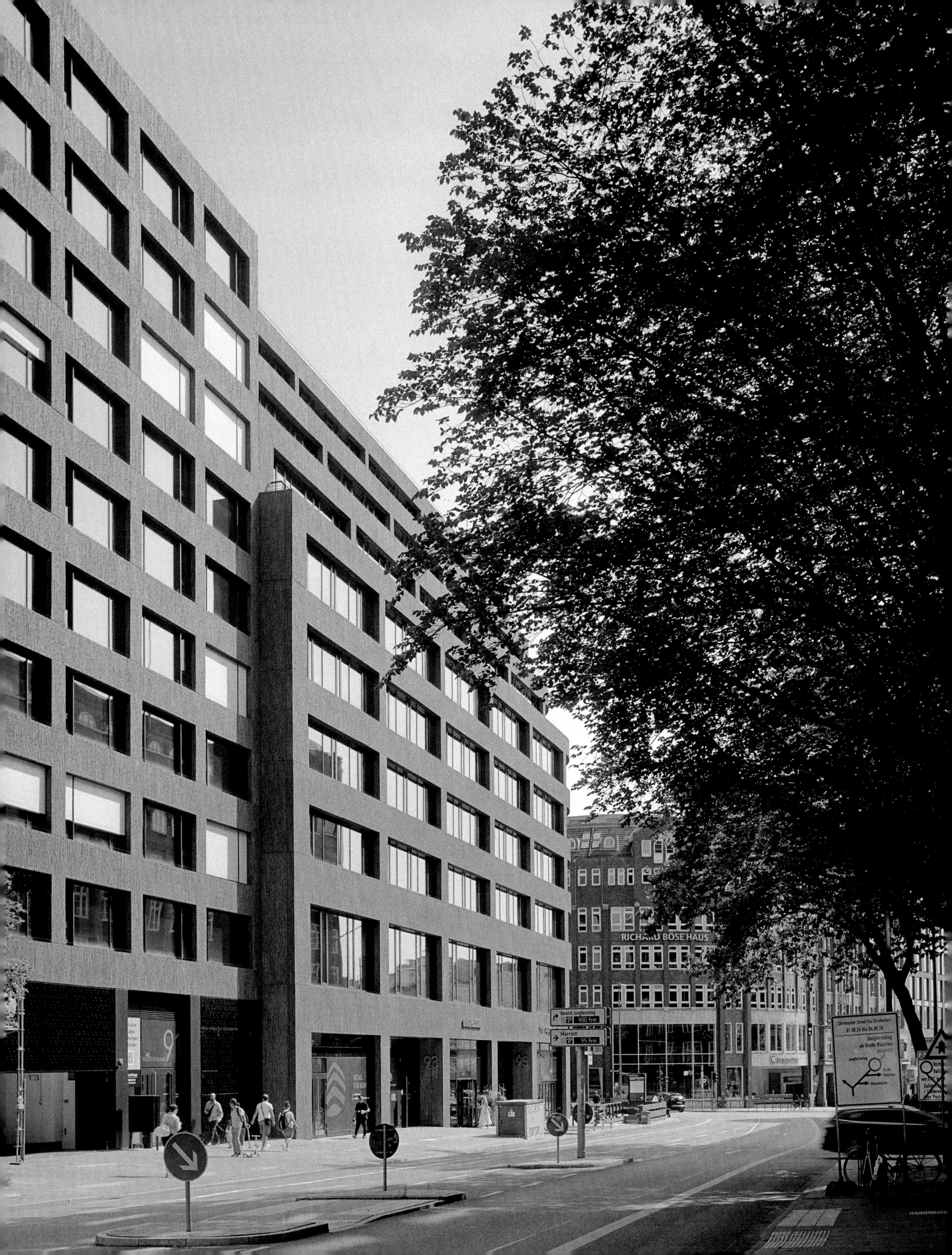
RICHARD BÖSE HAUS
Bereich Jungfernstieg
400 frei
Marriott
45 frei
93
95

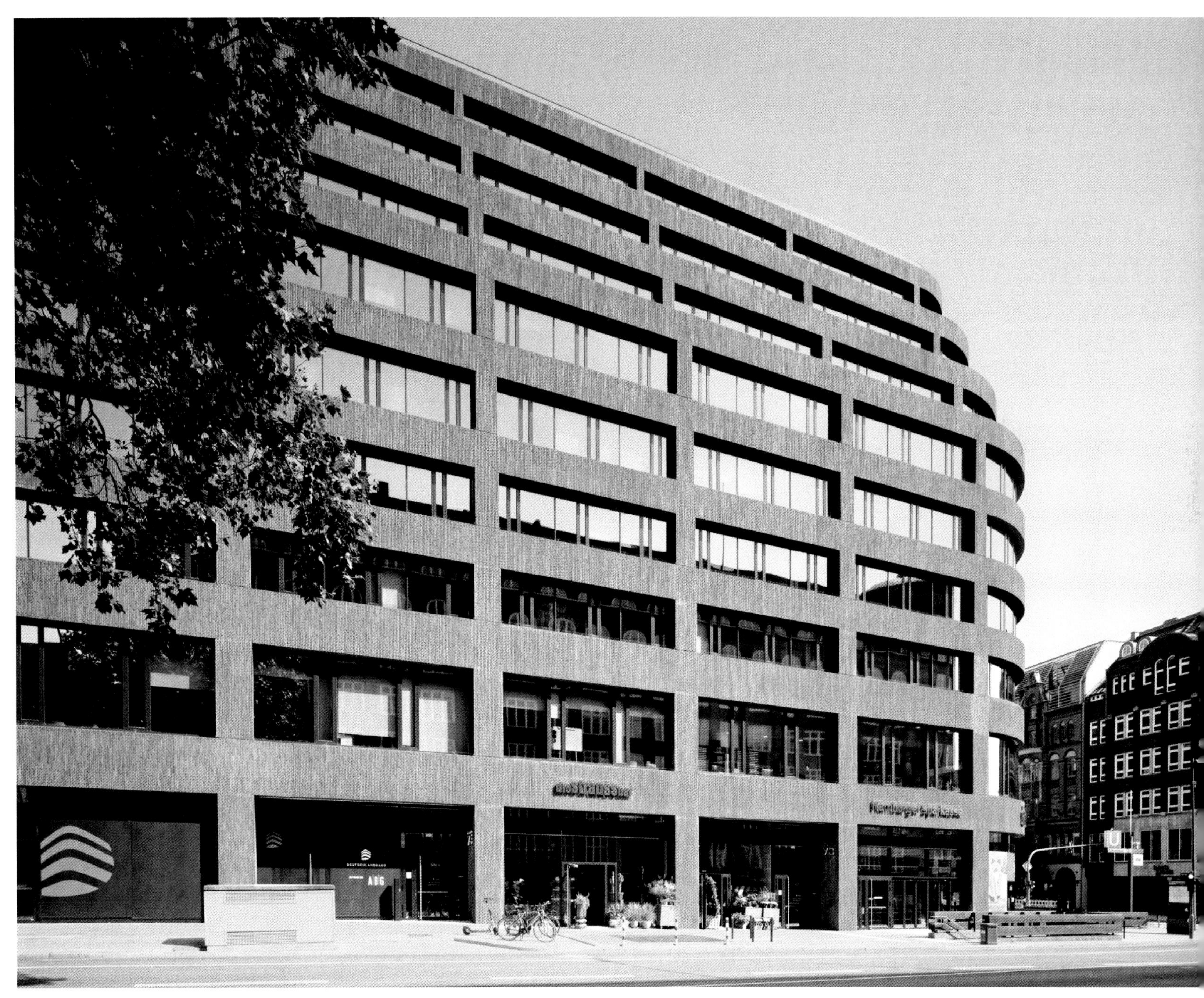

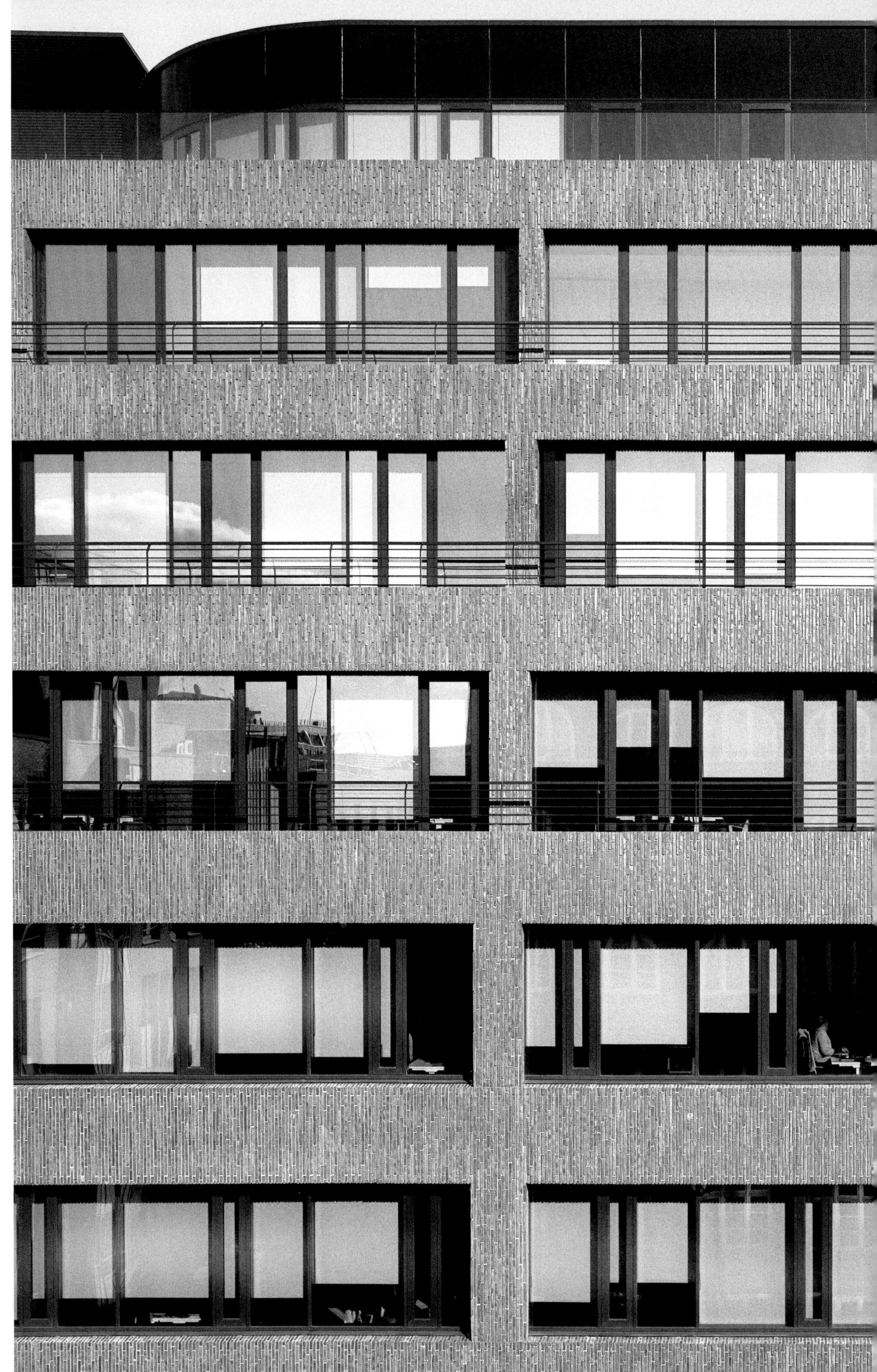

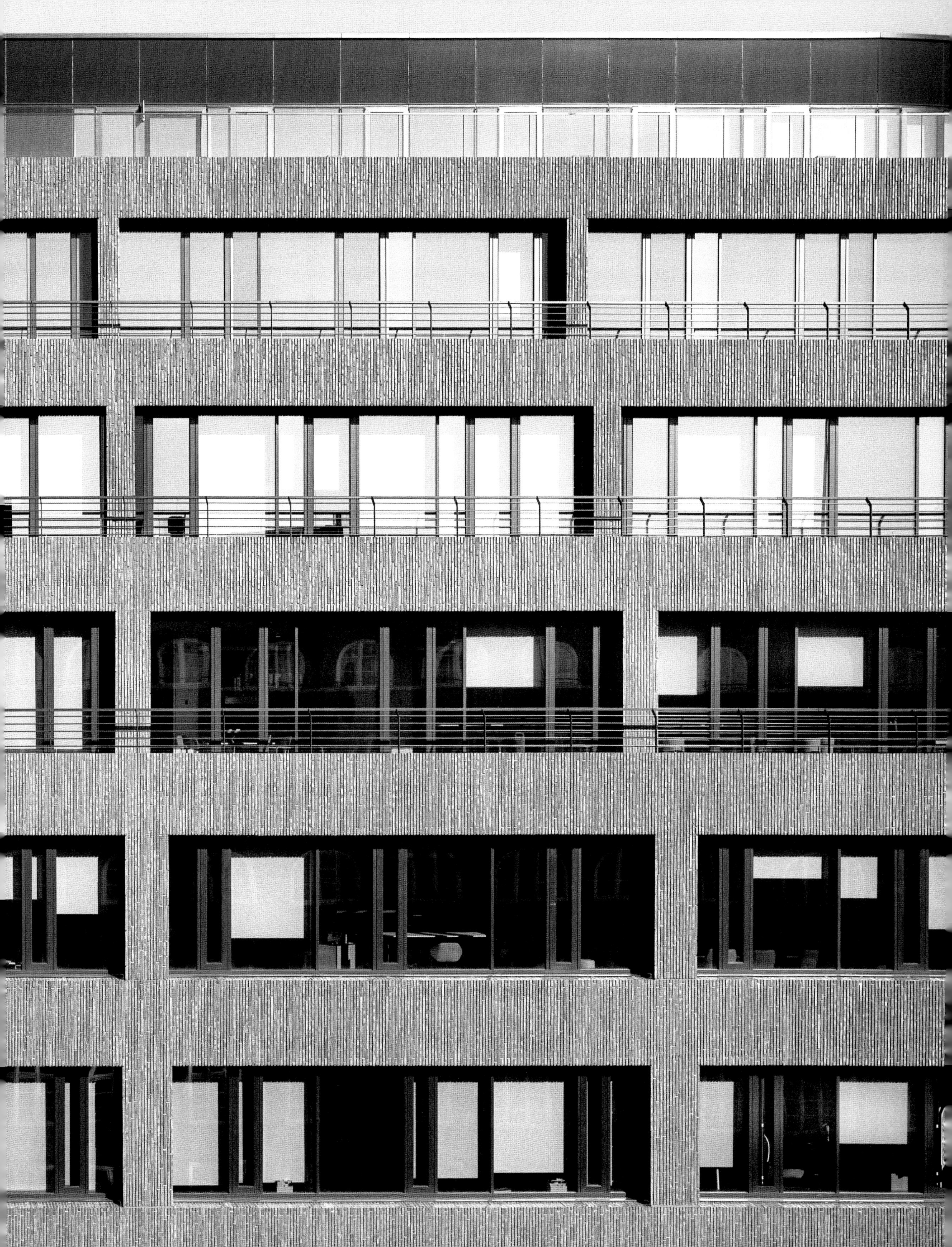

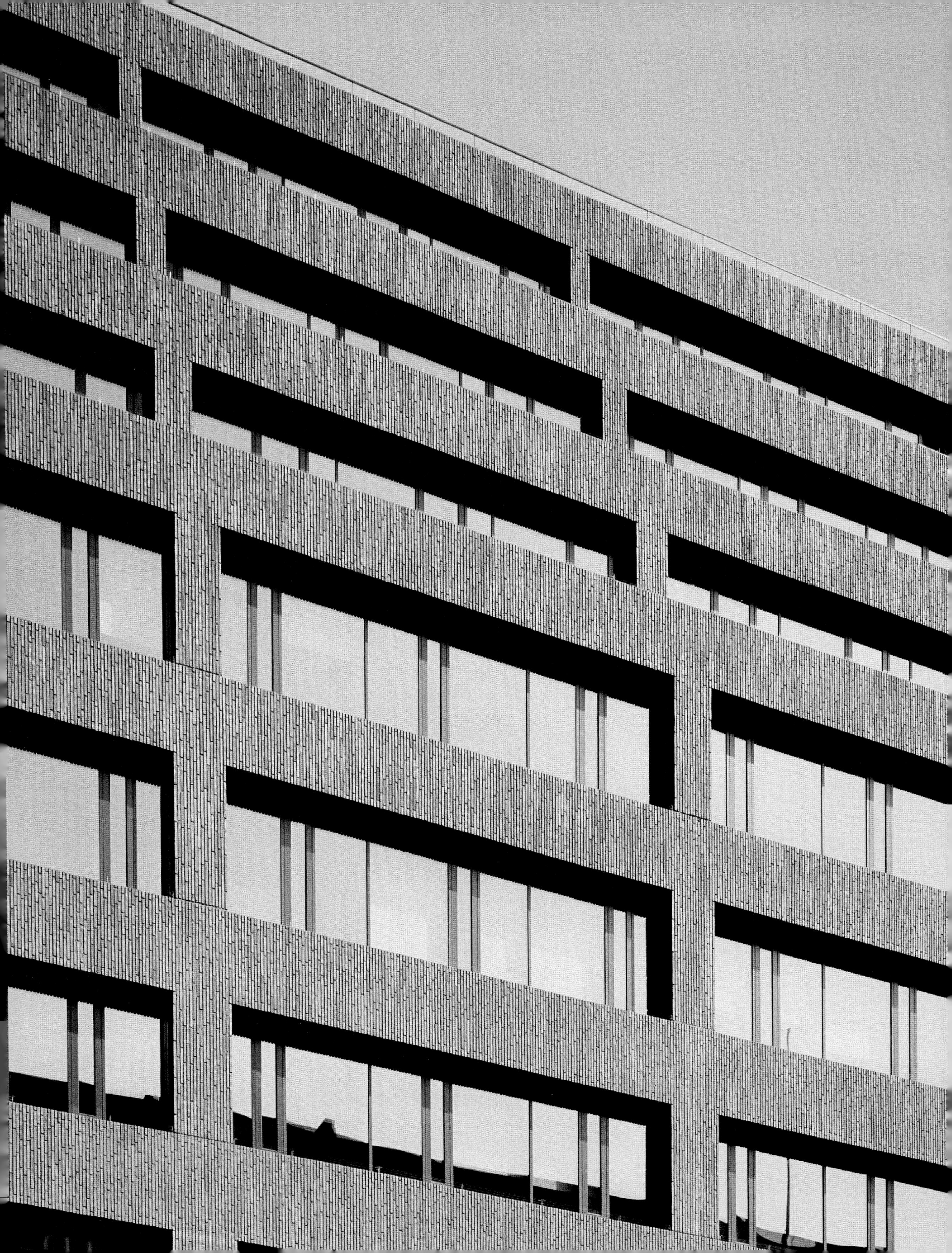

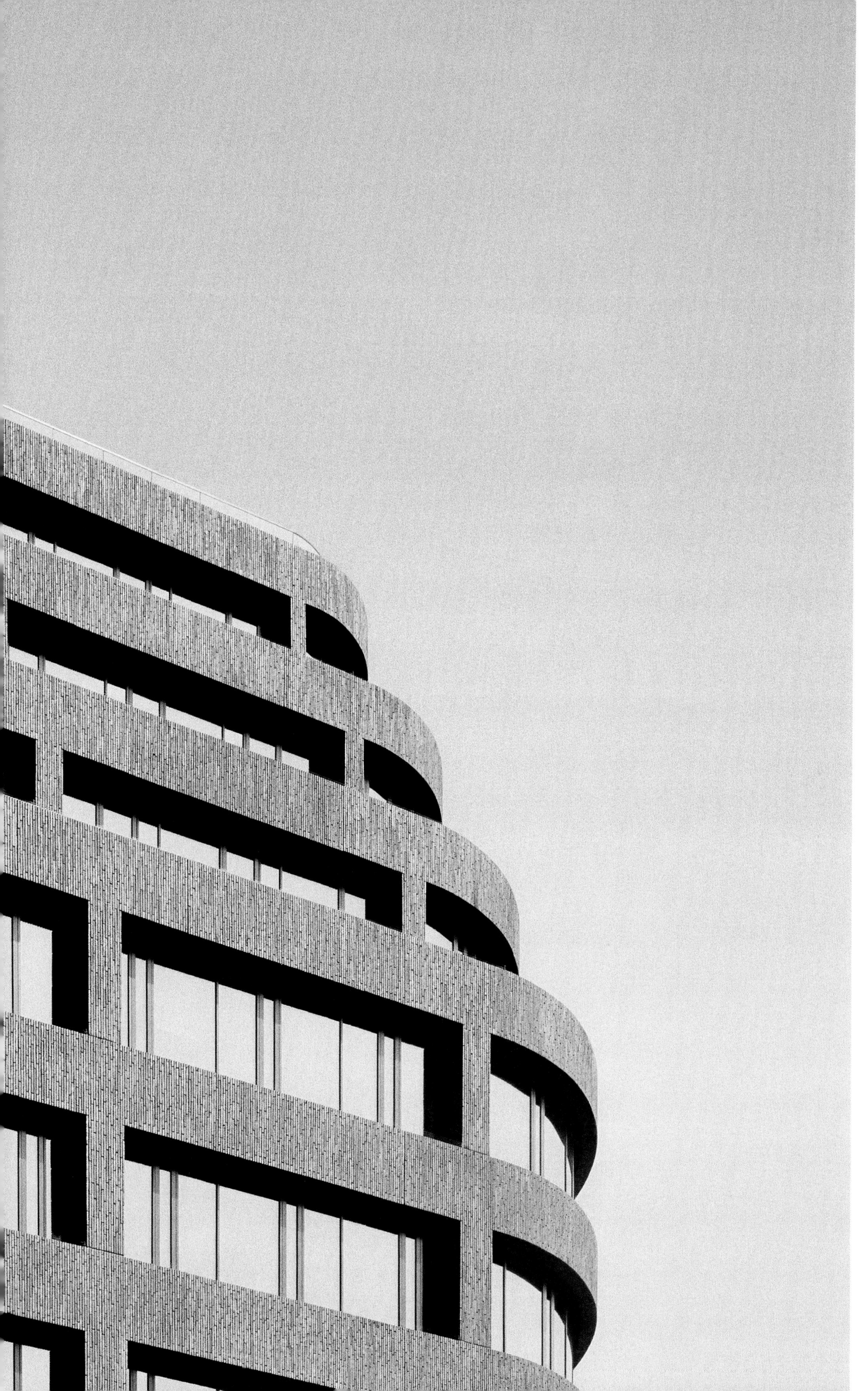

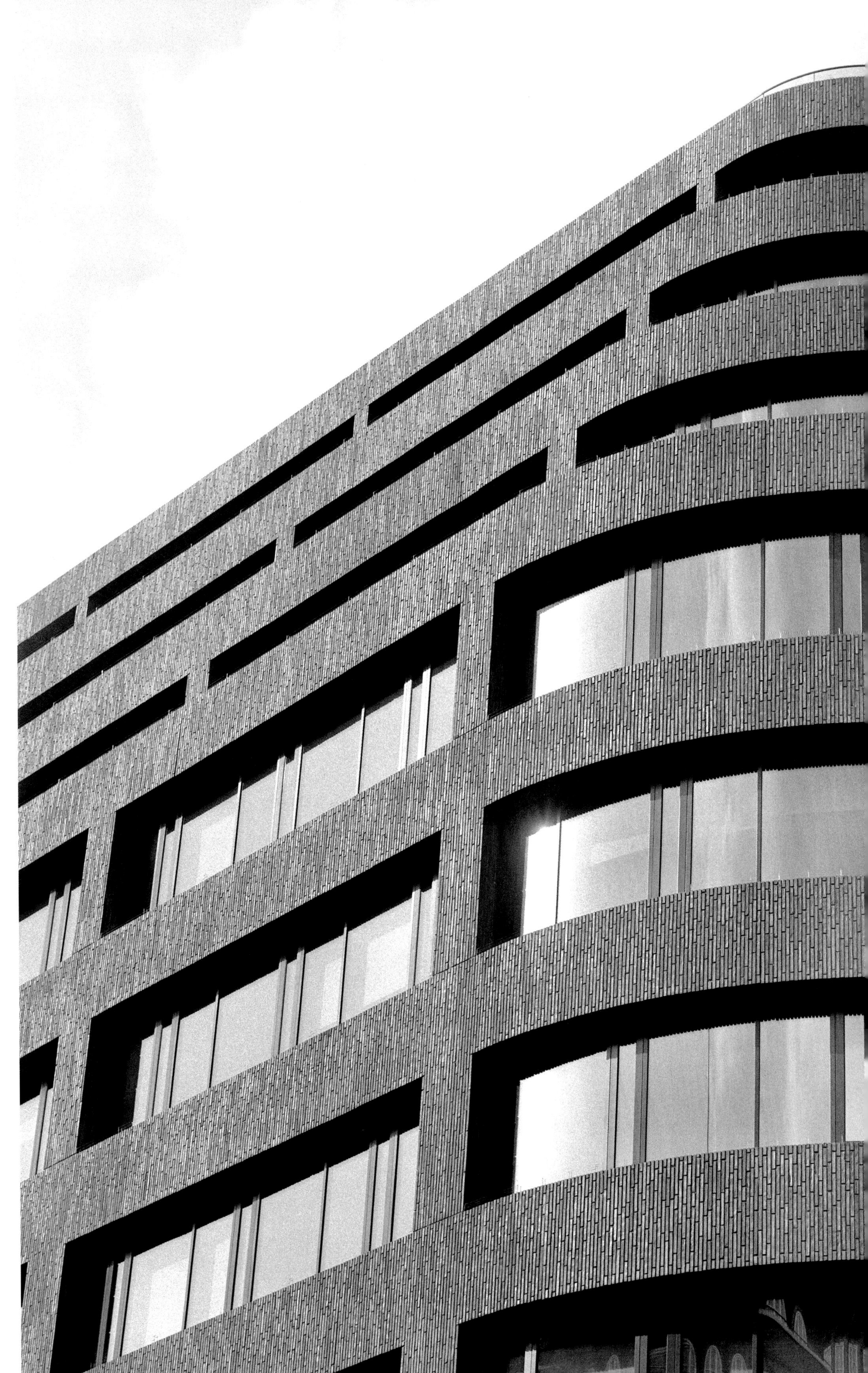

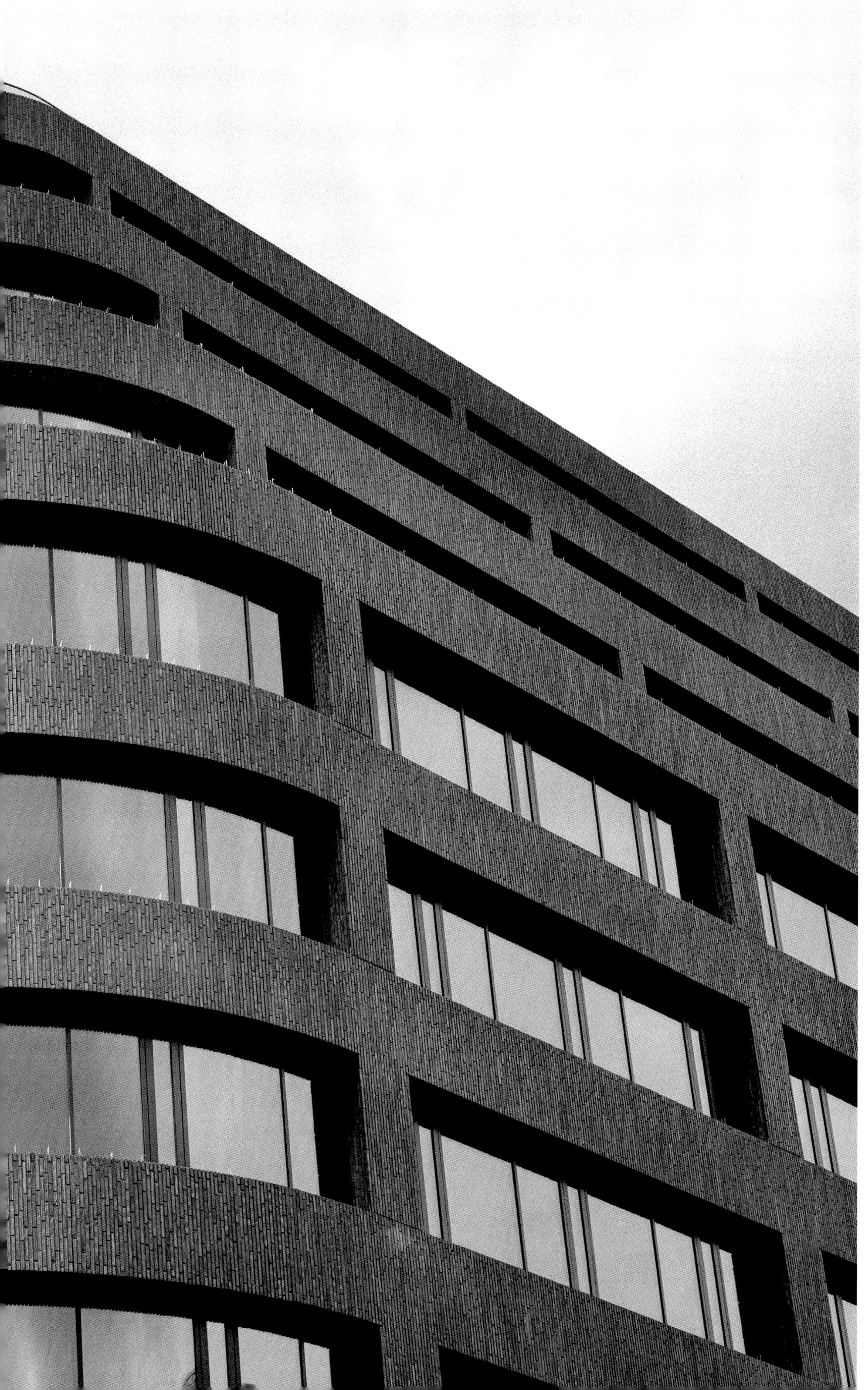

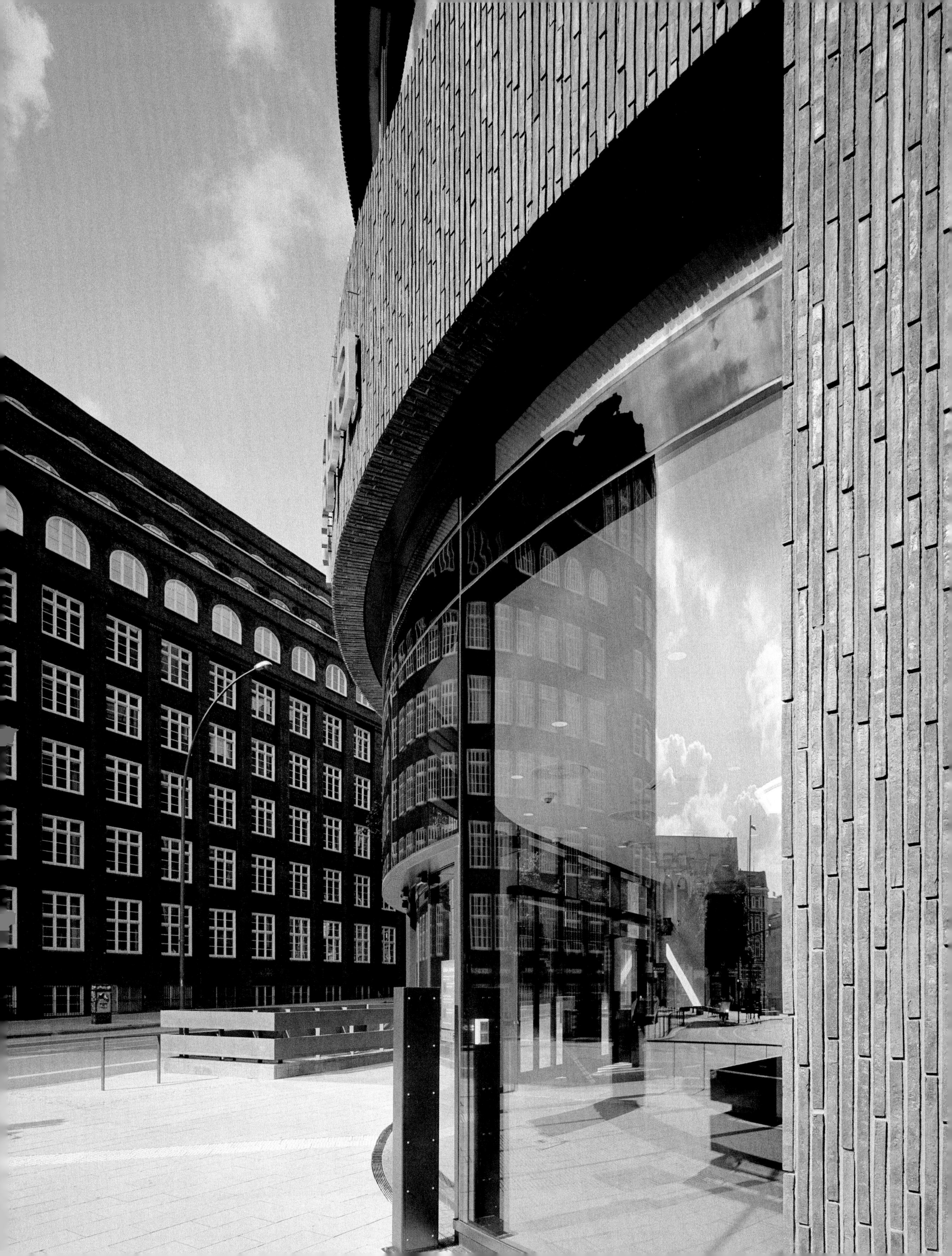

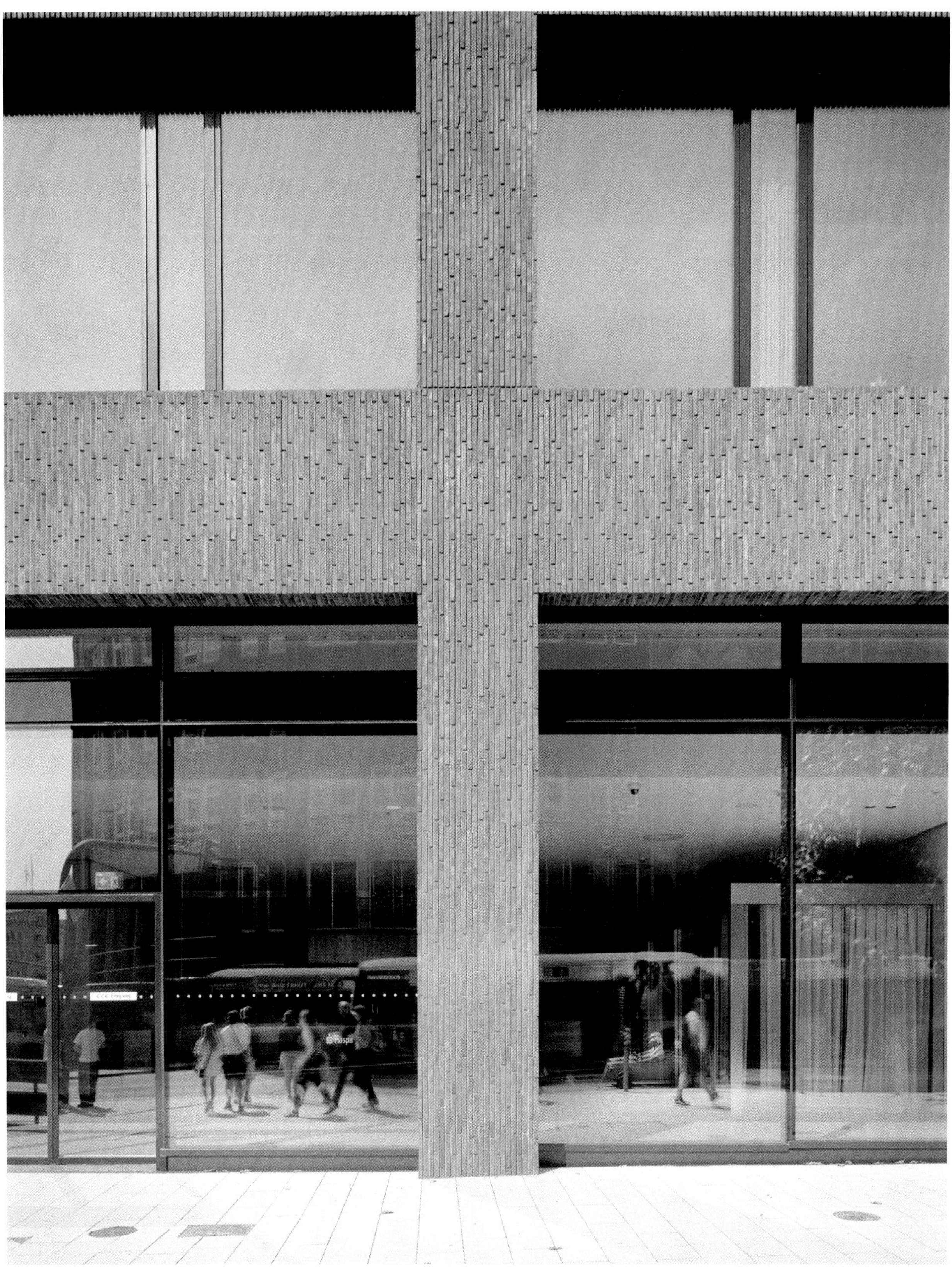

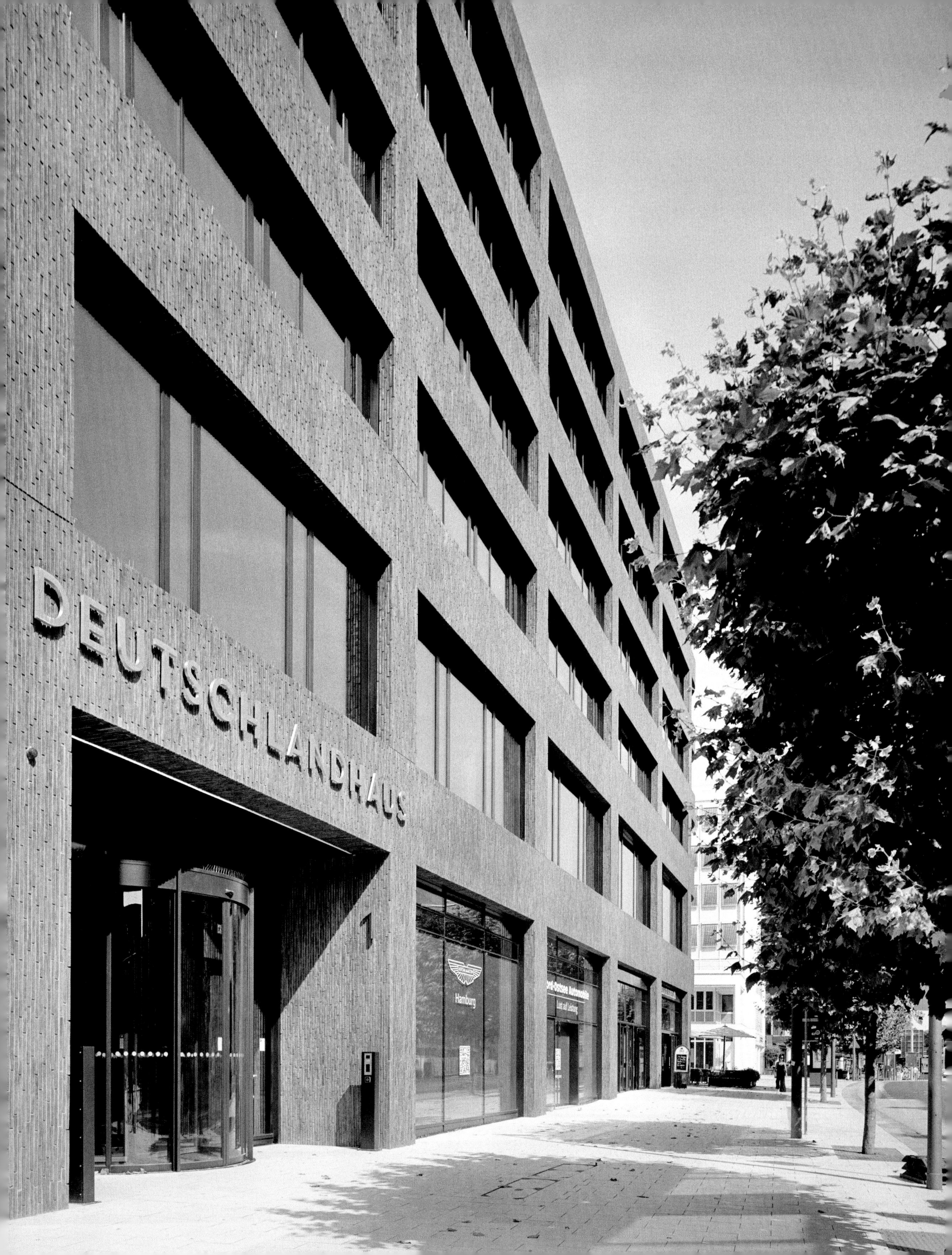
DEUTSCHLANDHAUS
Hamburg

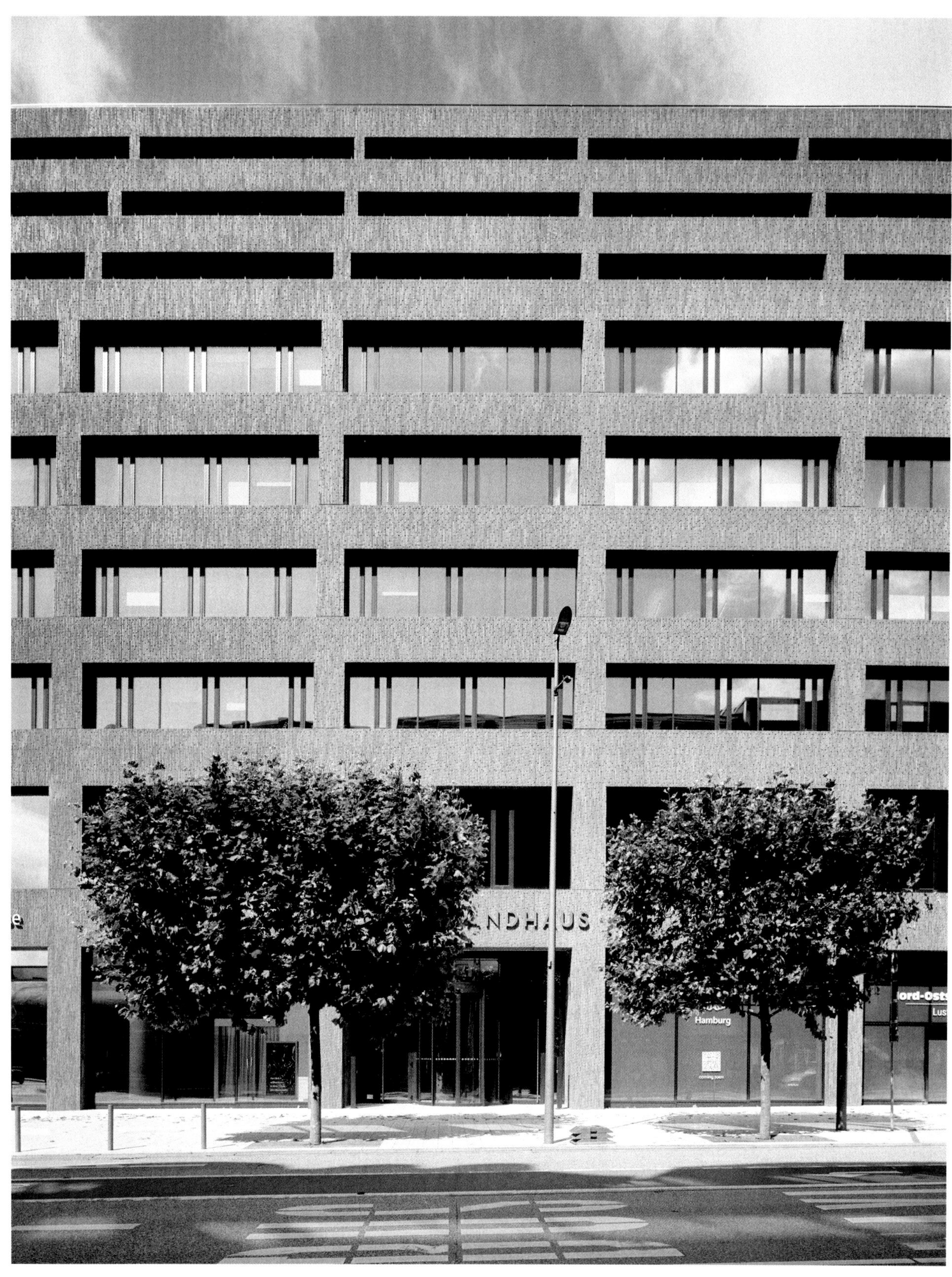
NDHAUS
Hamburg

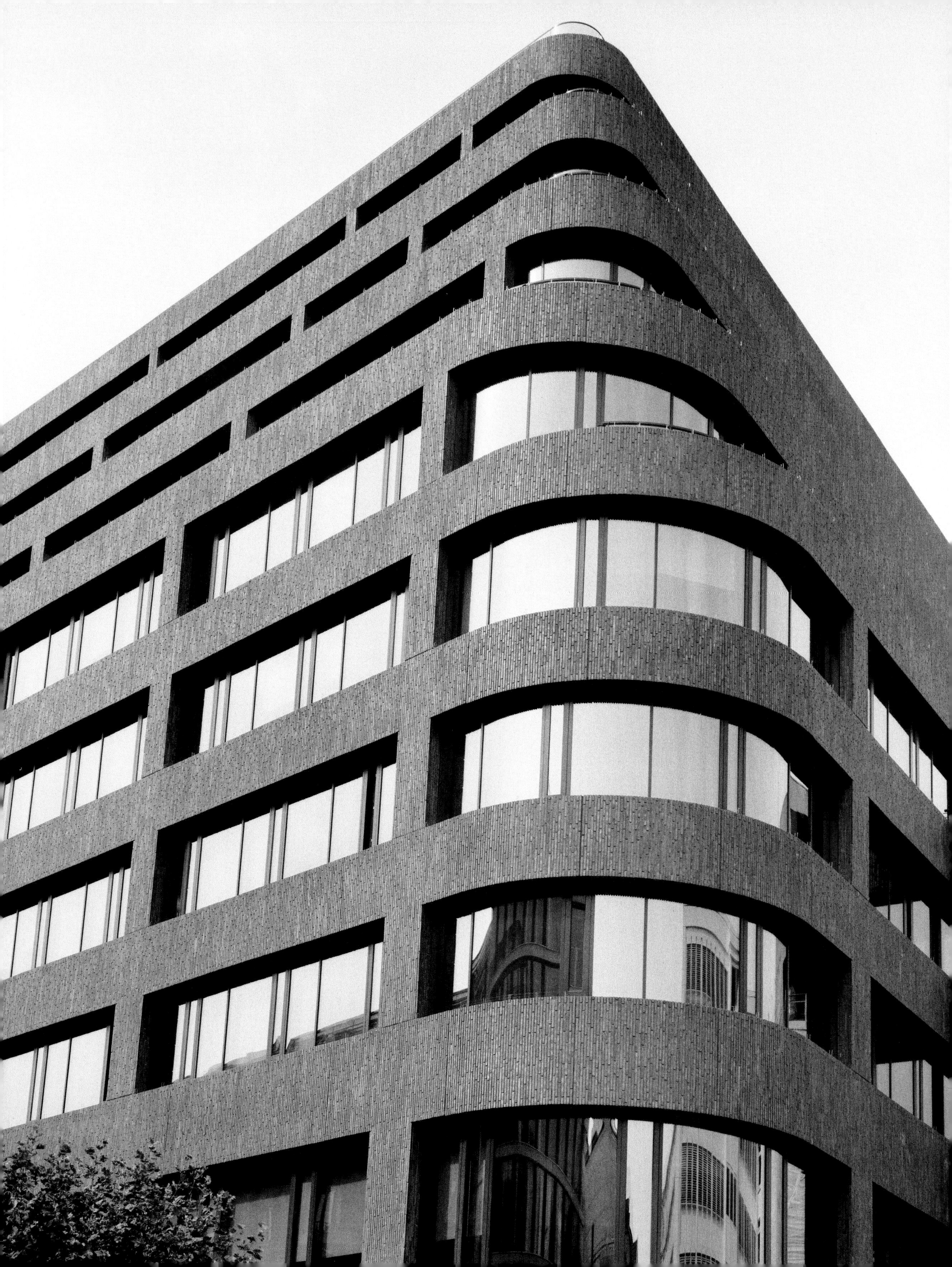

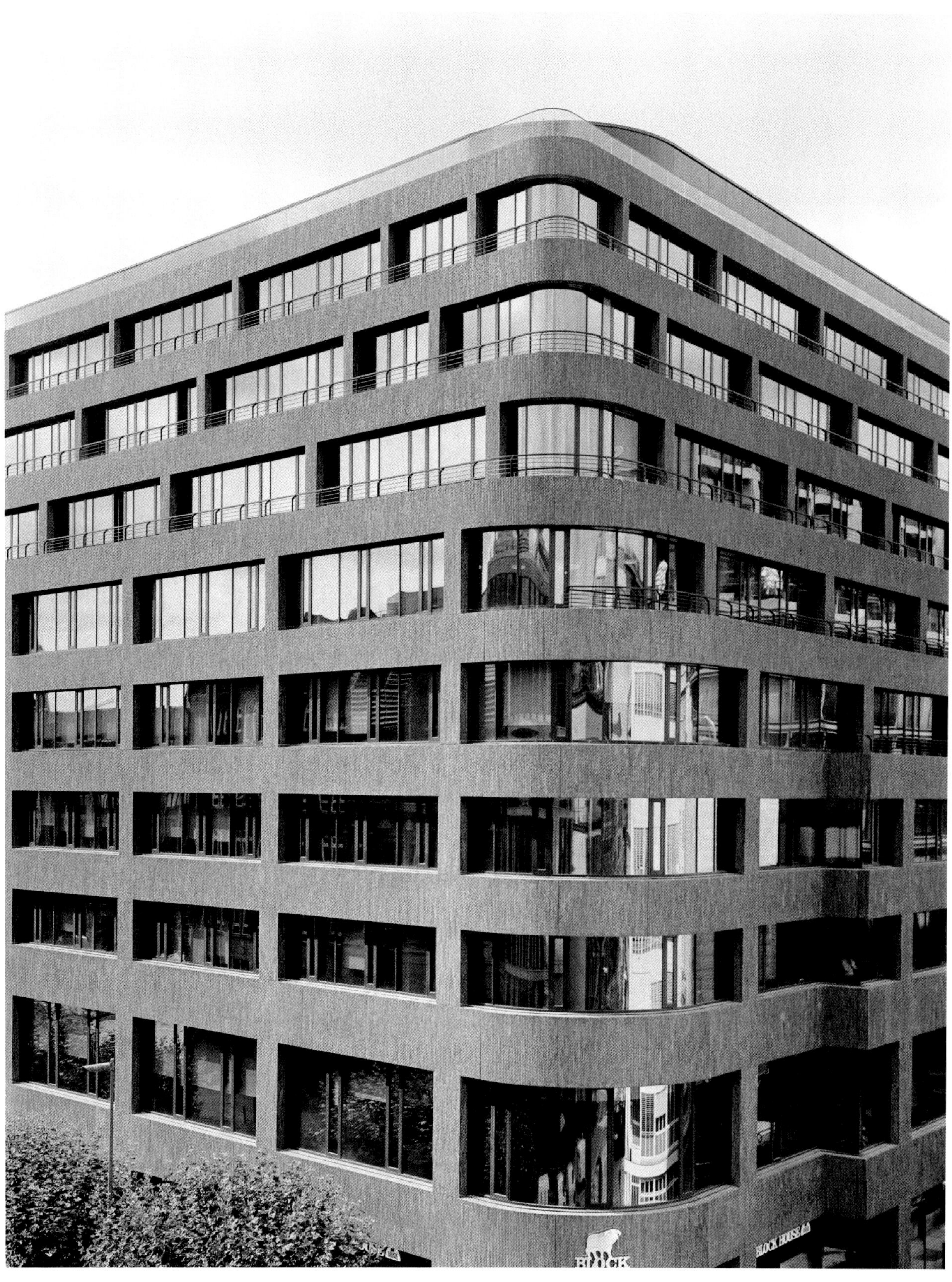
BLOCK HOUSE

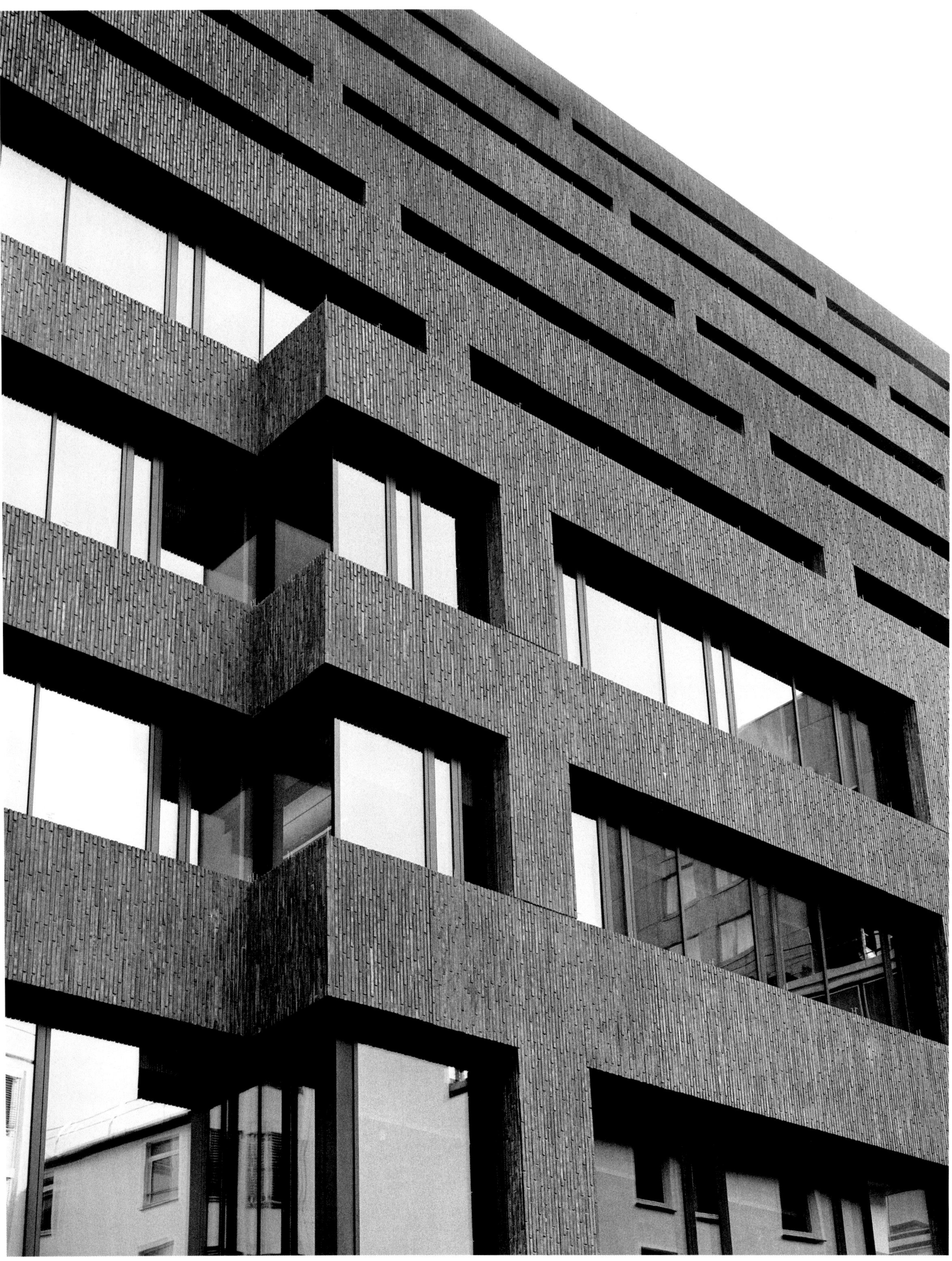

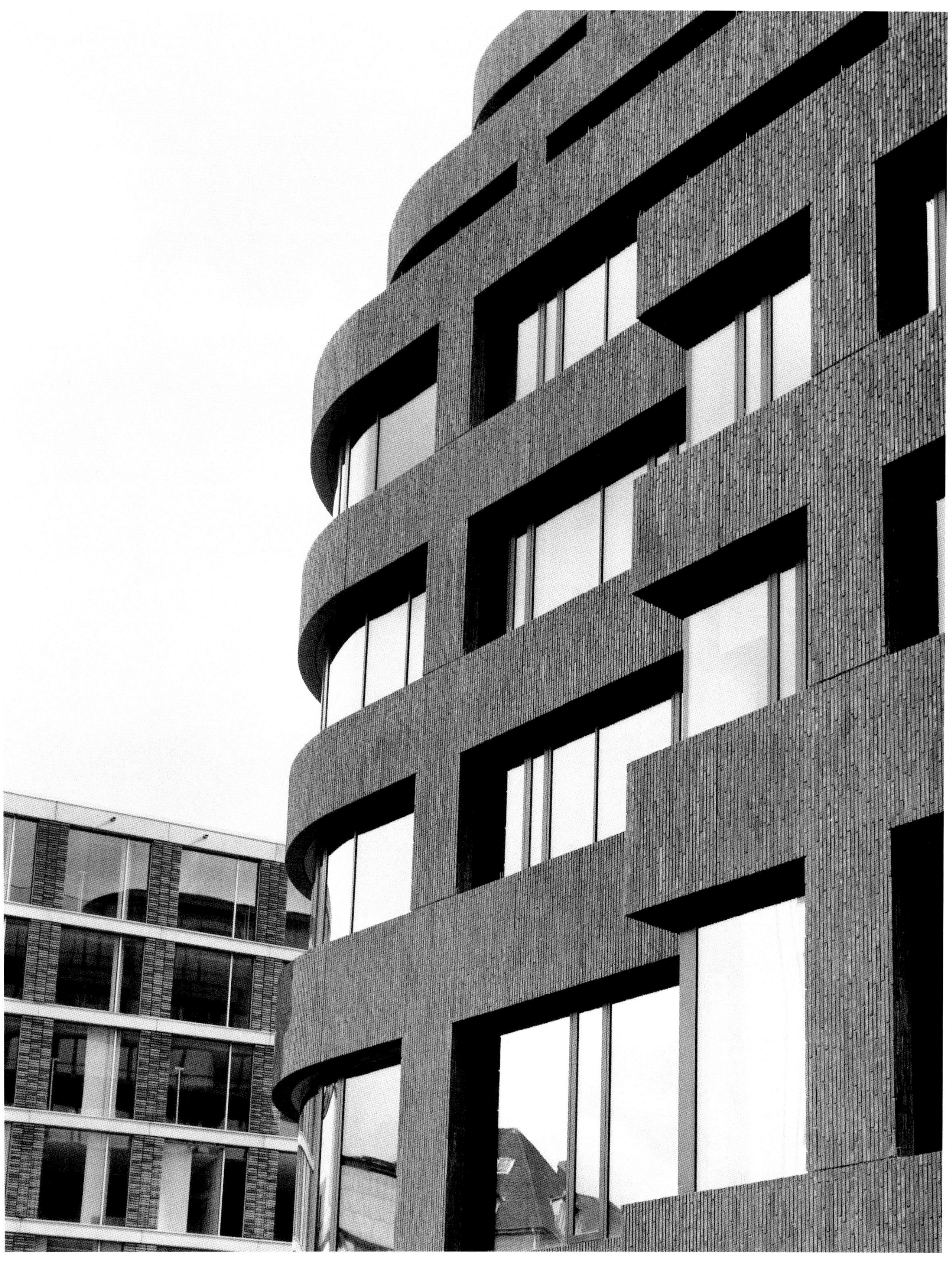

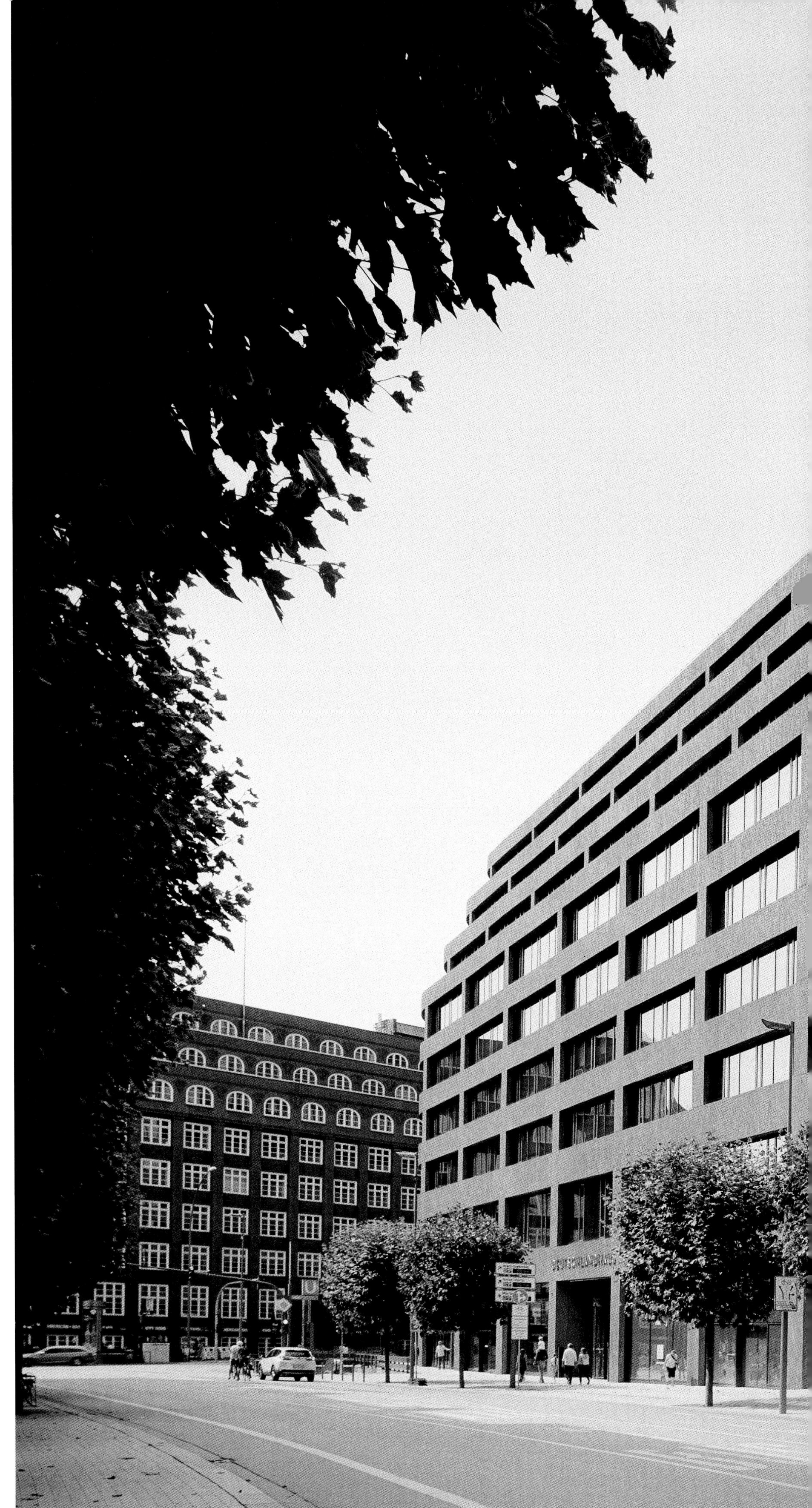

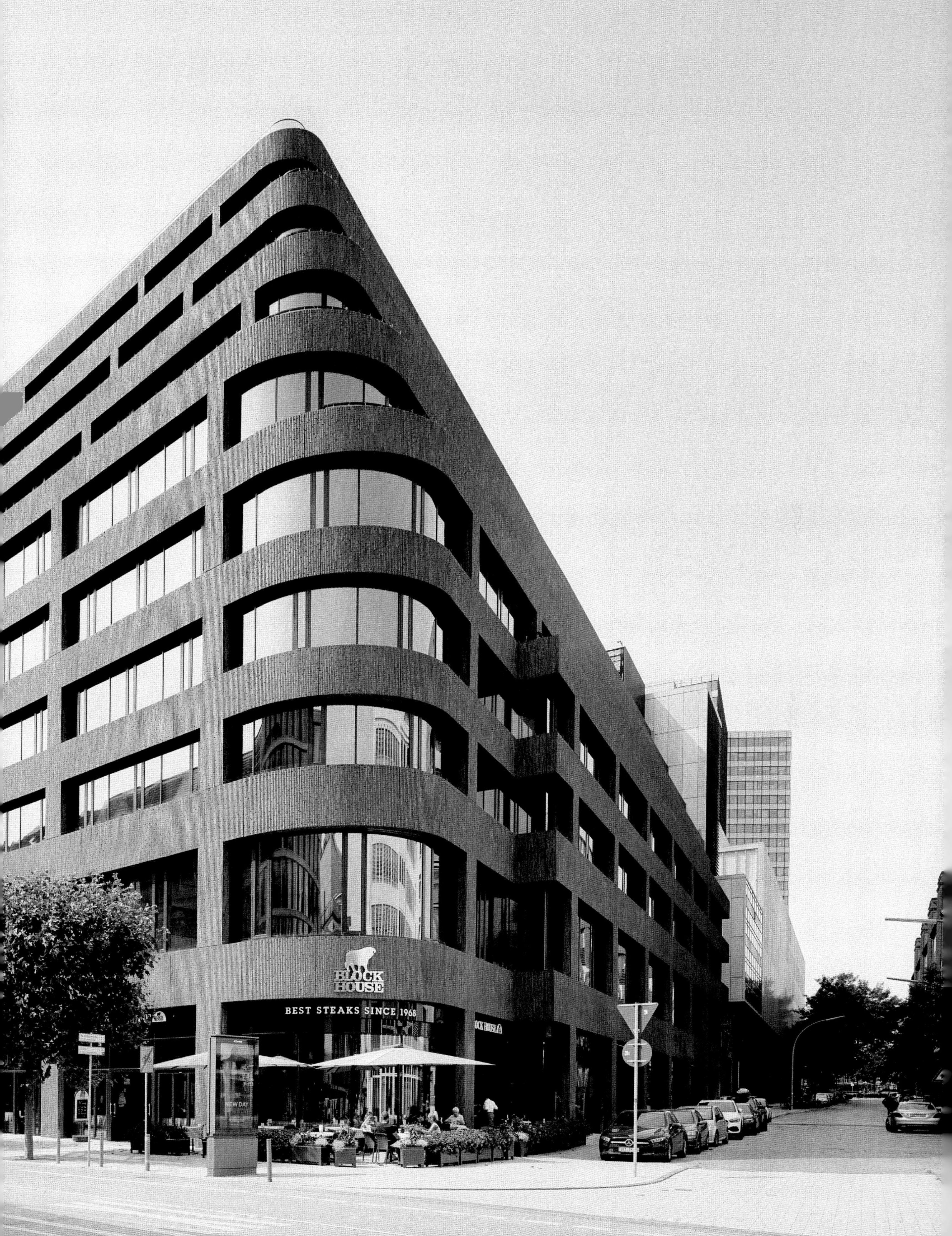
BLOCK HOUSE
BEST STEAKS SINCE 1968
NEW DAY

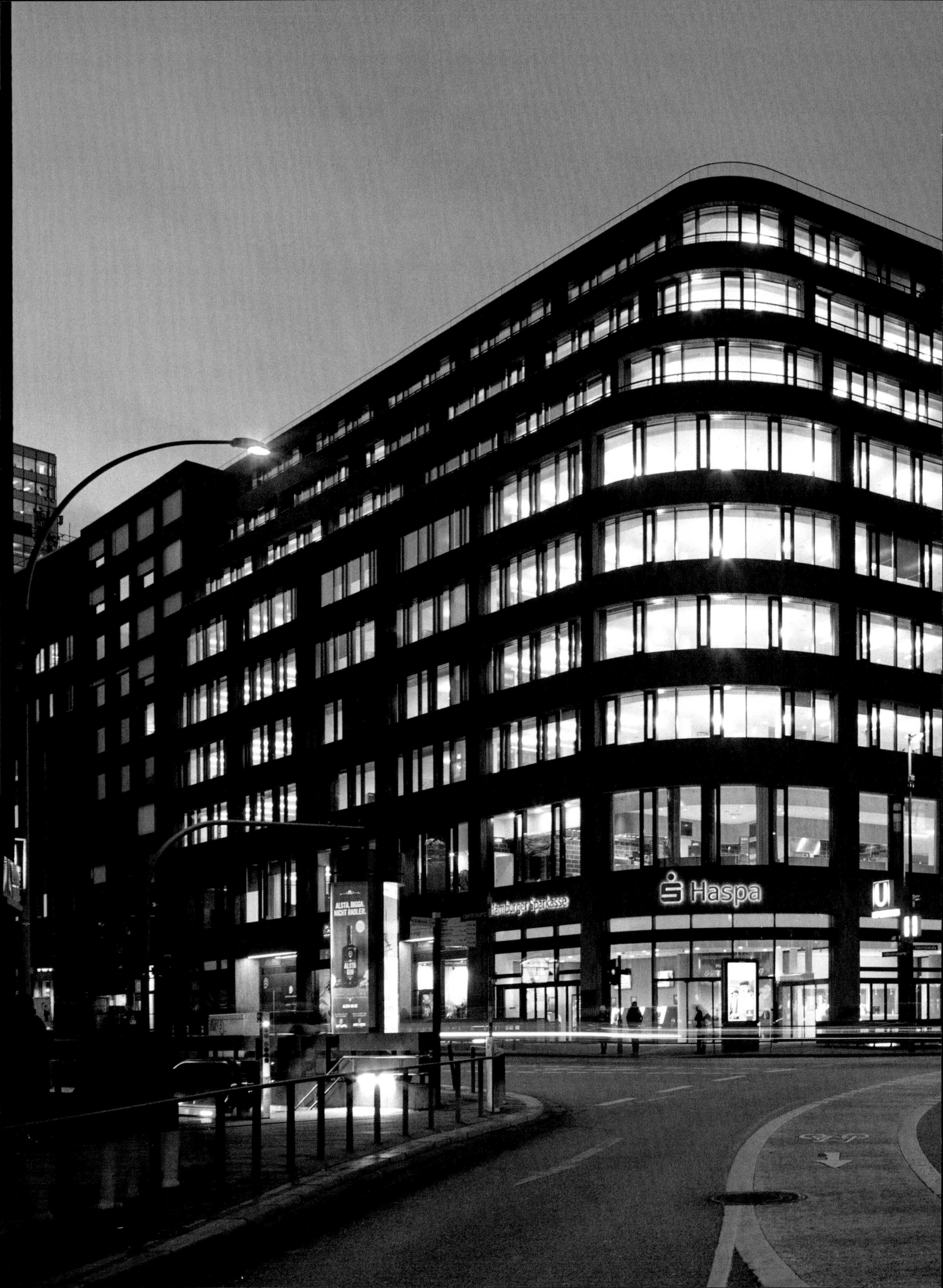
ALSTA, DIGGA.
NICHT RADLER.
ALSTA
GIN
Hamburger Sparkasse
Haspa
U

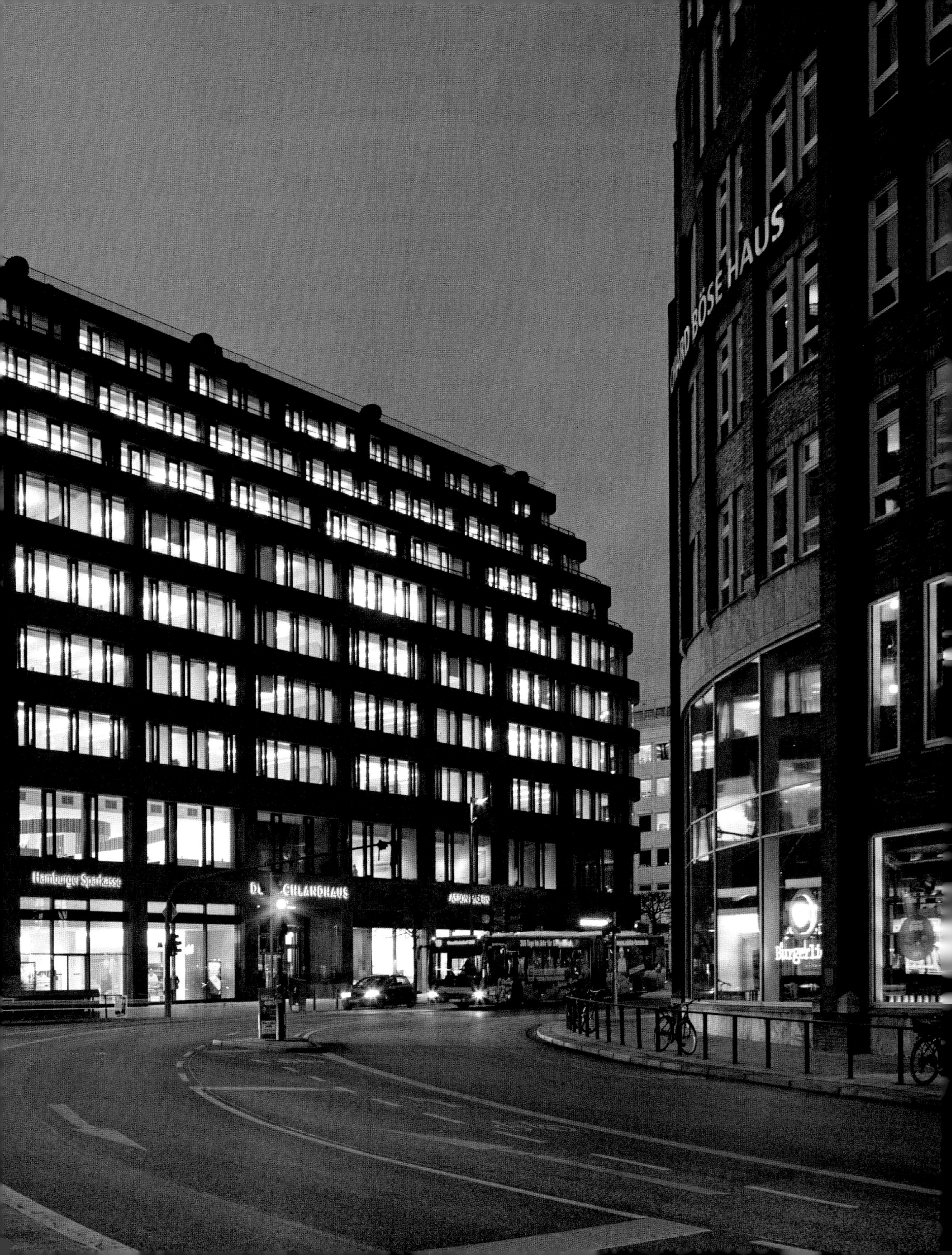
BÖSE HAUS
Hamburger Sparkasse

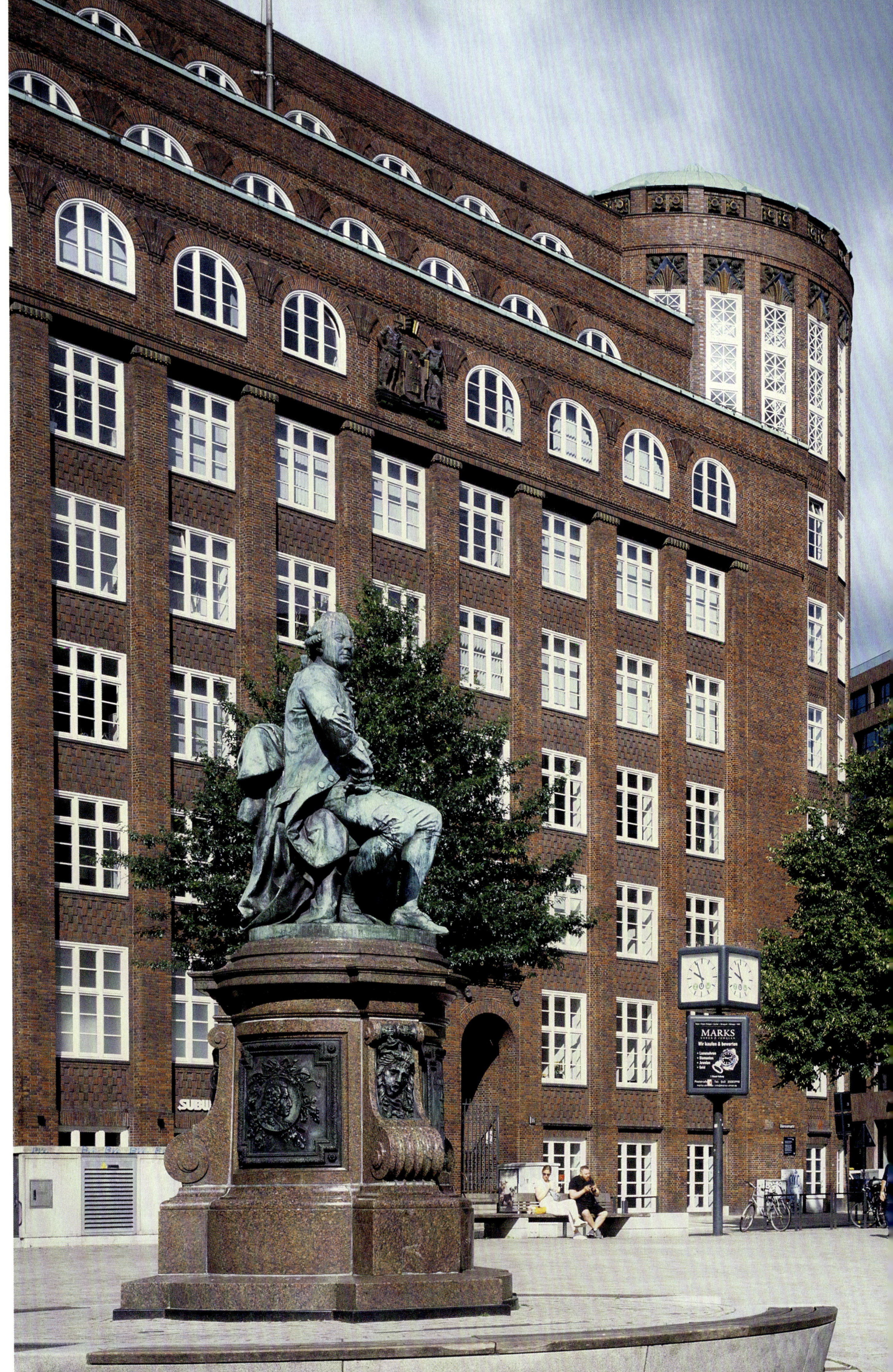
MARKS
Wir kaufen & bewerten

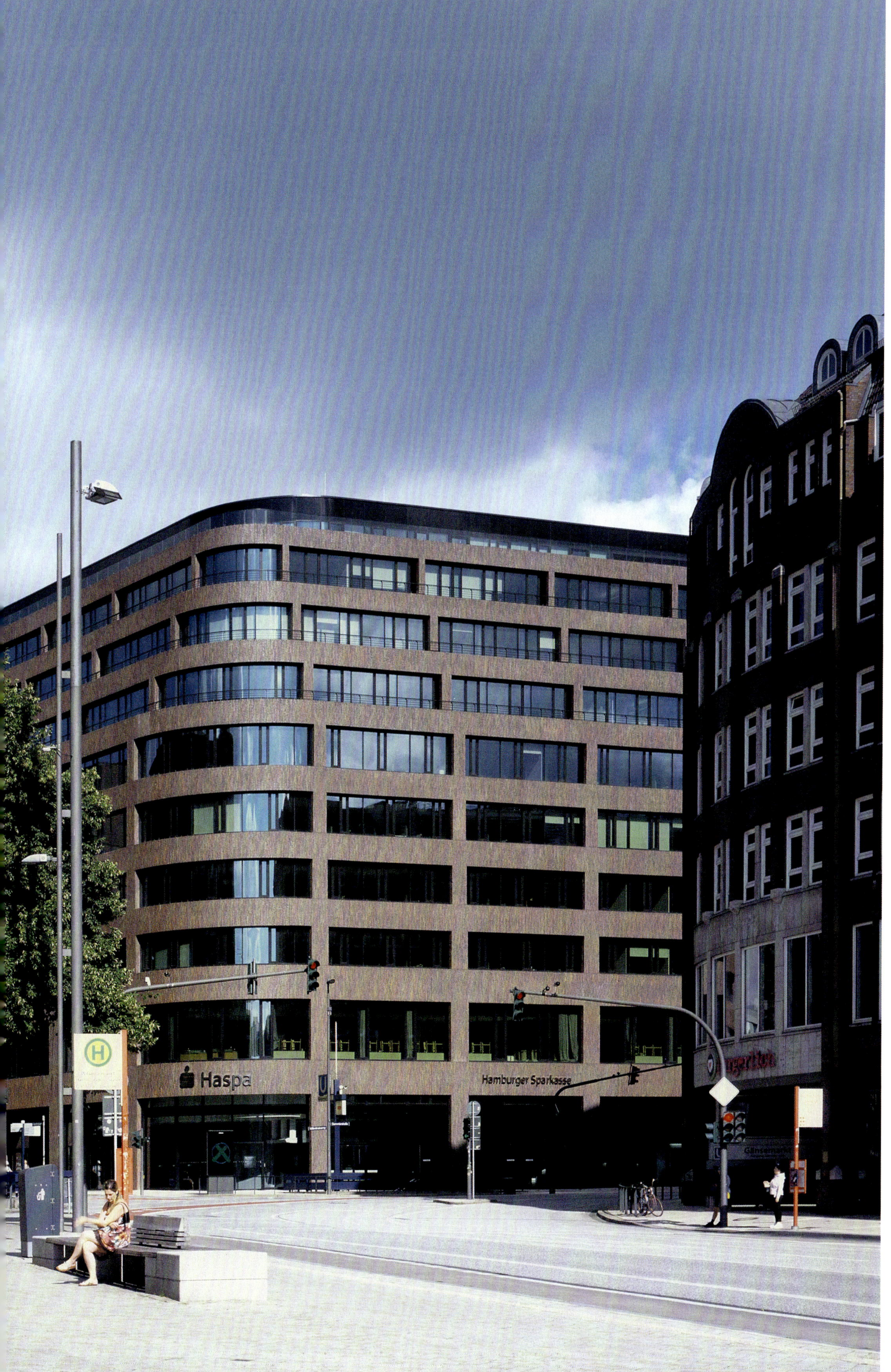
Haspa
Hamburger Sparkasse

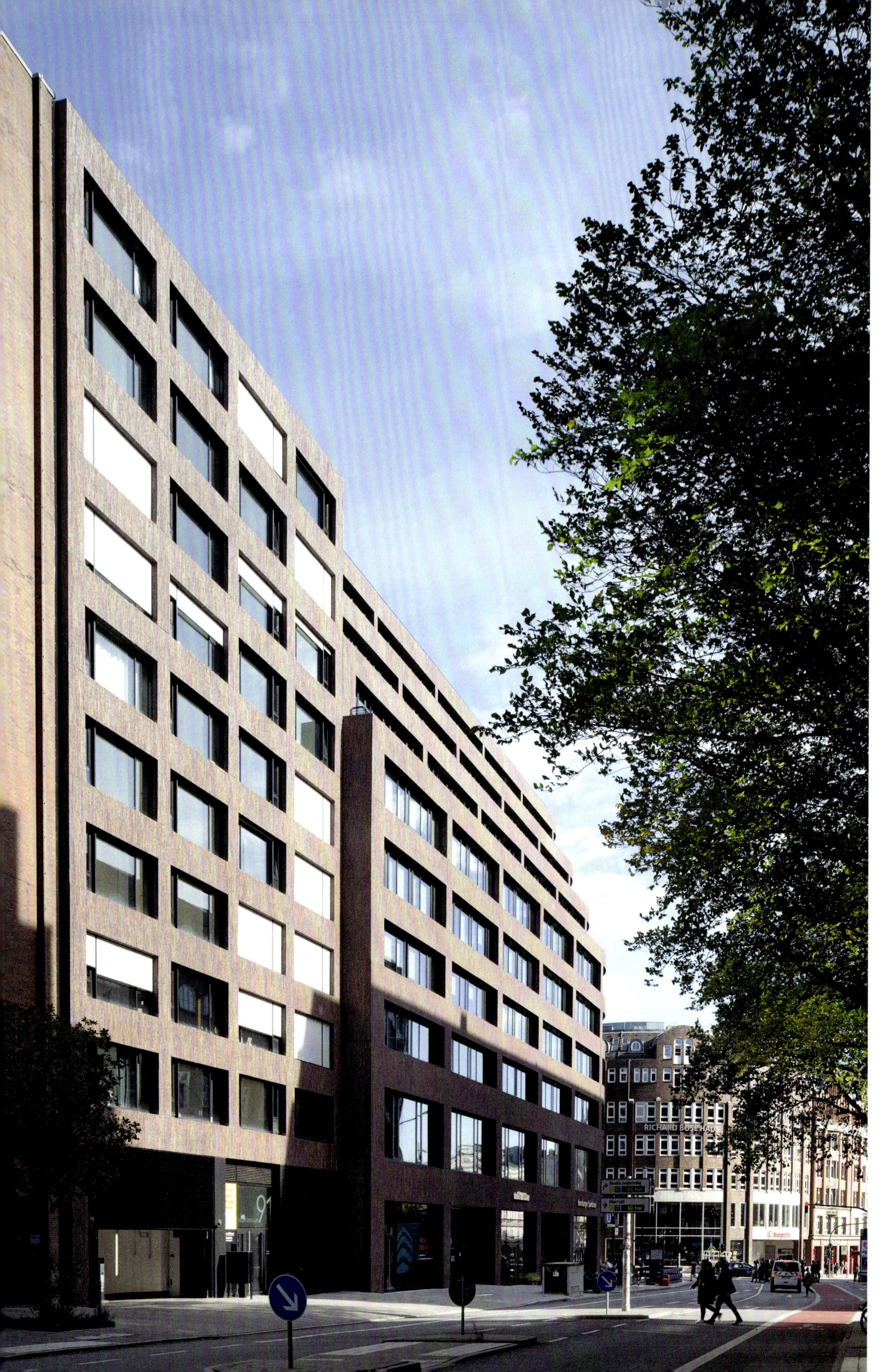
RICHARD BÖSE HAUS
Marriott
60 frei

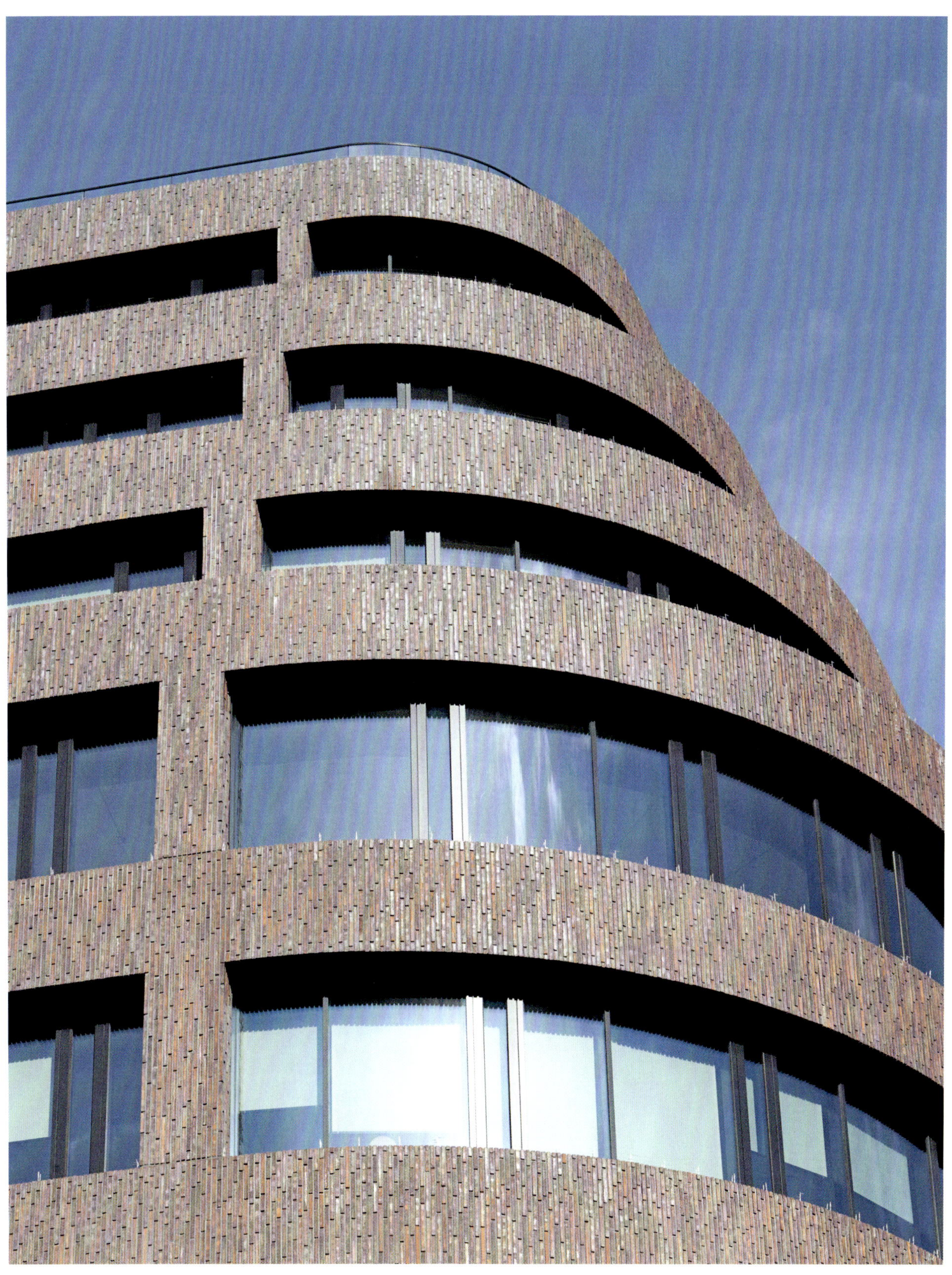

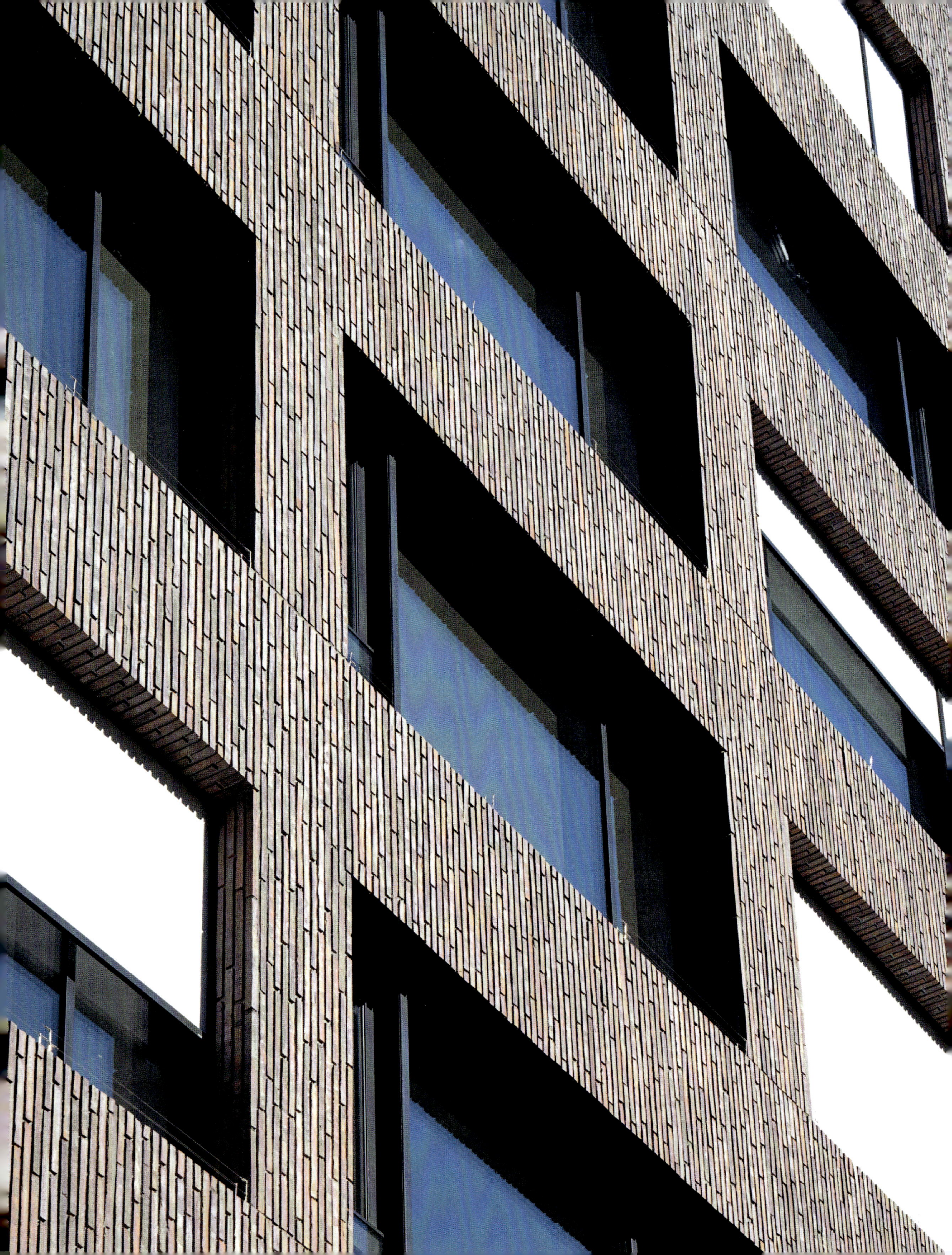

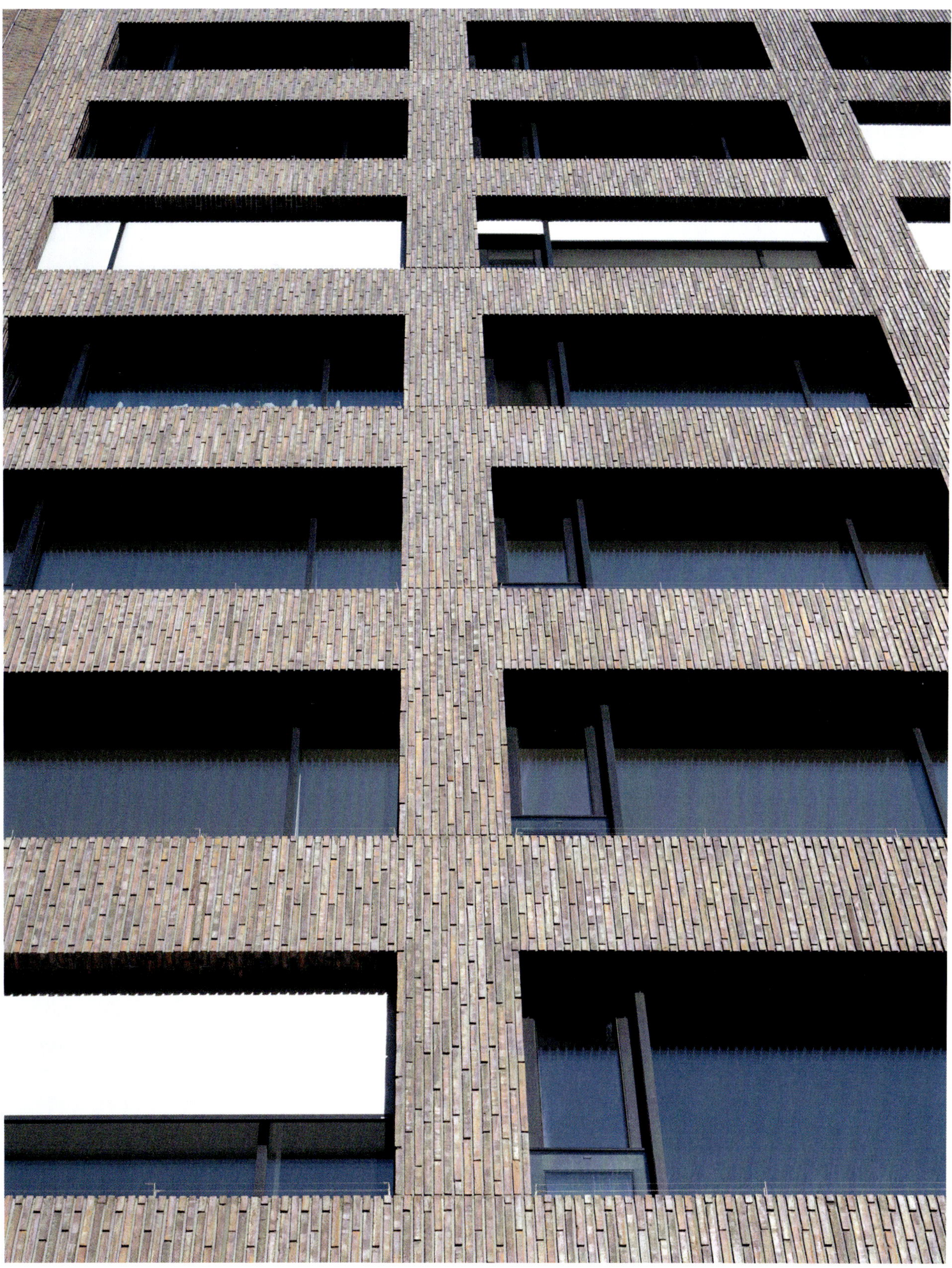

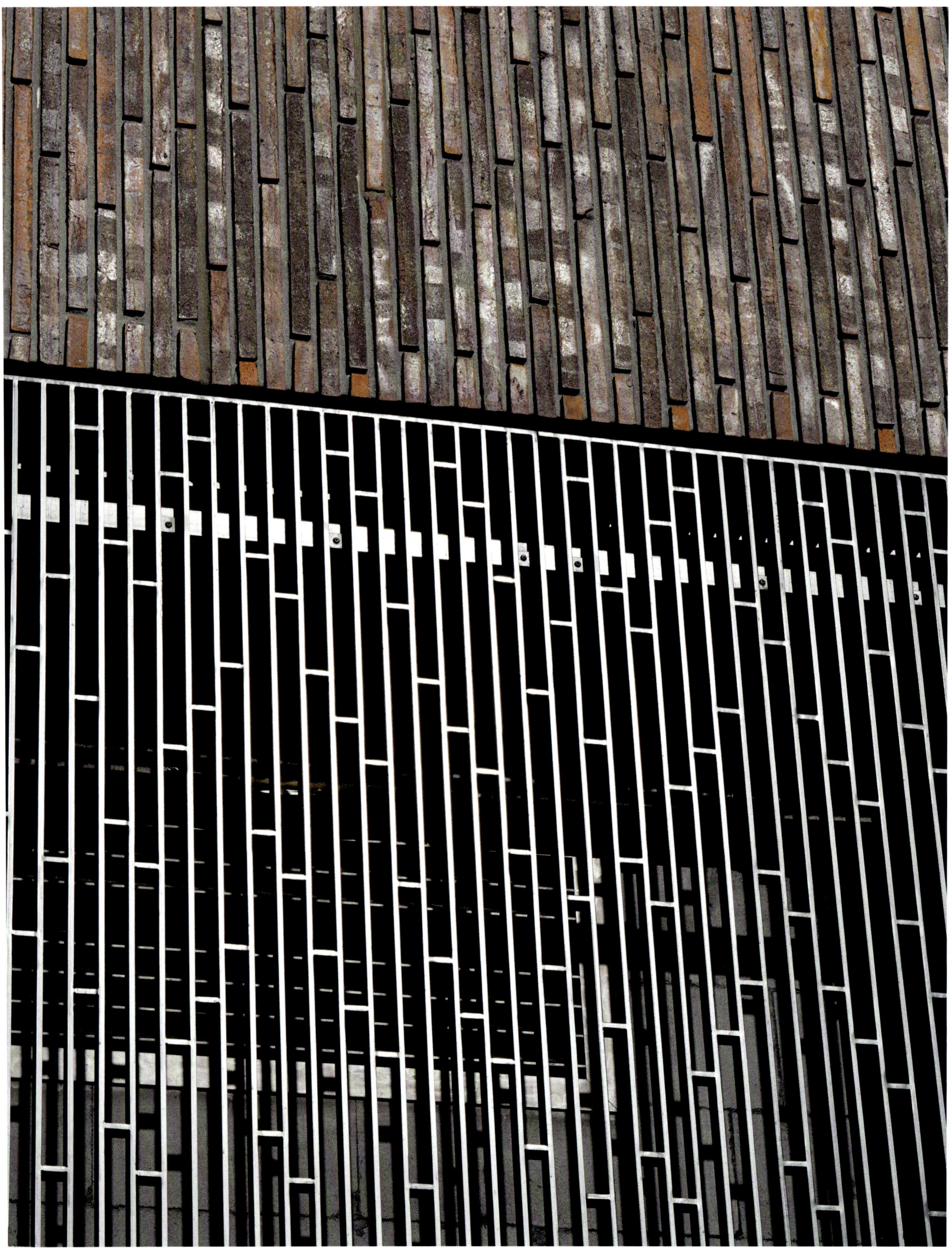

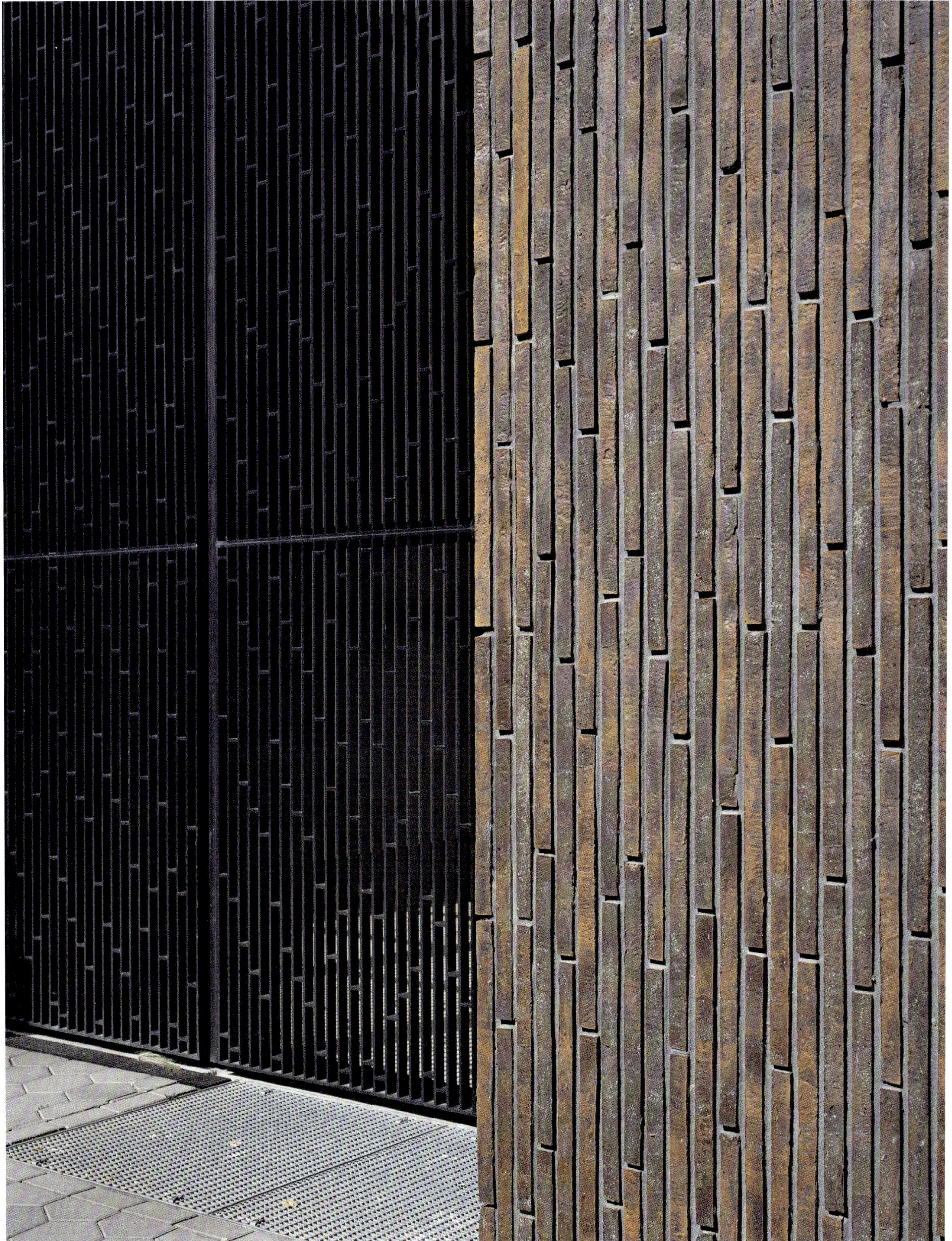

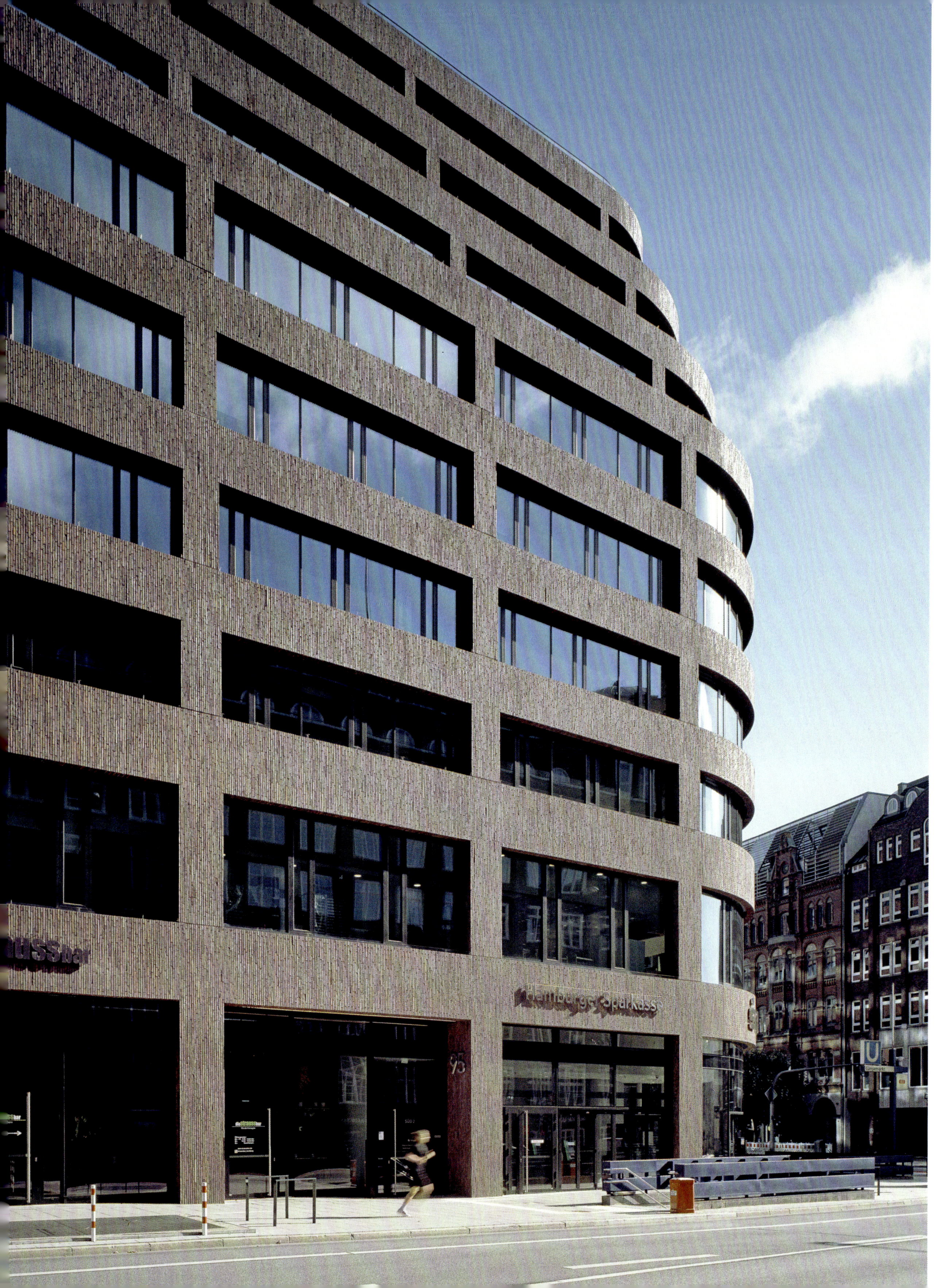

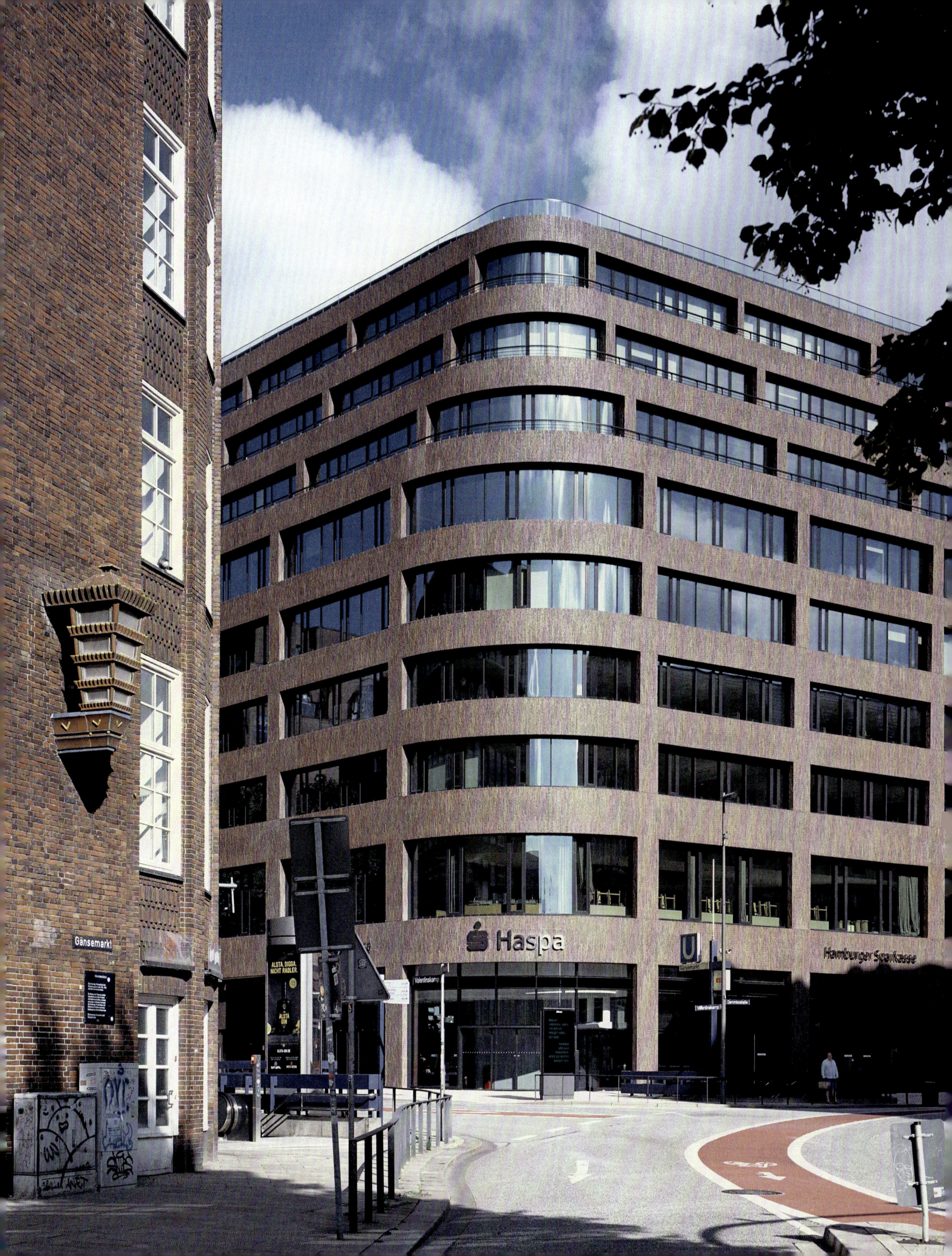
Gänsemarkt
Haspa
Hamburger Sparkasse
ALSTA, DIGGA.
NICHT RADLER.
Valentinskamp

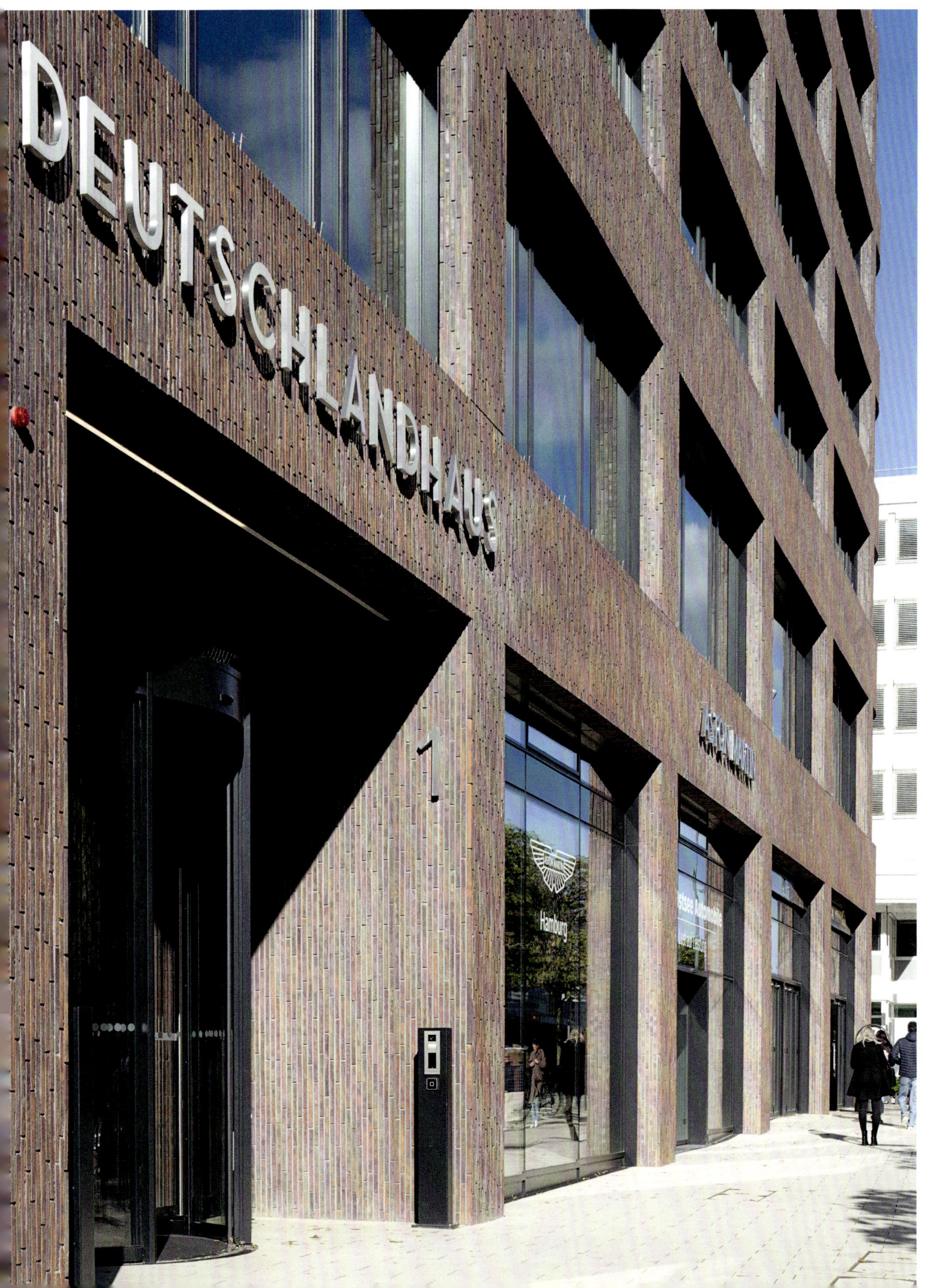
DEUTSCHLANDHAUS
1
Hamburg

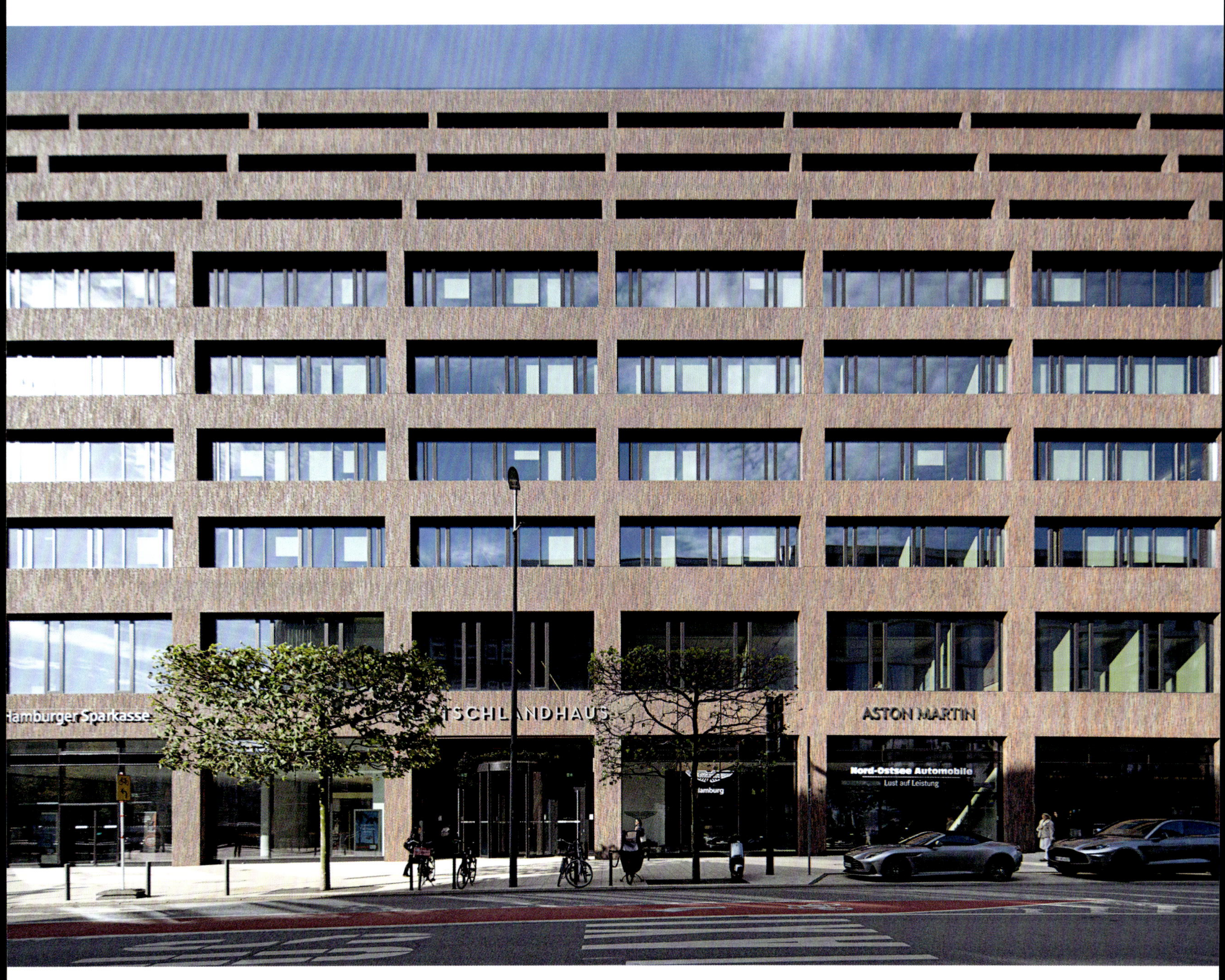
Hamburger Sparkasse
ASTON MARTIN
Nord-Ostsee Automobile
Lust auf Leistung

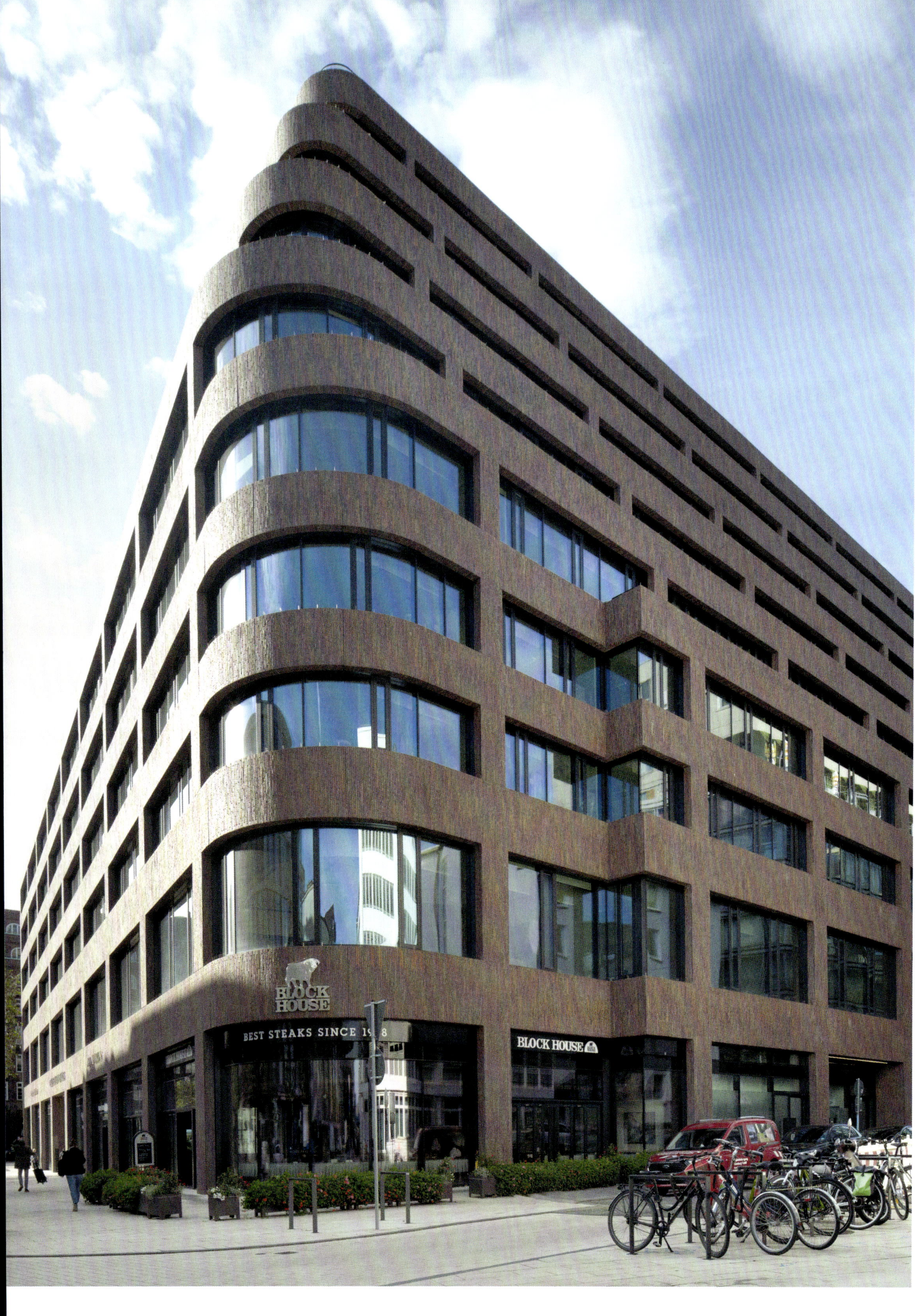
BLOCK HOUSE
BLOCK HOUSE

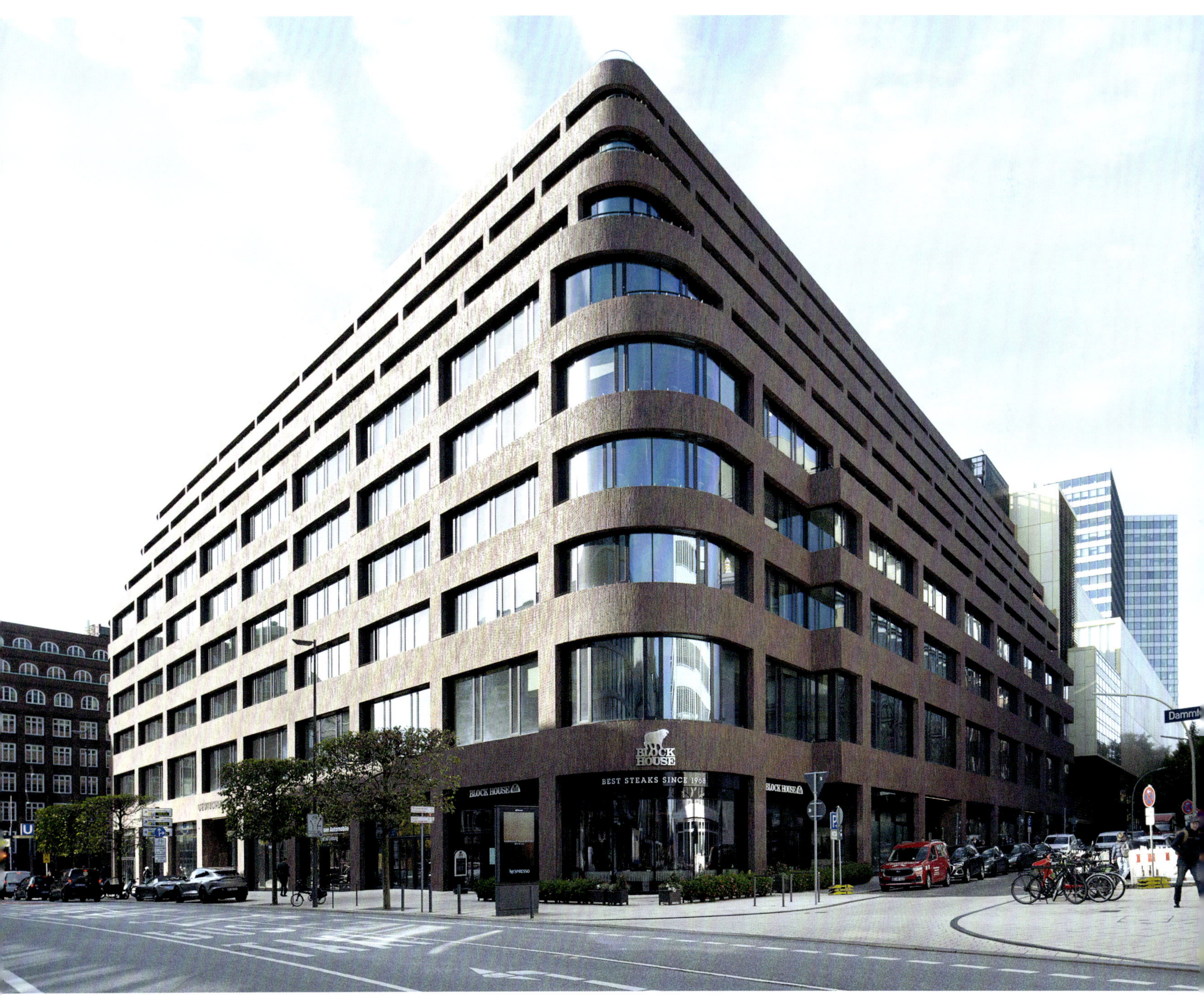
BLOCK HOUSE
BEST STEAKS SINCE 1968
BLOCK HOUSE
BLOCK HOUSE

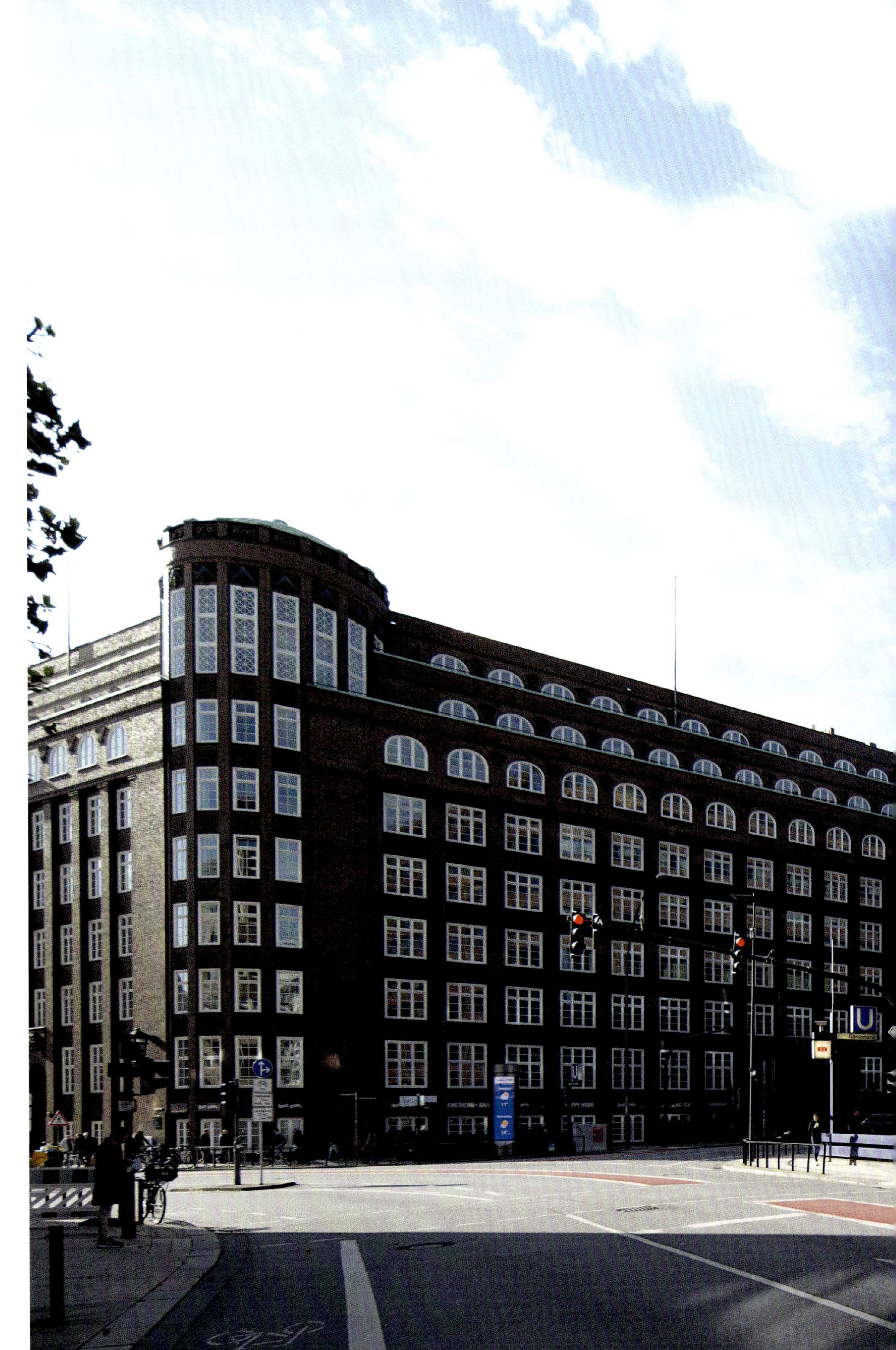

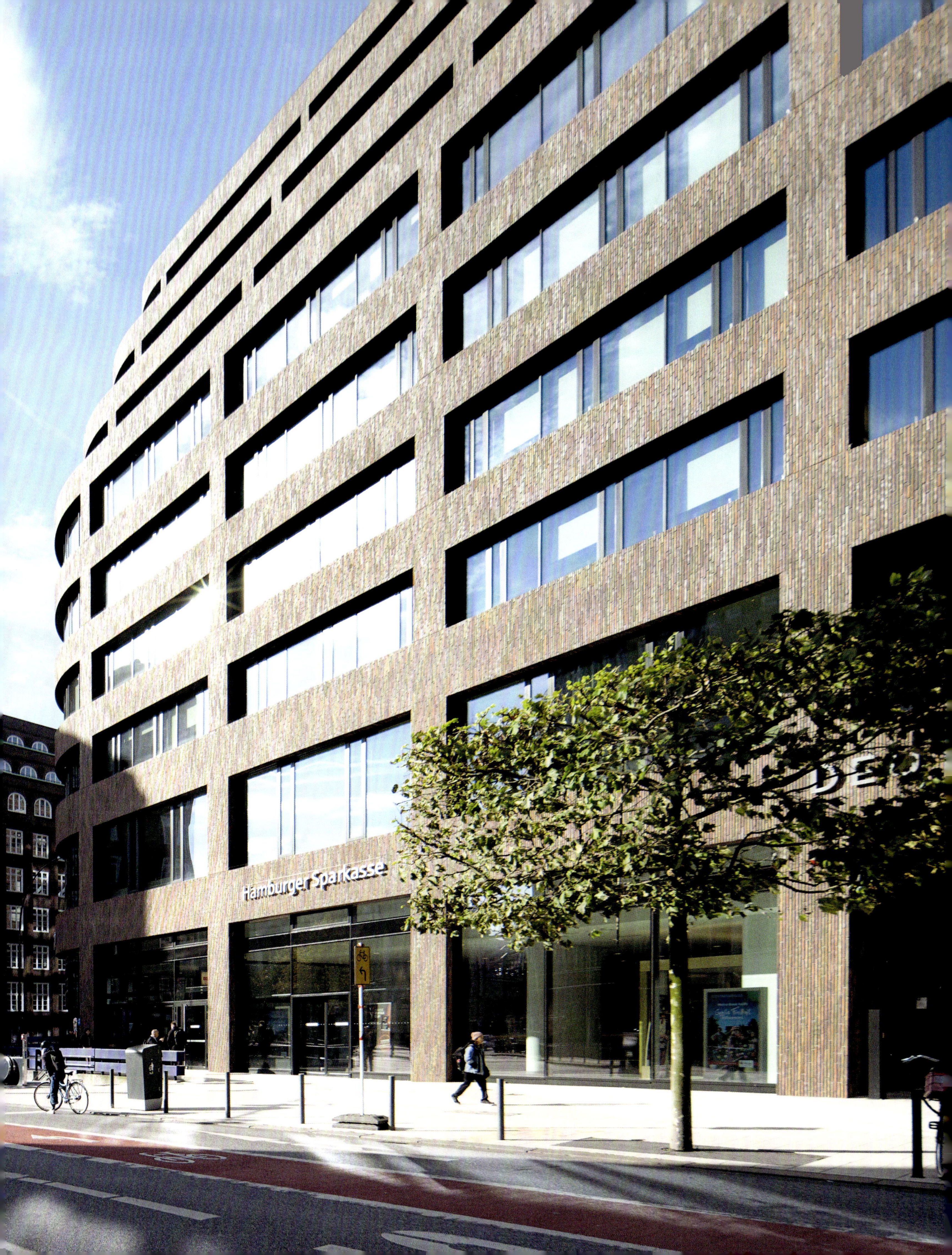
Hamburger Sparkasse

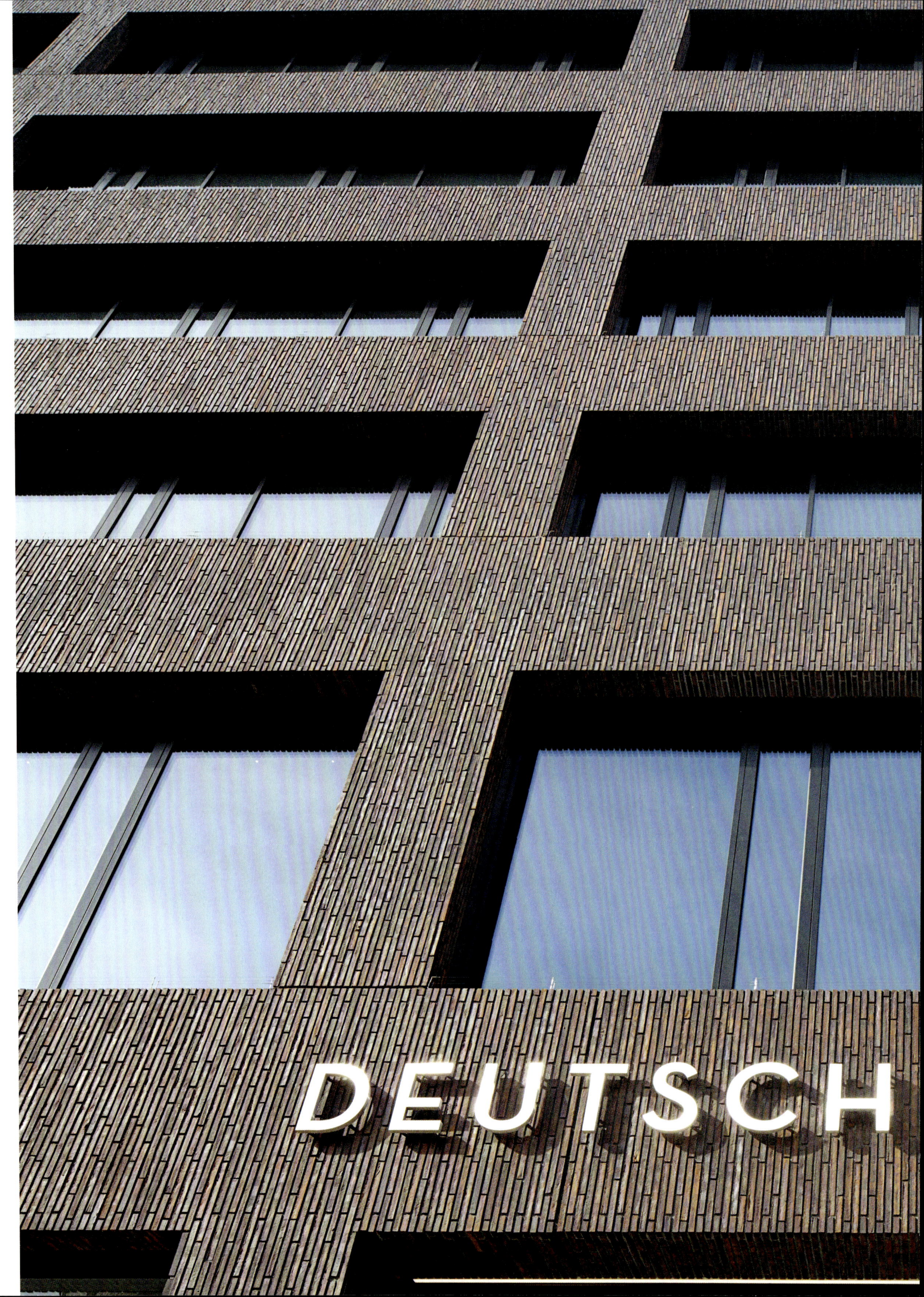
DEUTSCH

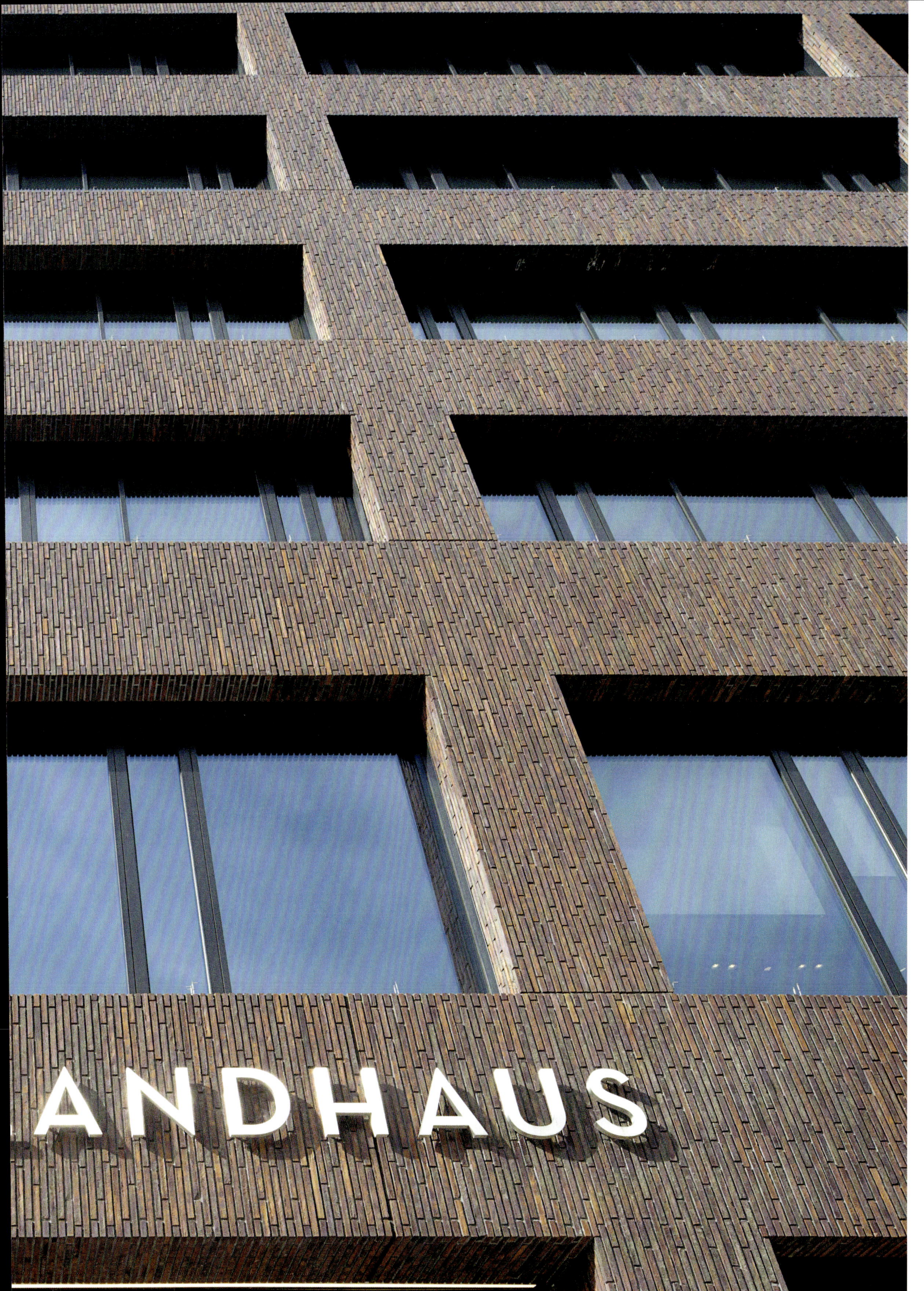
ANDHAUS

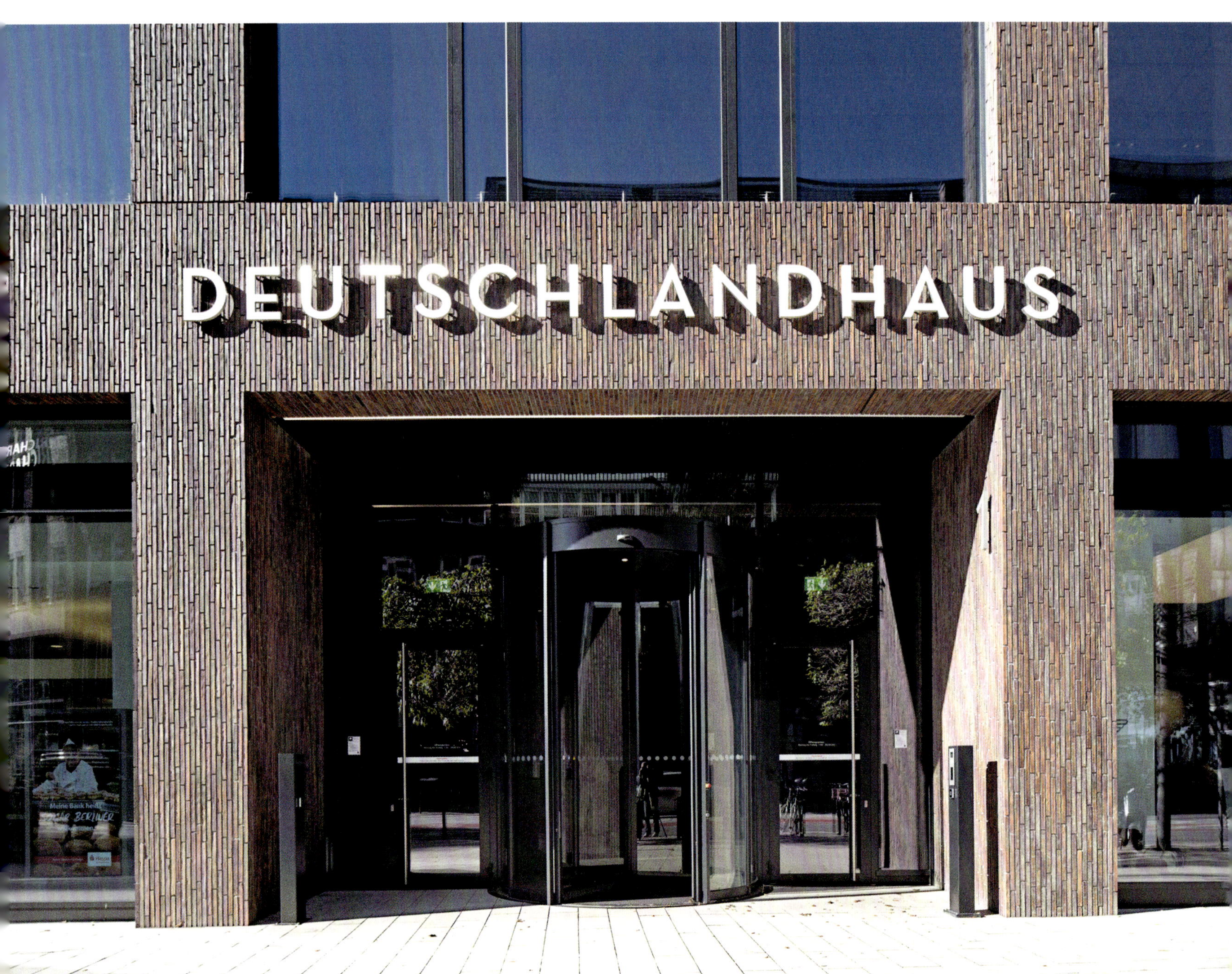
DEUTSCHLANDHAUS

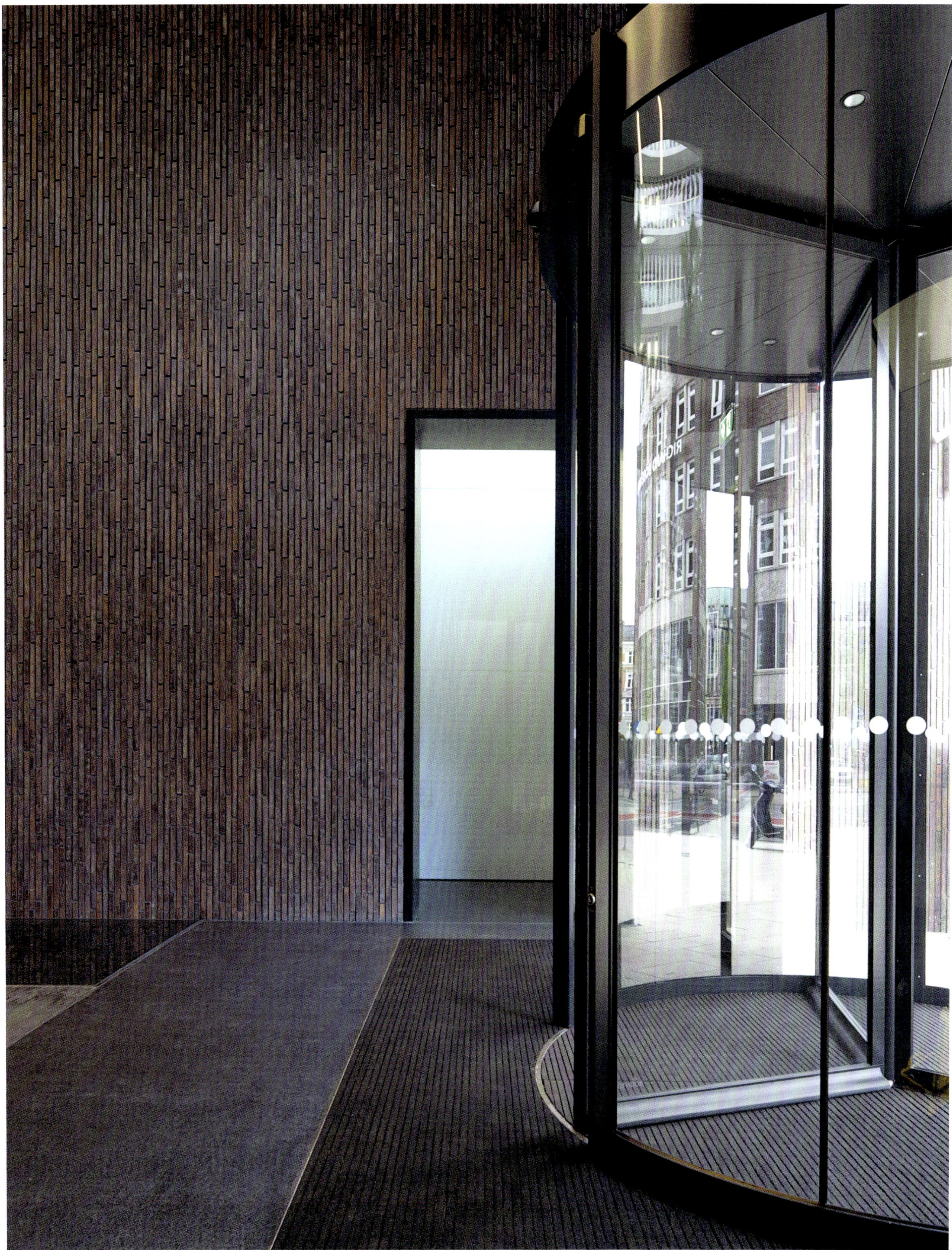

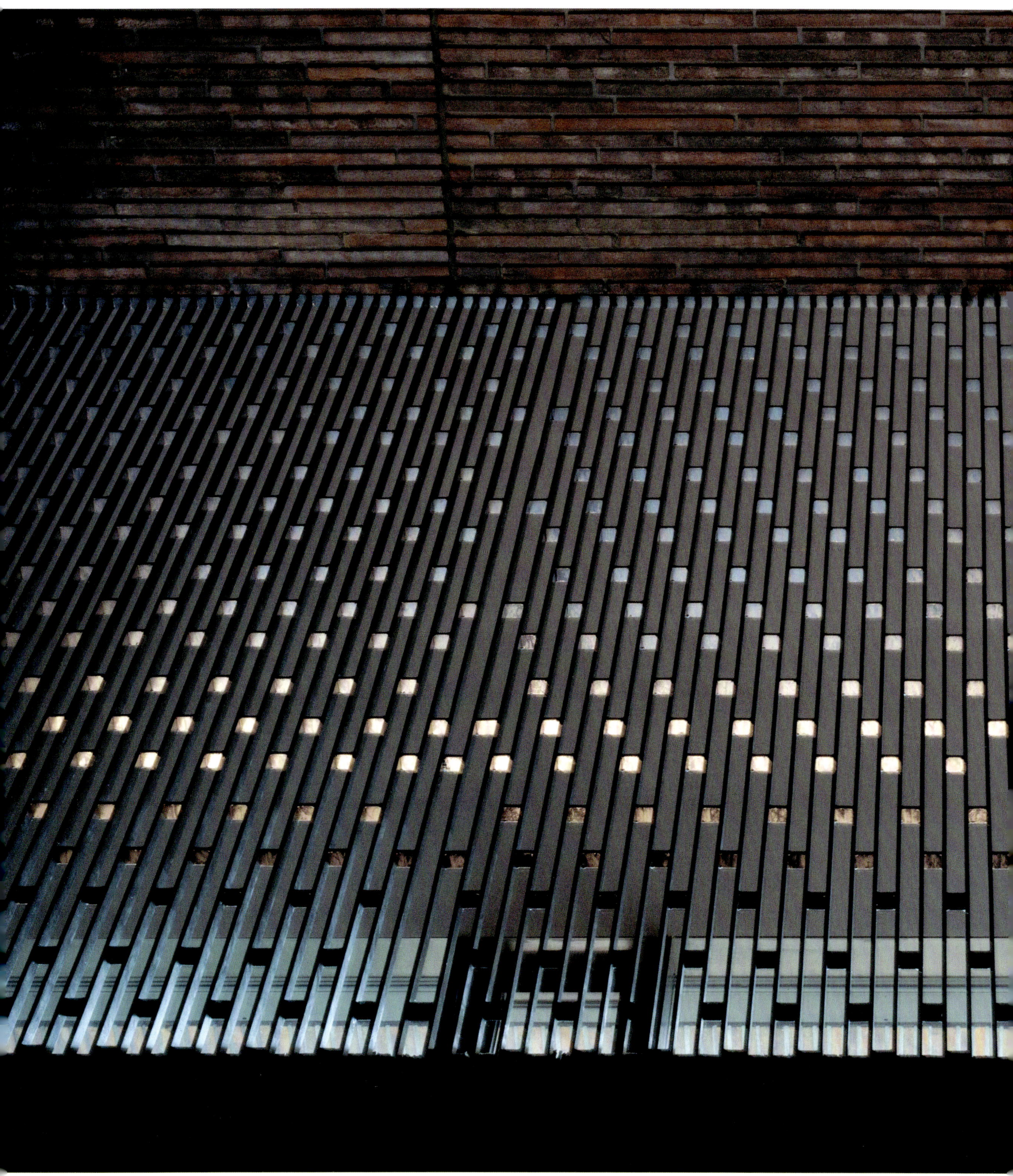

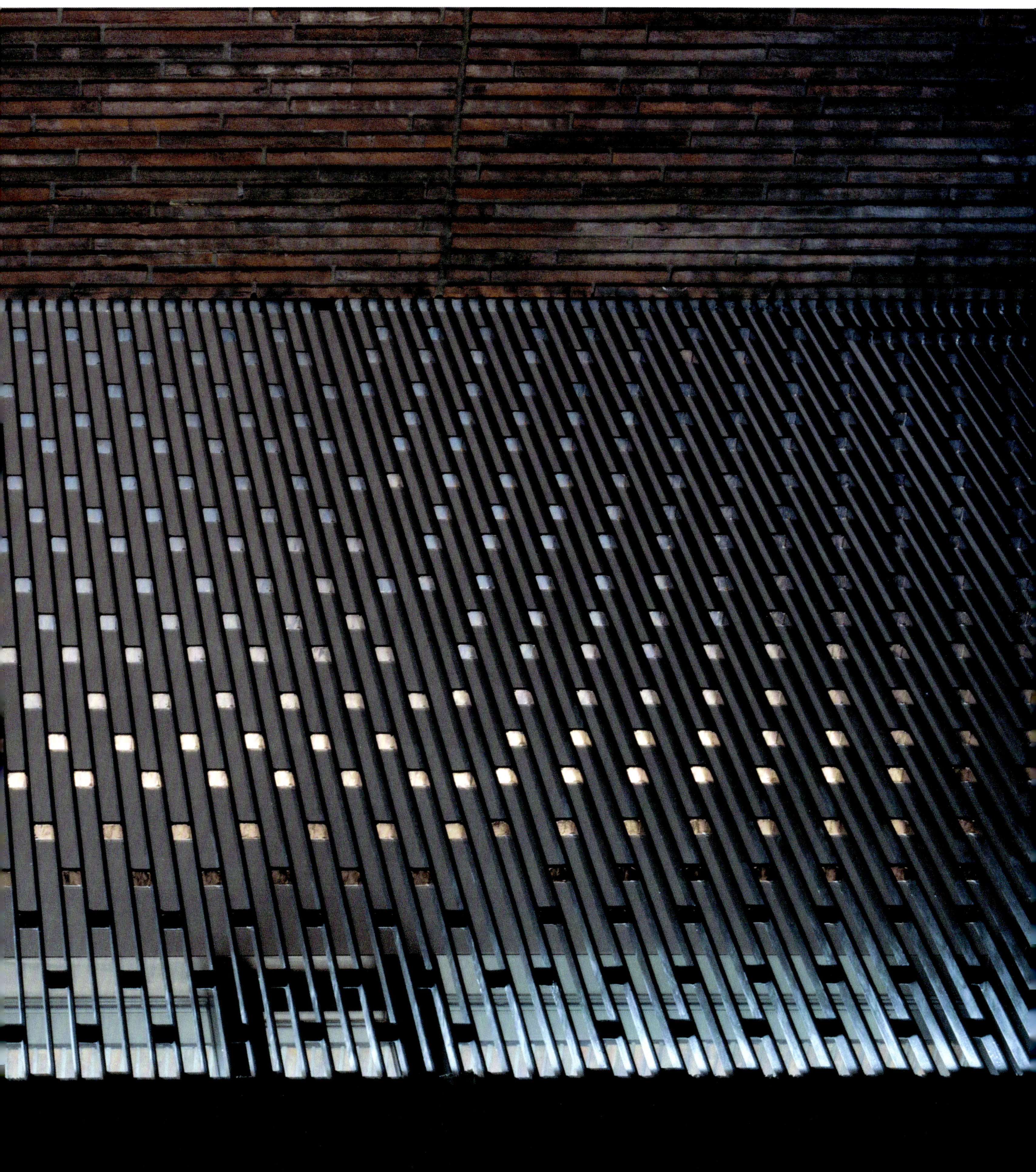

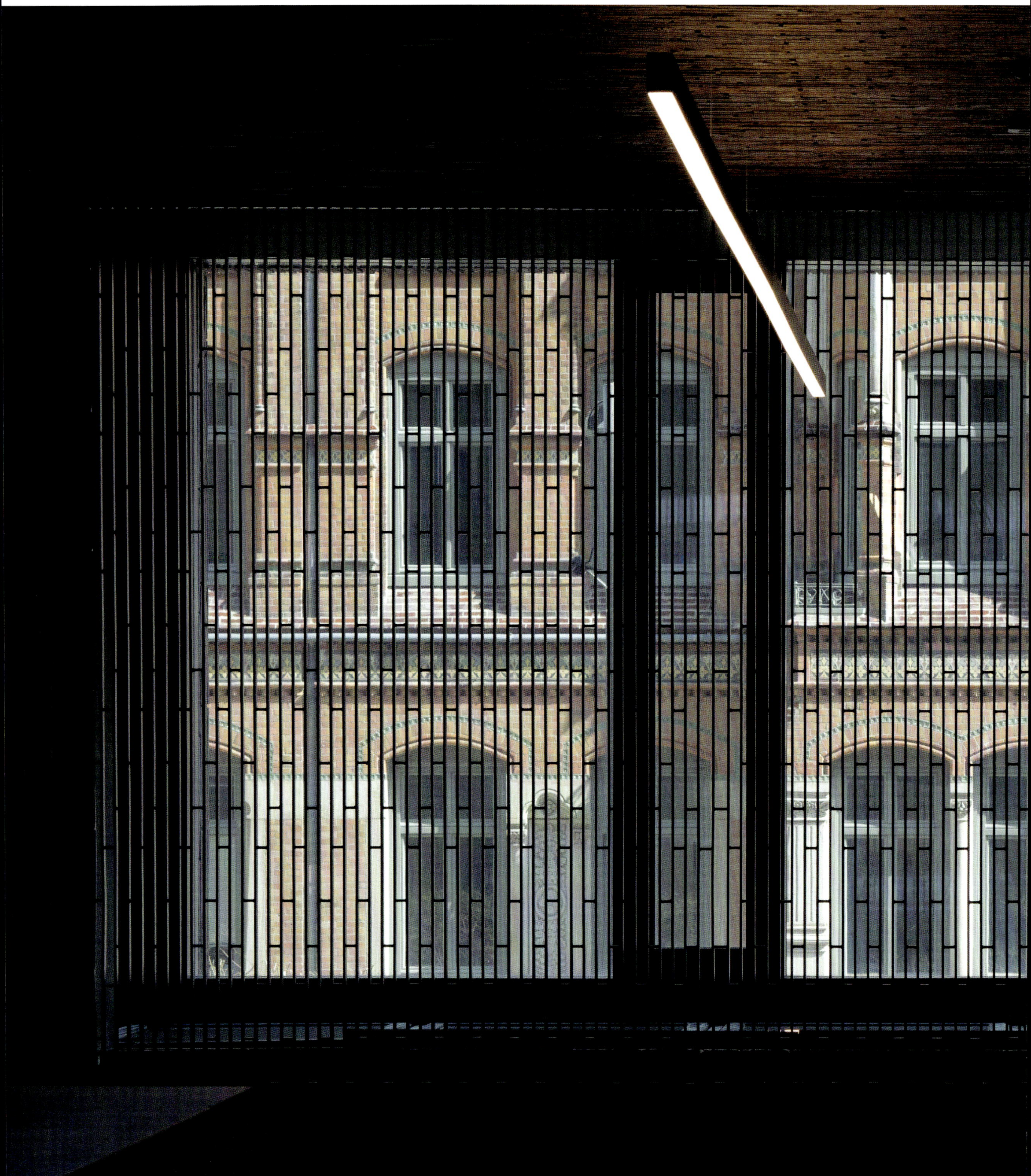

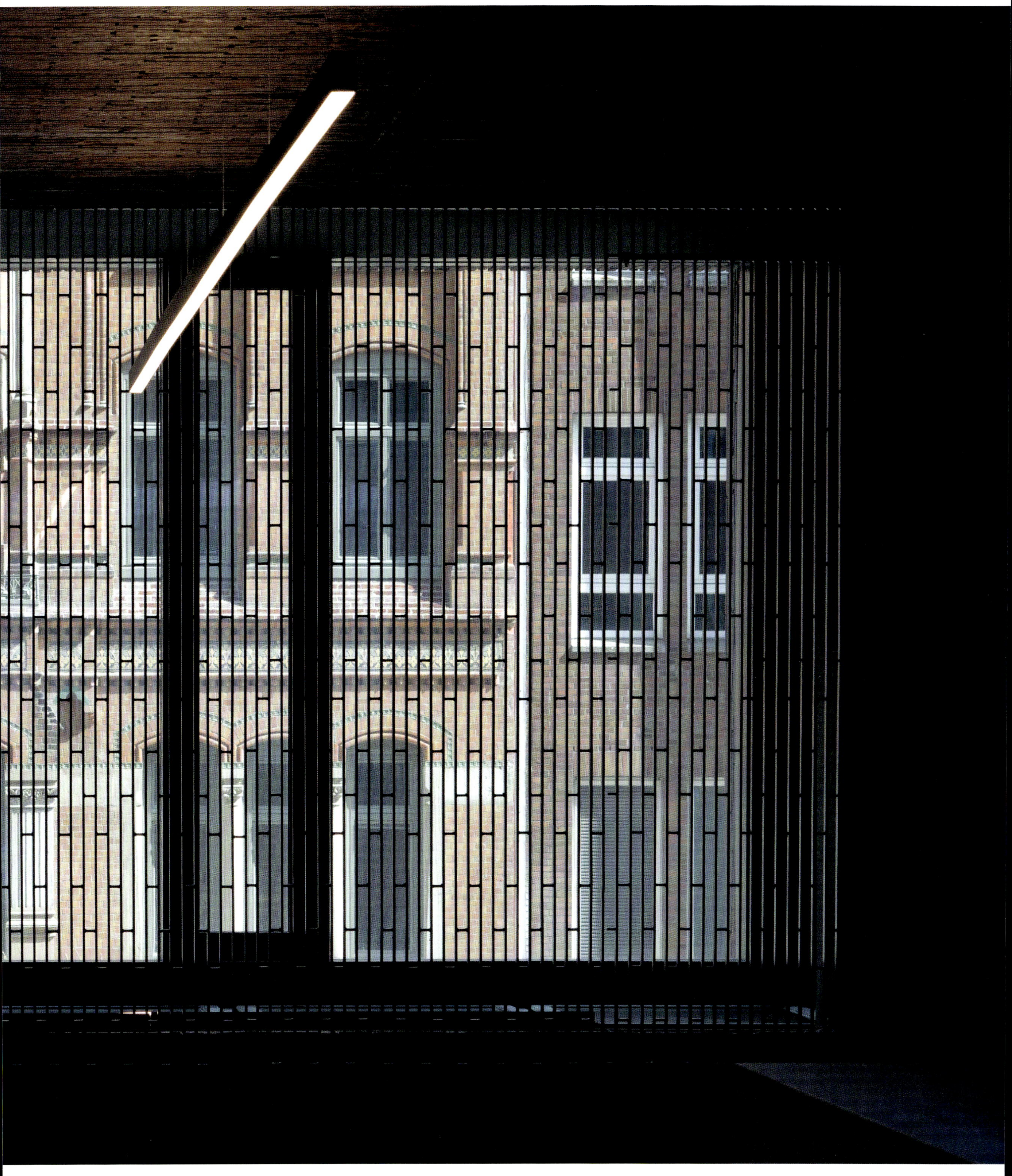

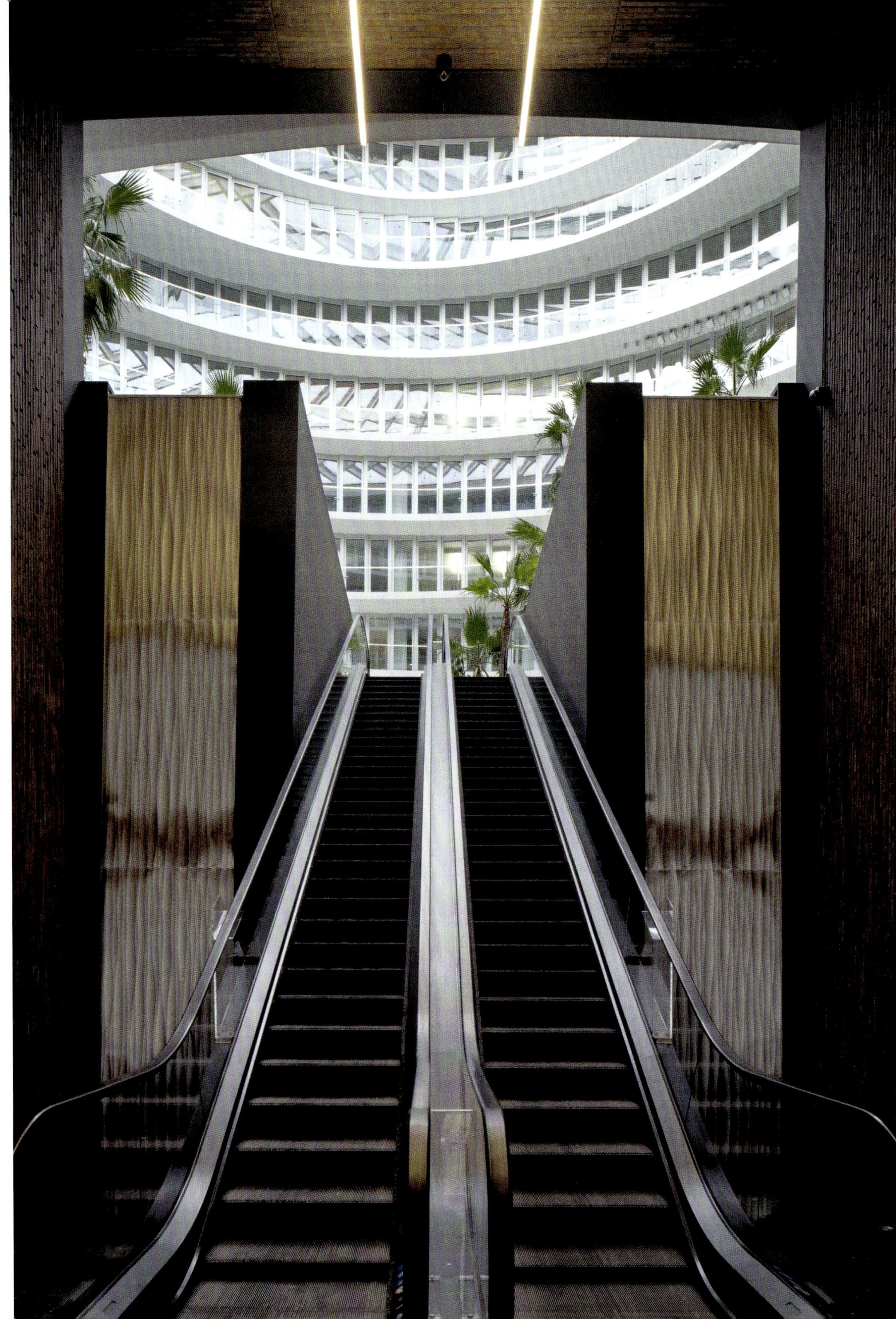

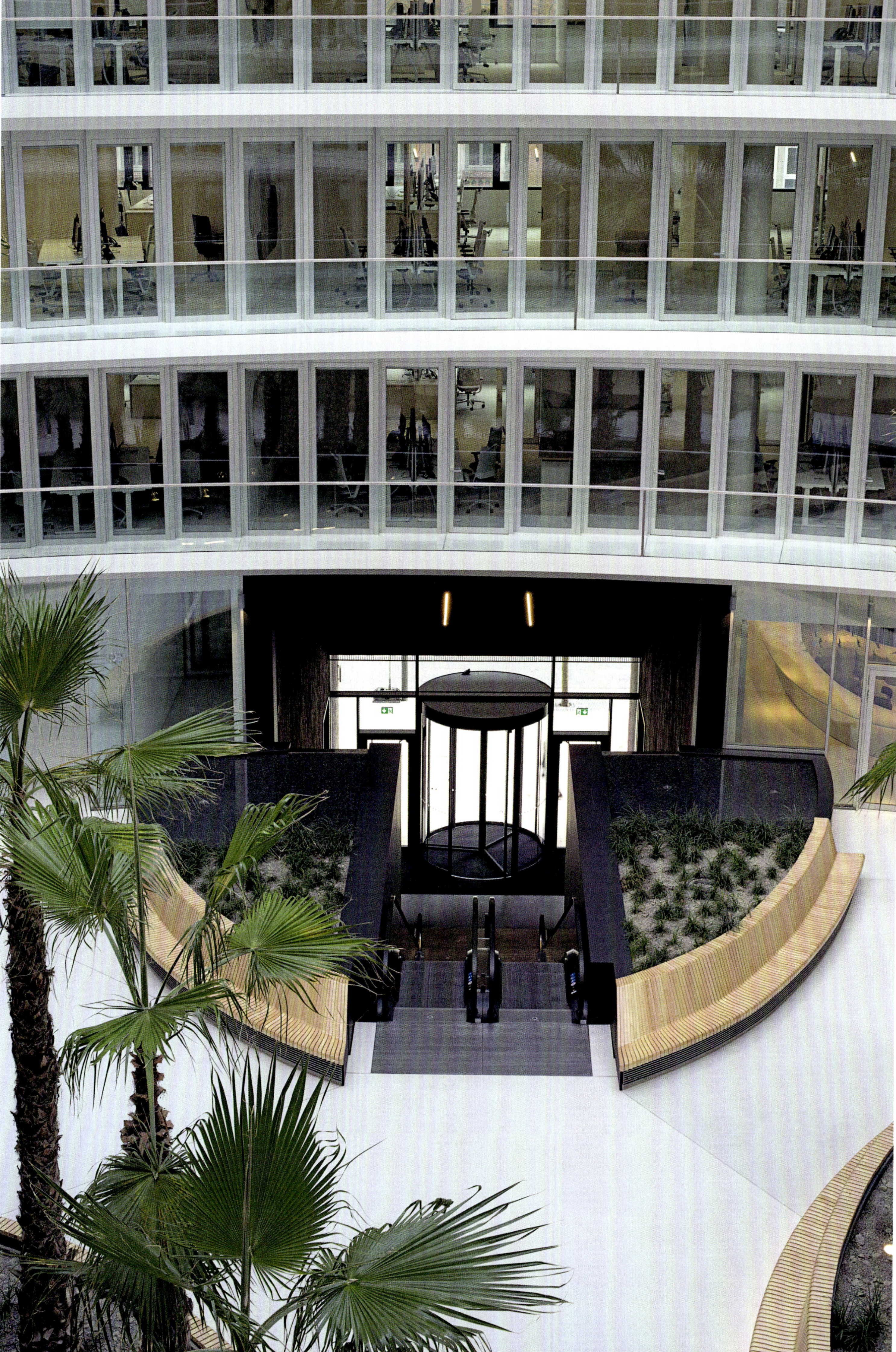

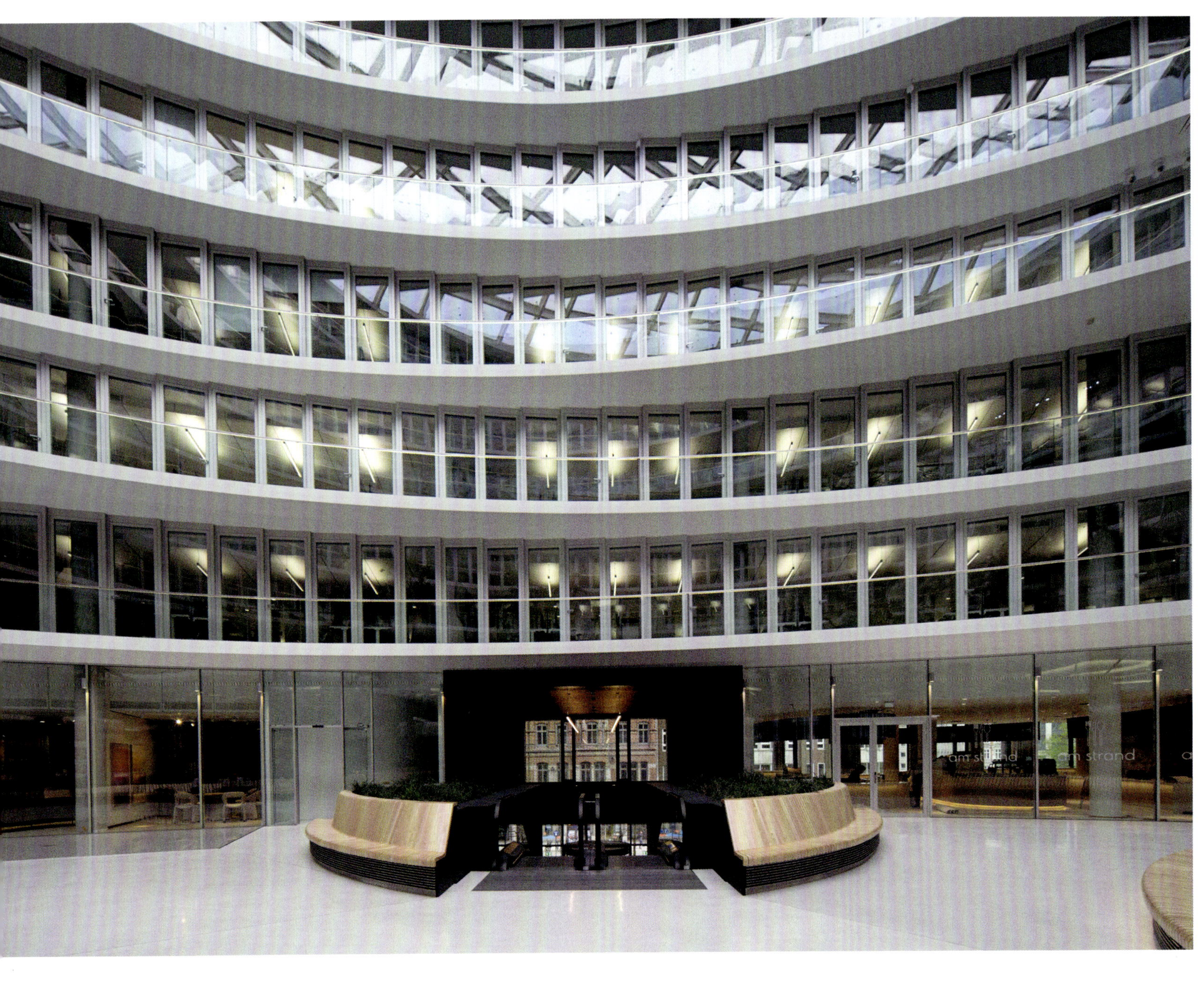
am strand

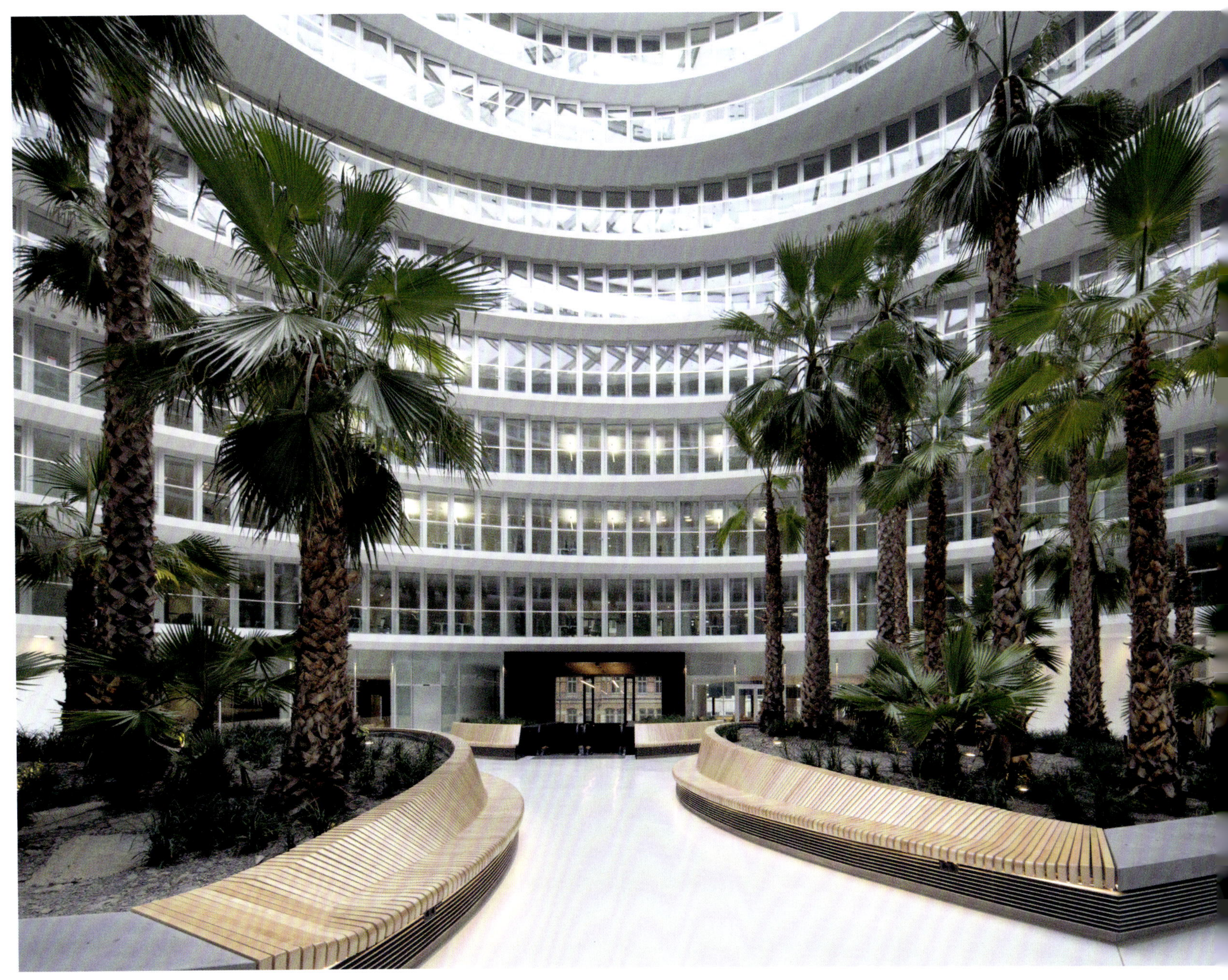

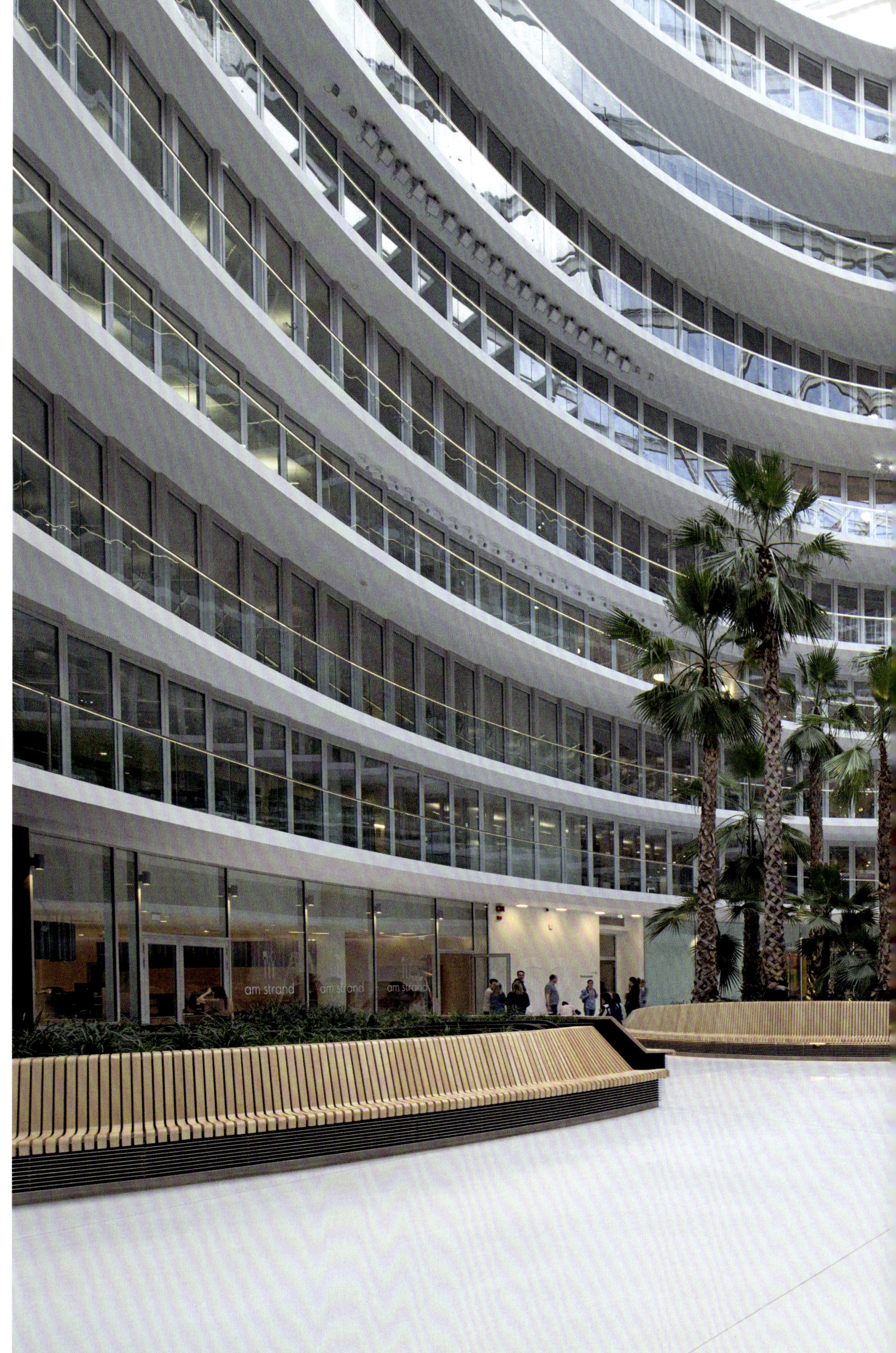
am strand
am strand
am strand

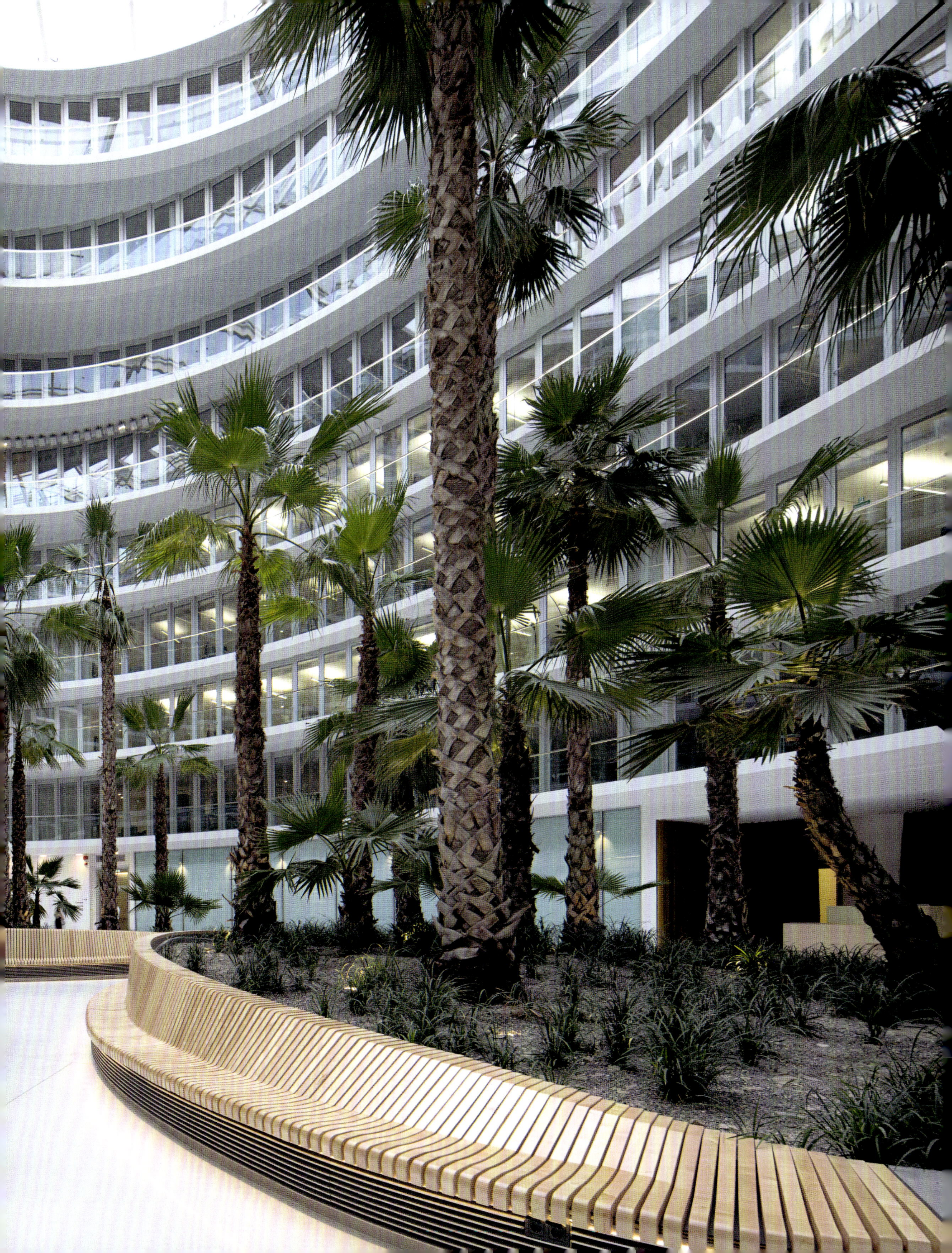

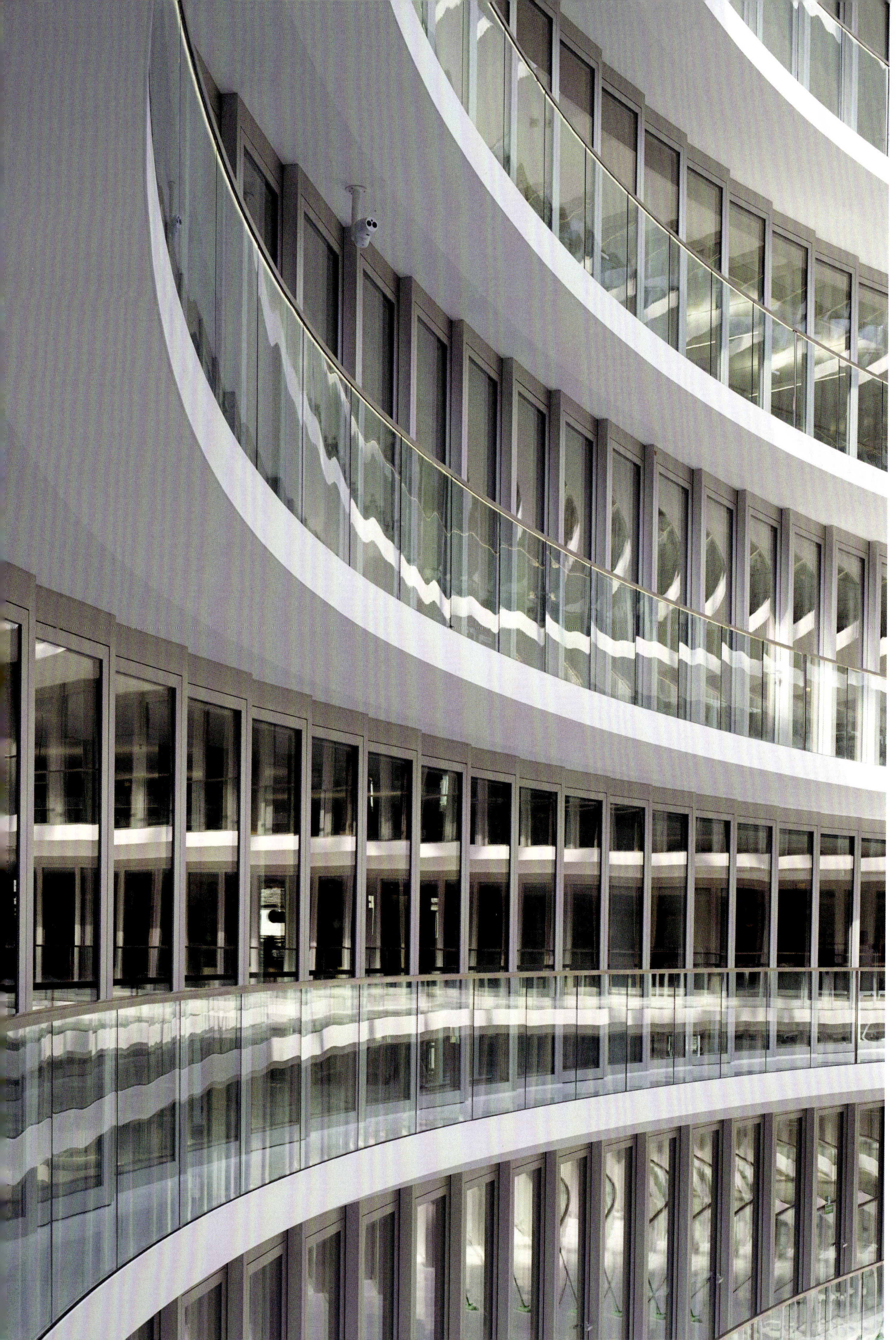

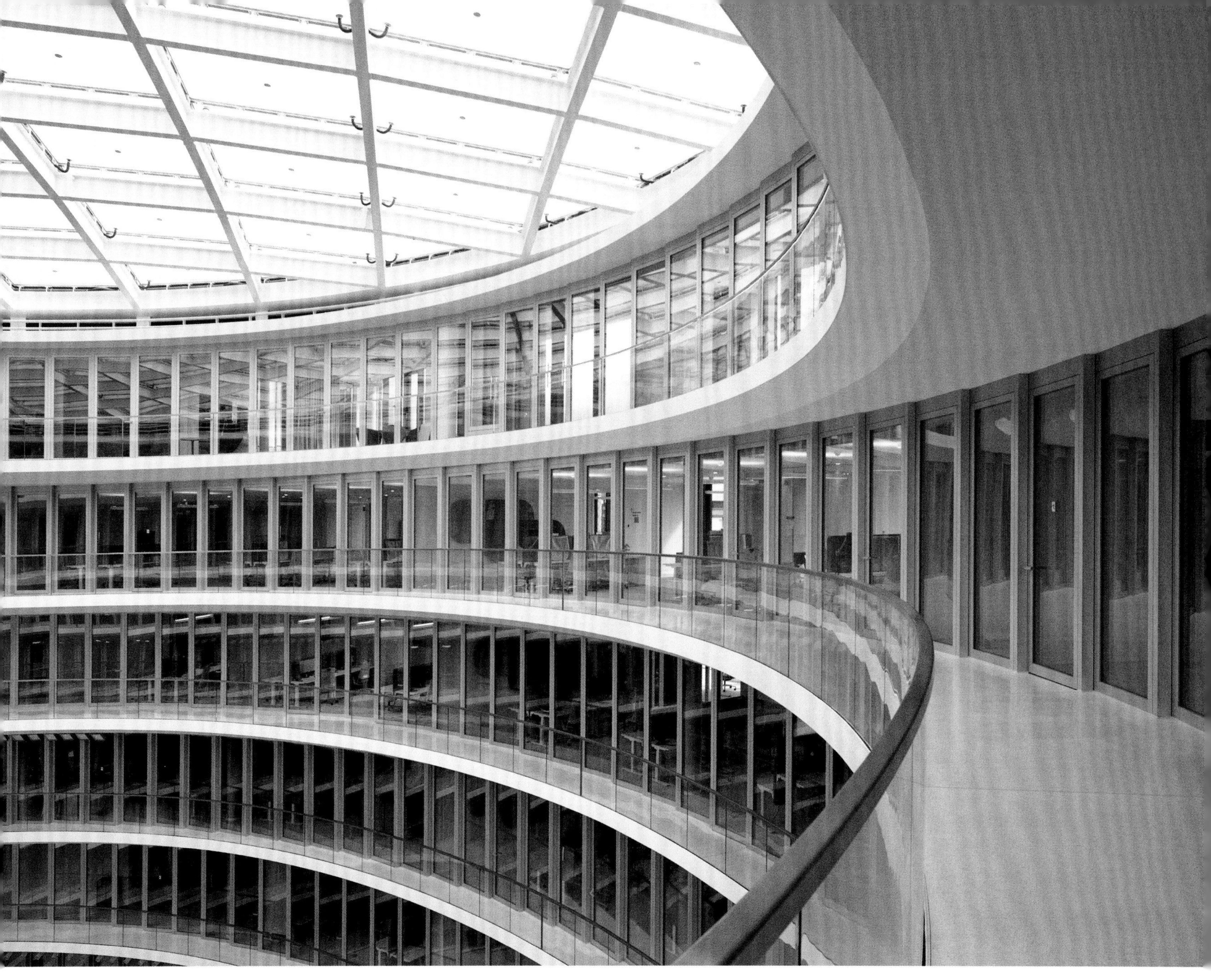

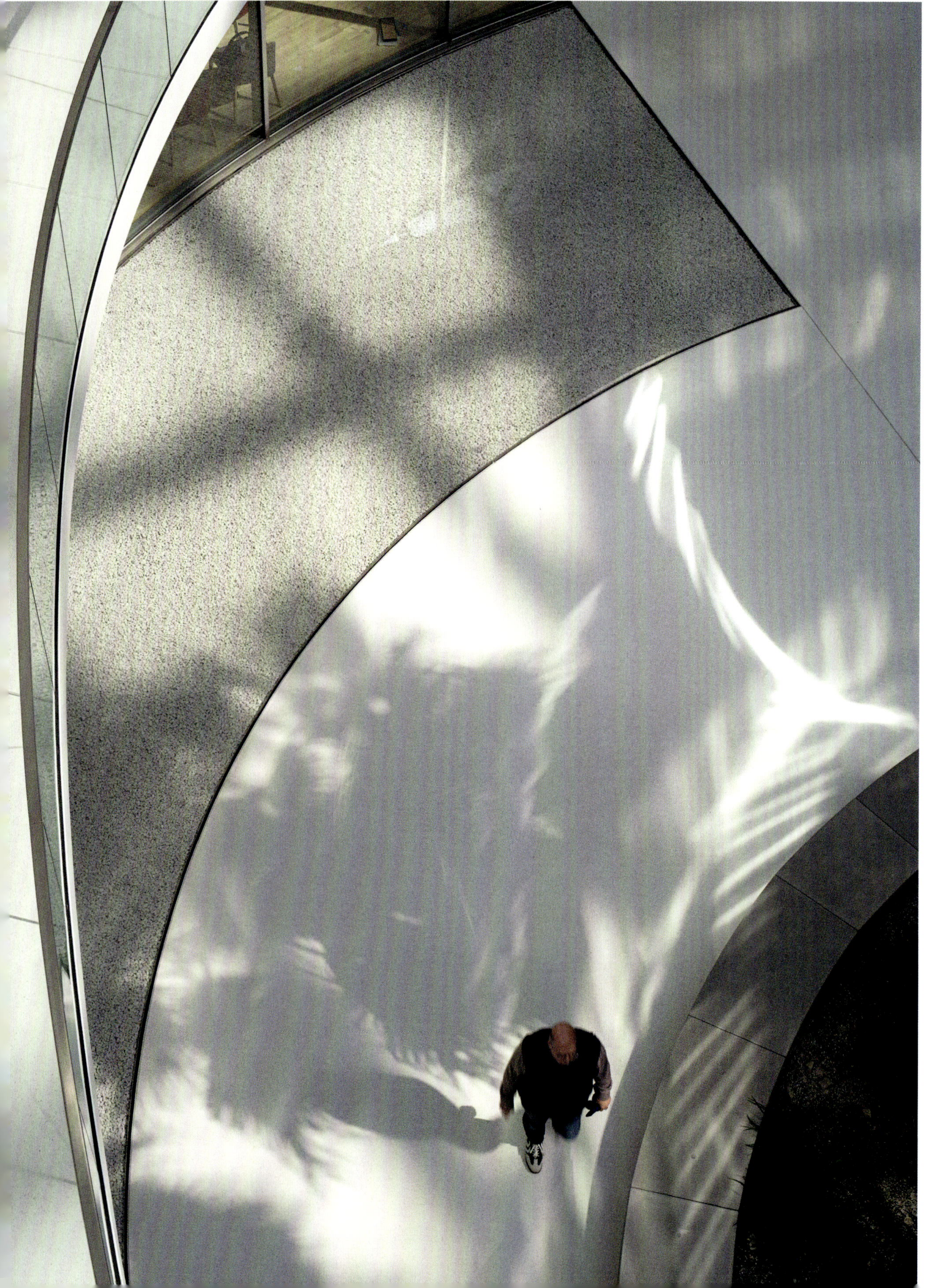

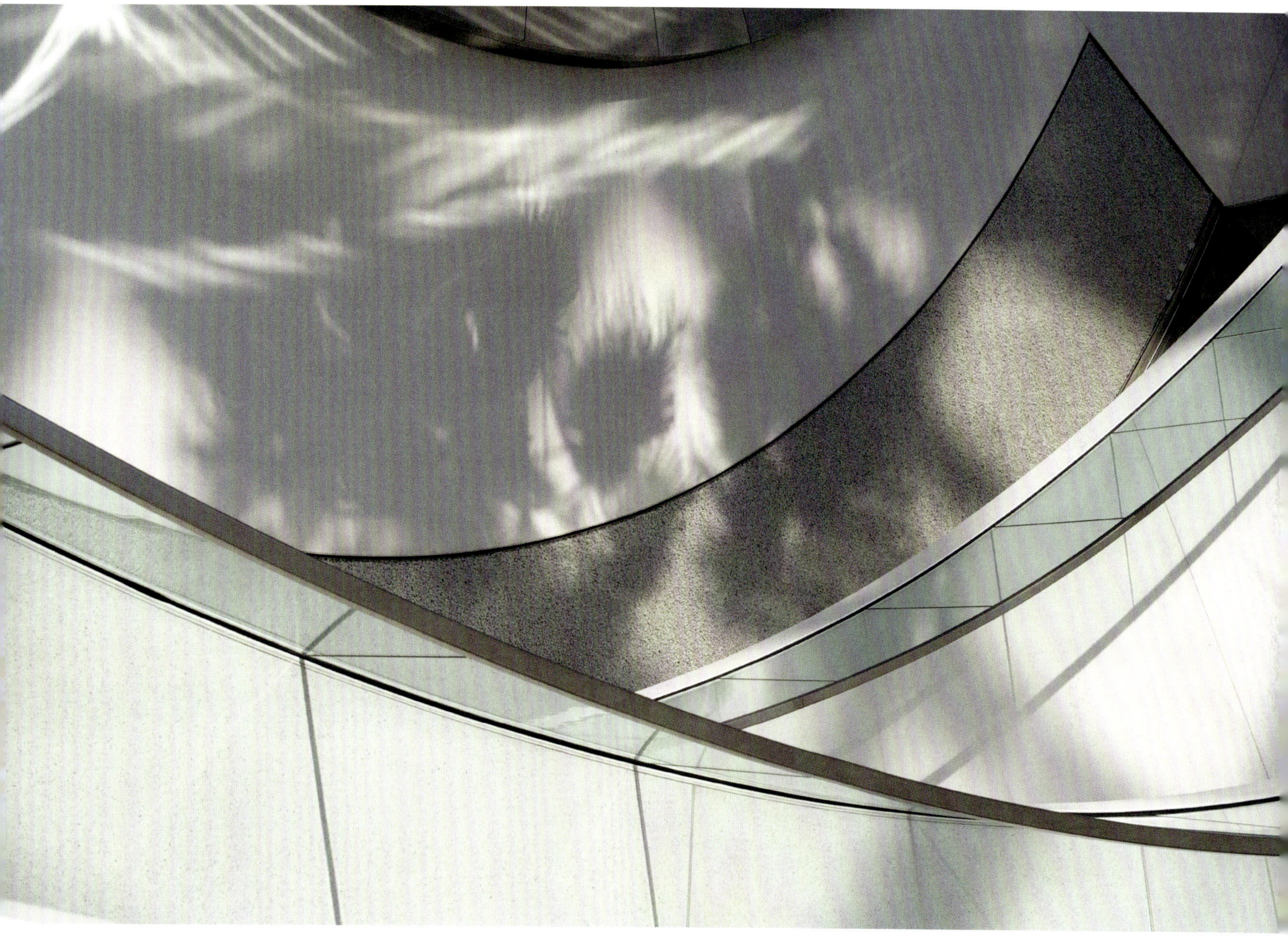

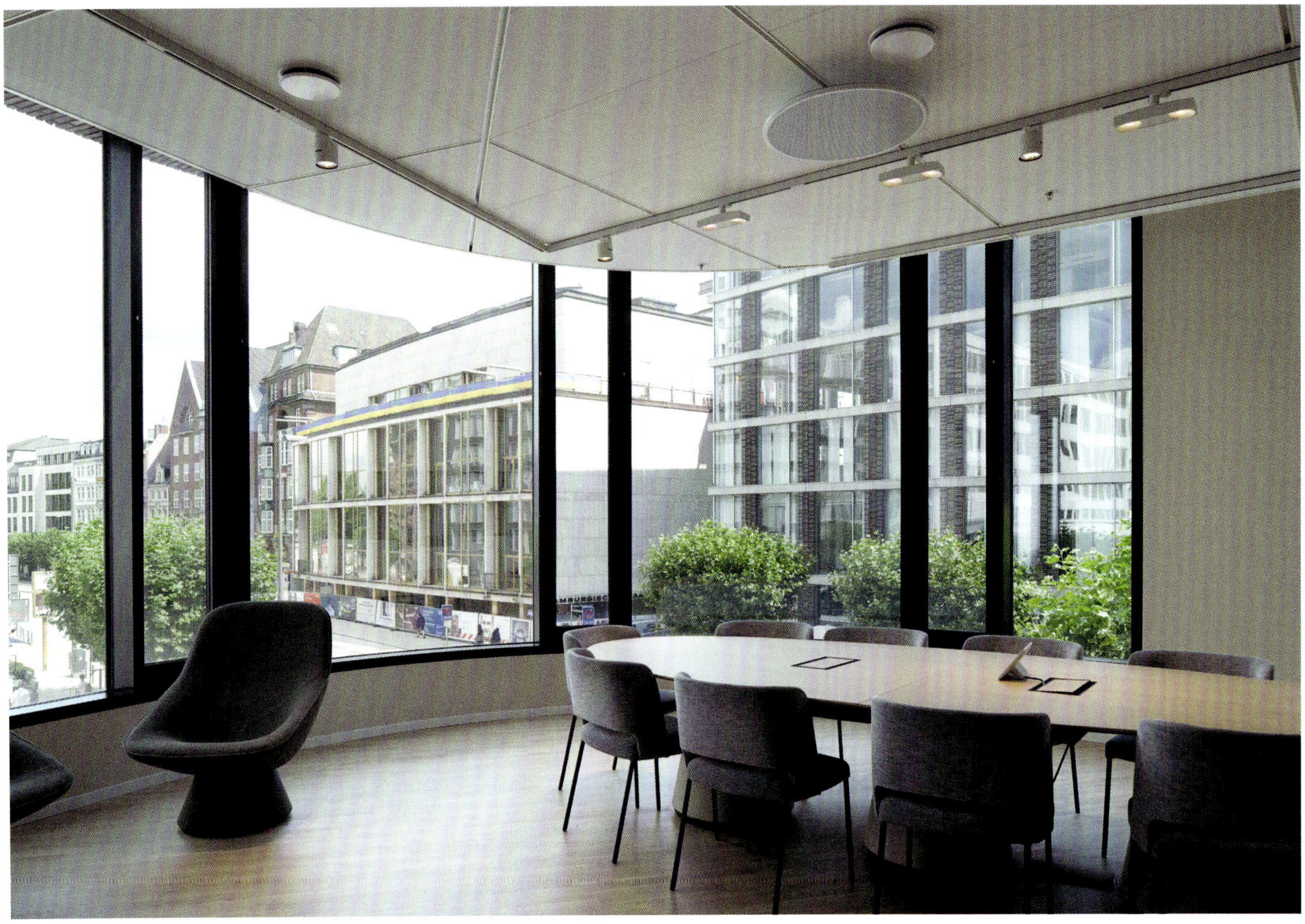

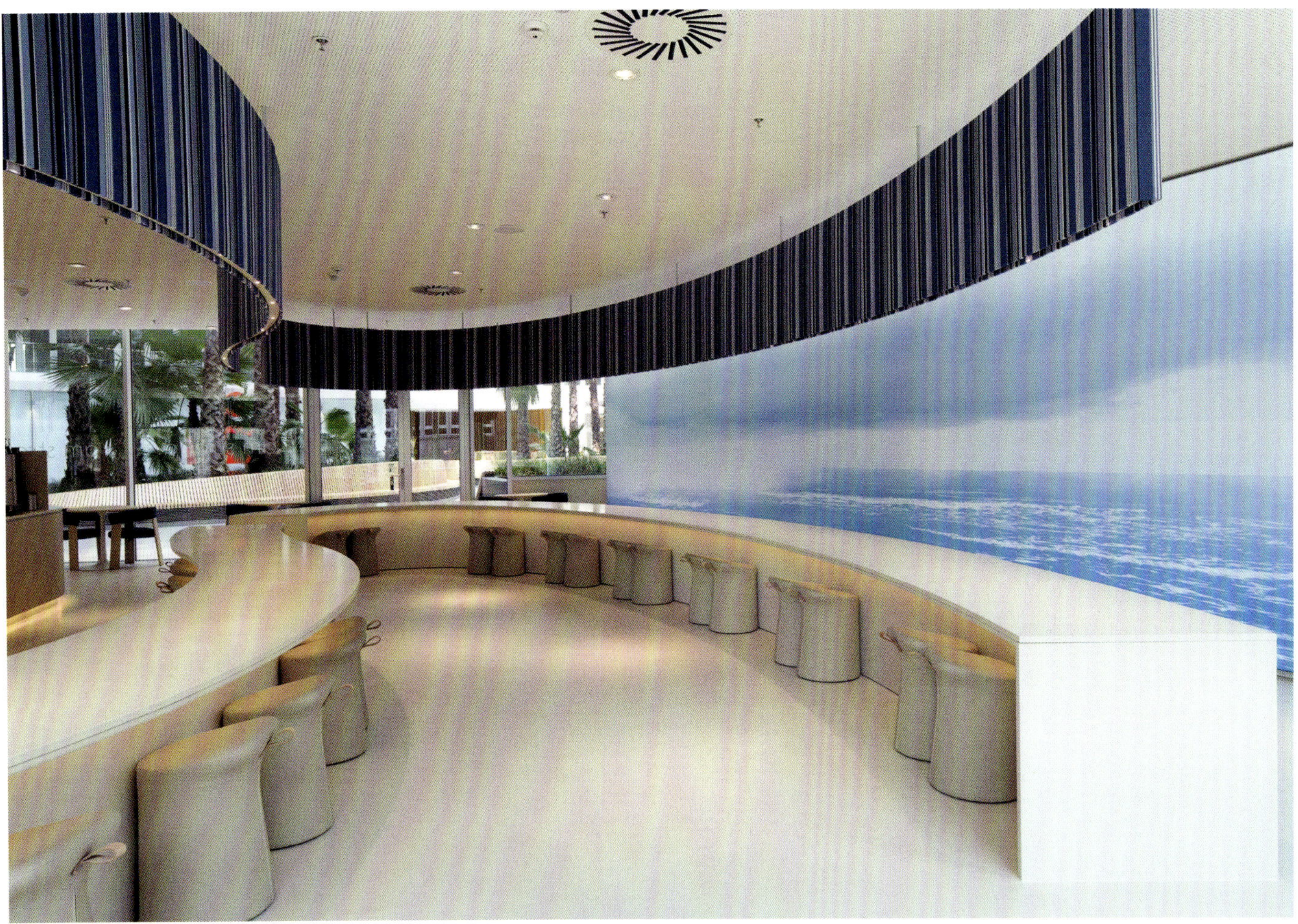

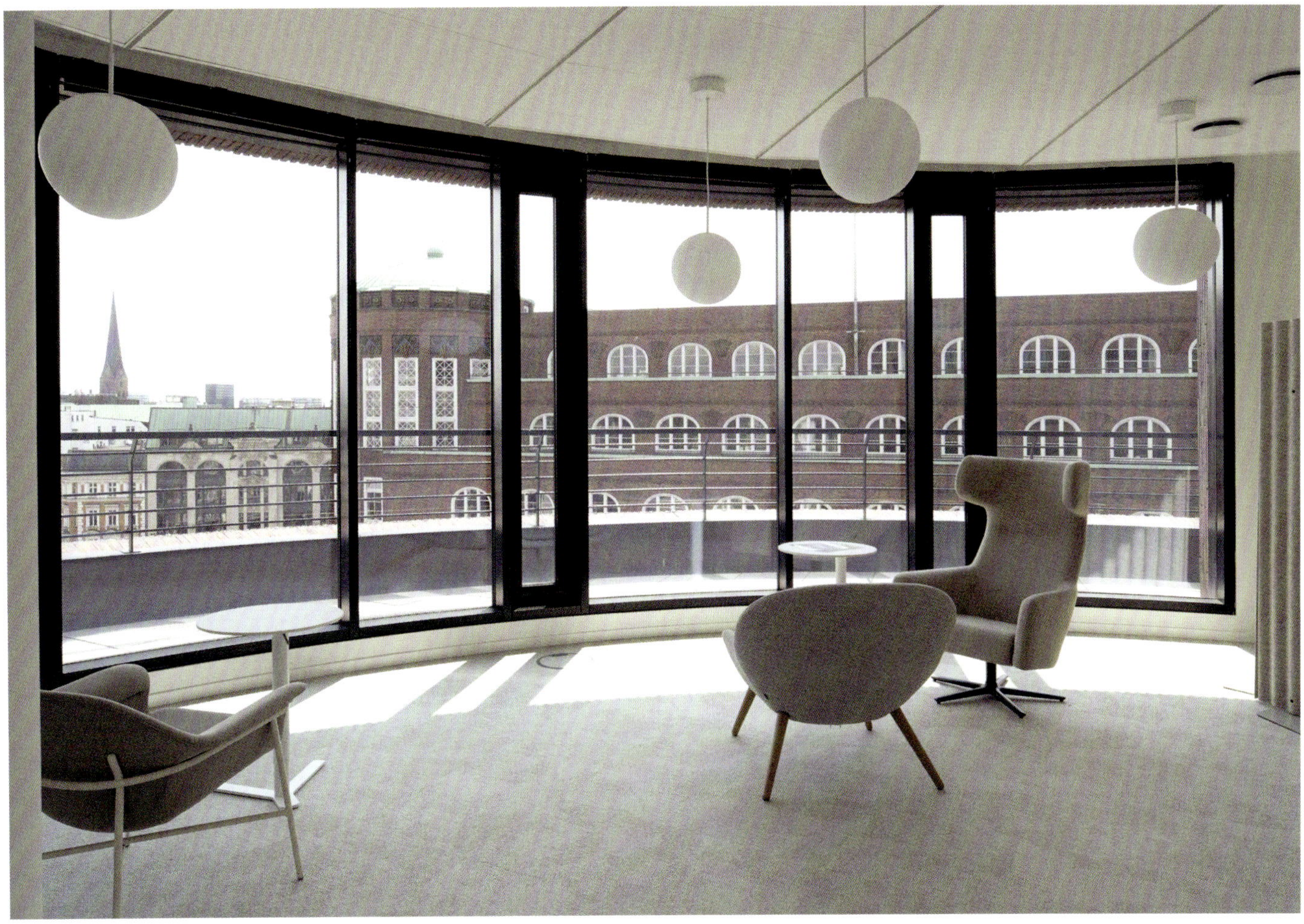

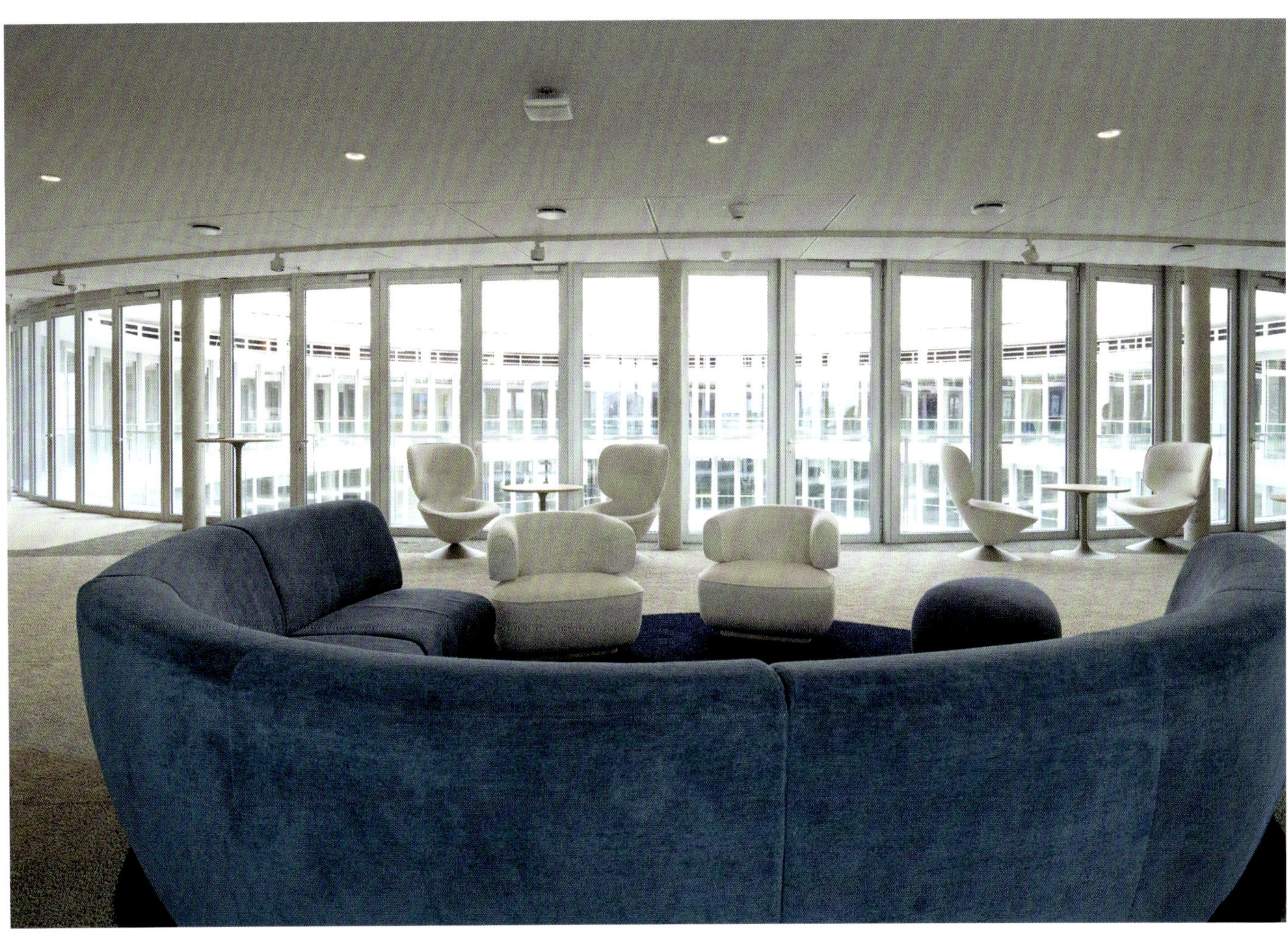

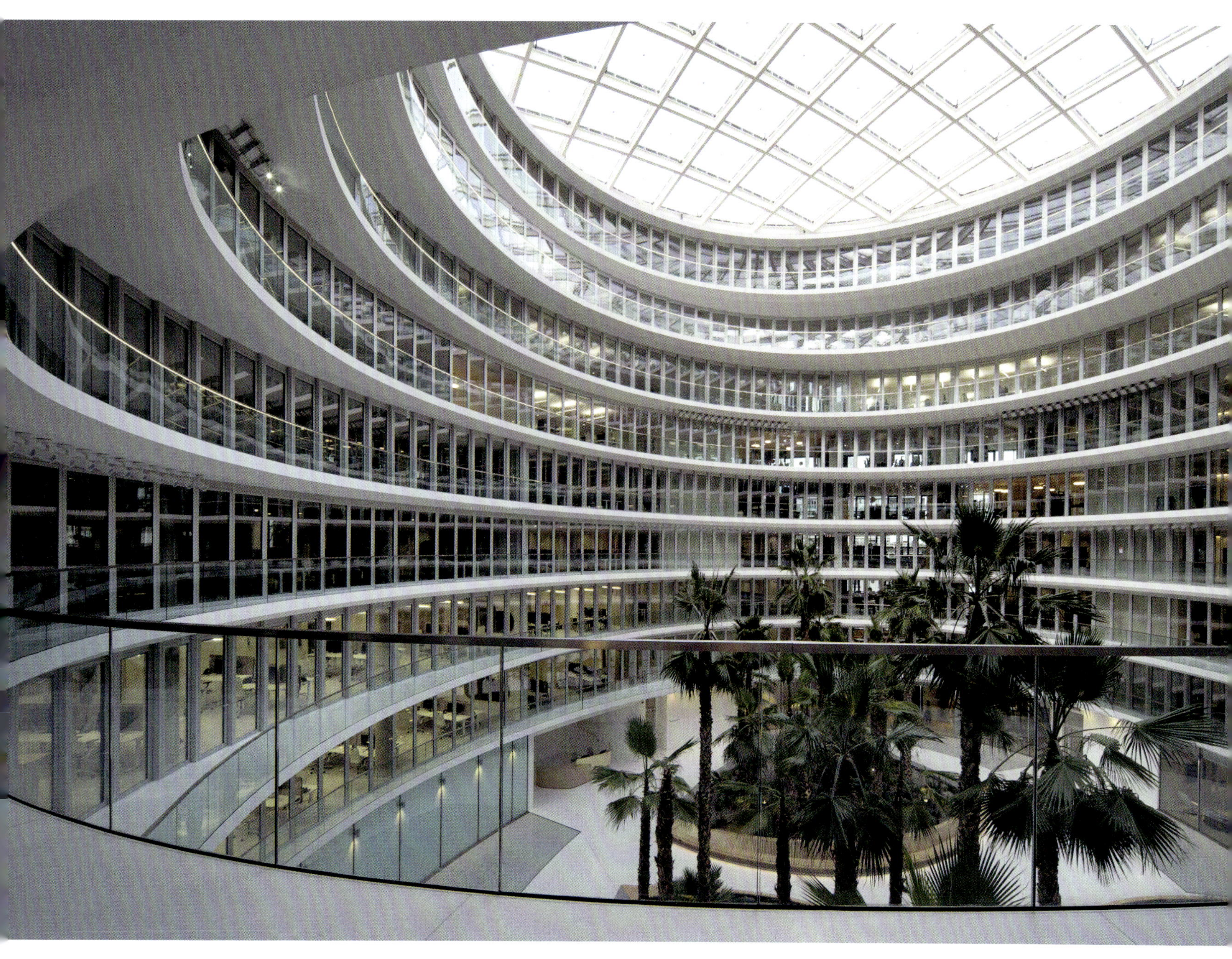

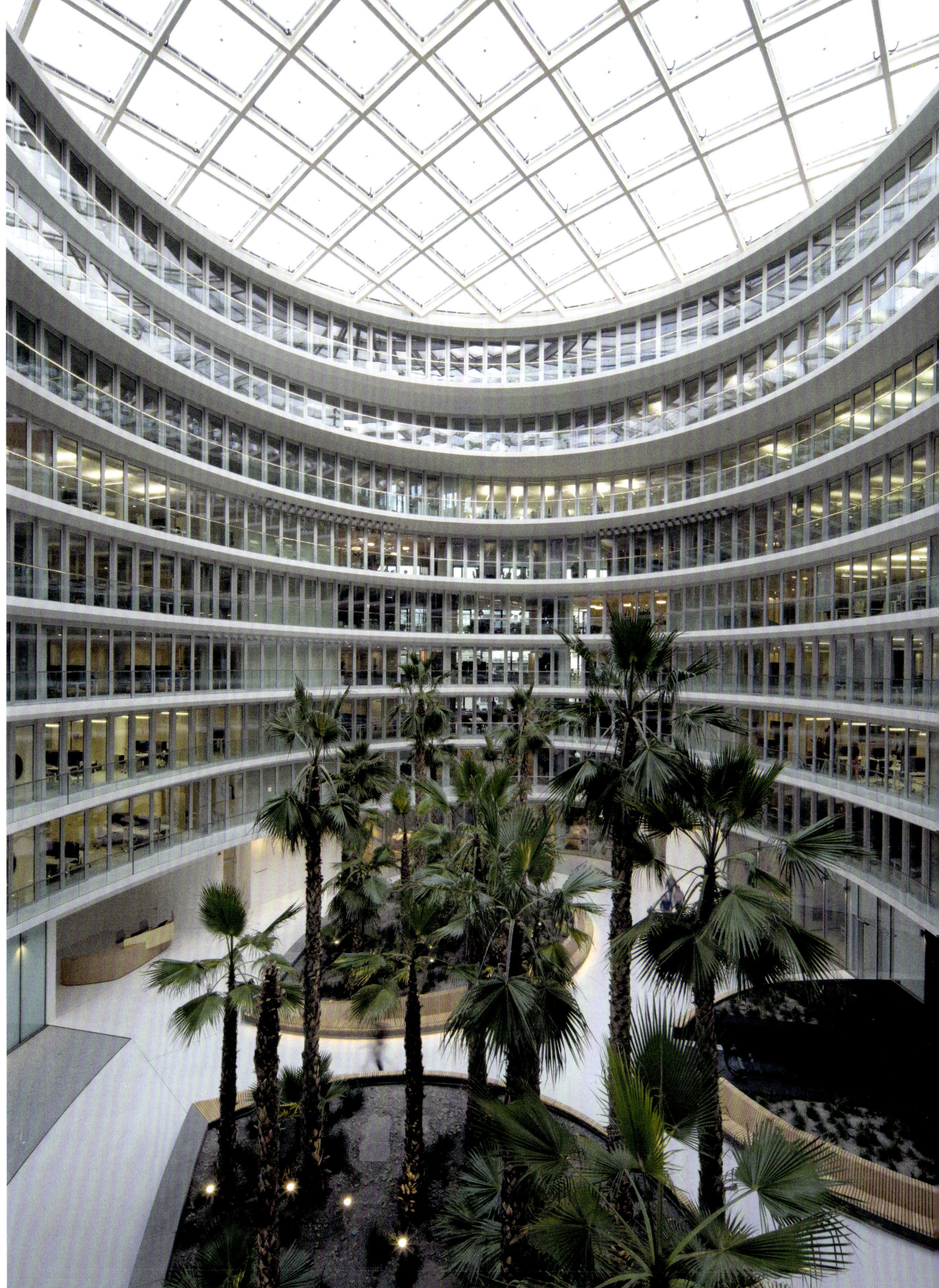

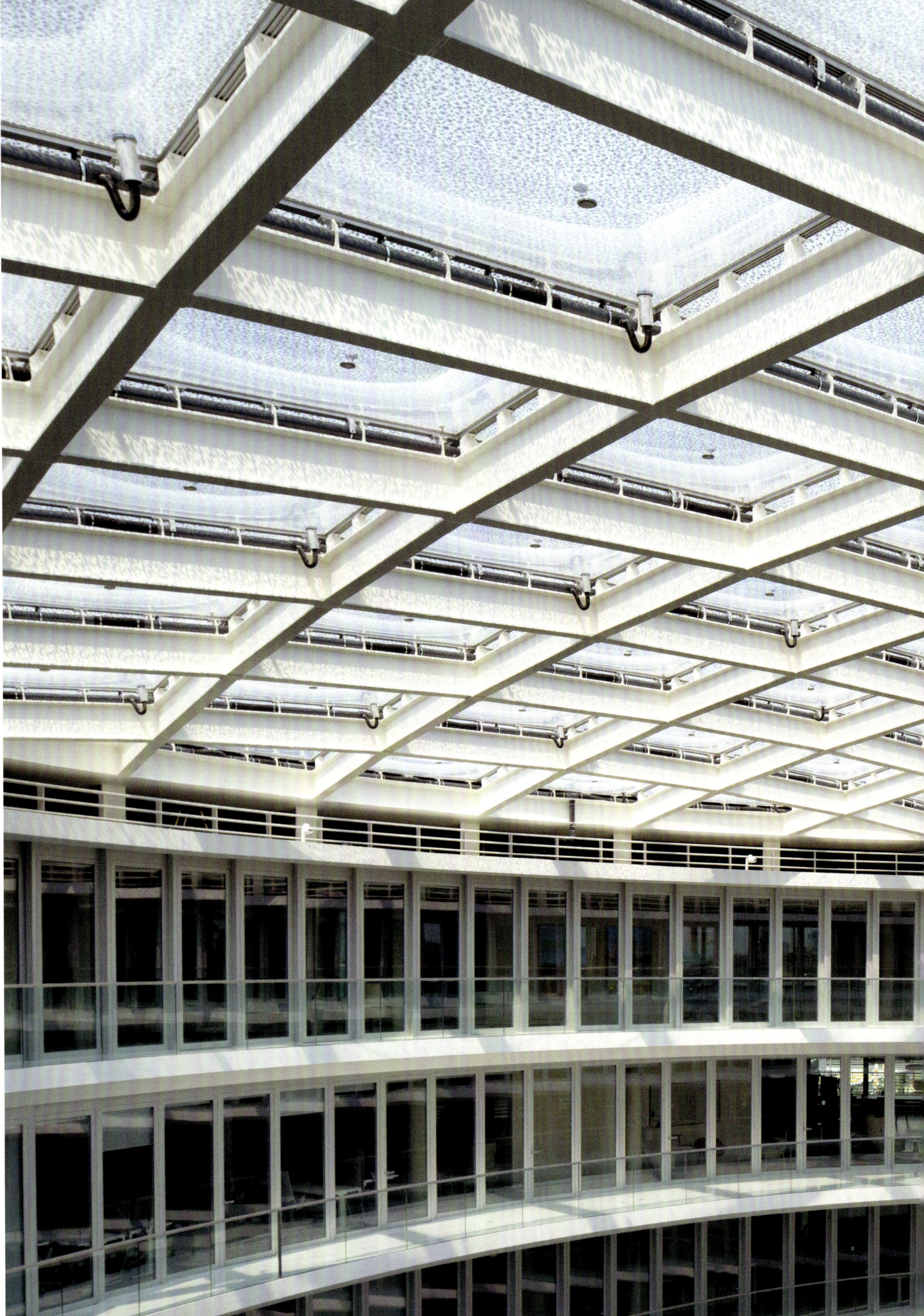

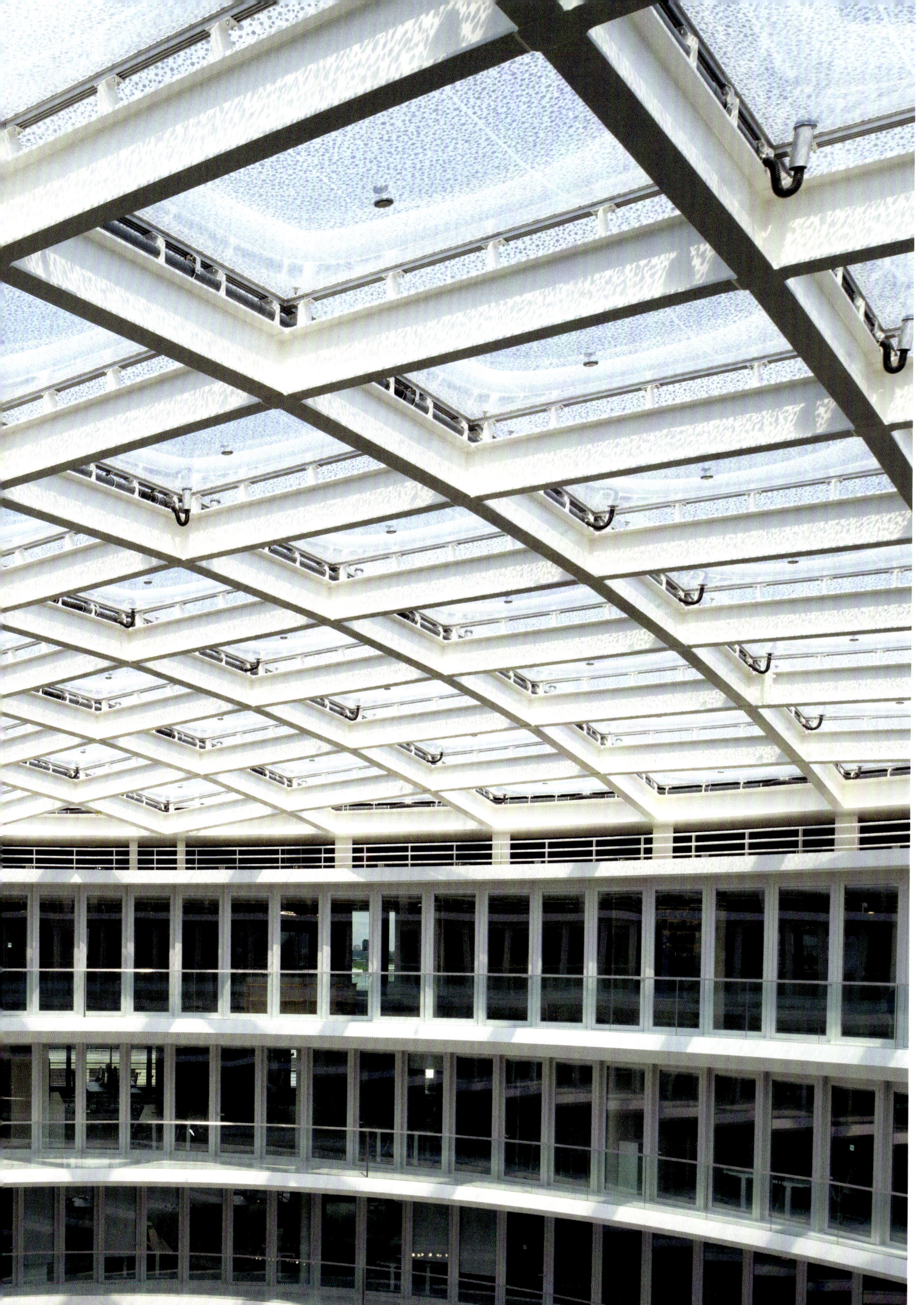

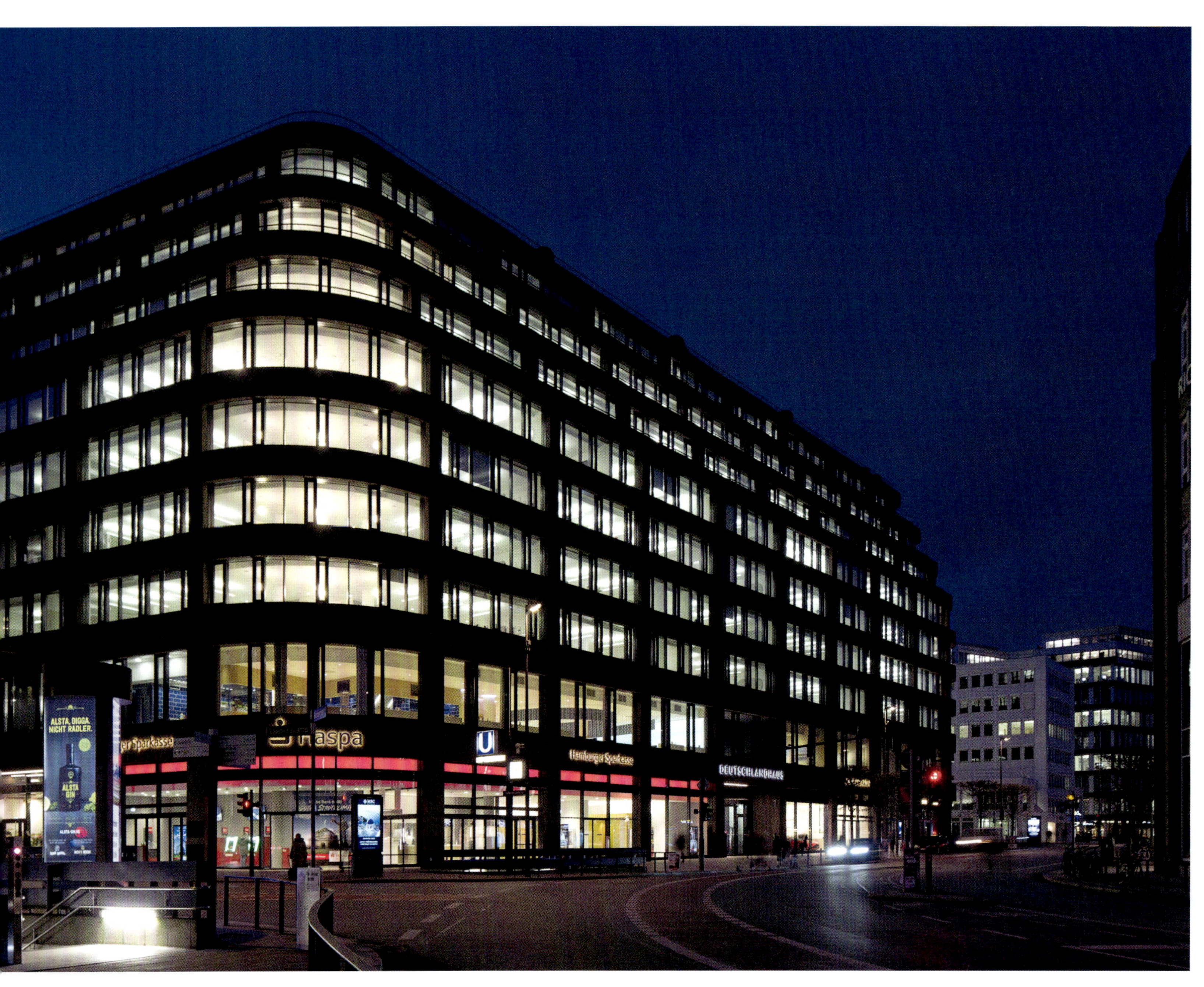
ALSTA, DIGGA.
NICHT RADLER.
ALSTA
GIN
U
Hamburger Sparkasse
DEUTSCHLANDHAUS

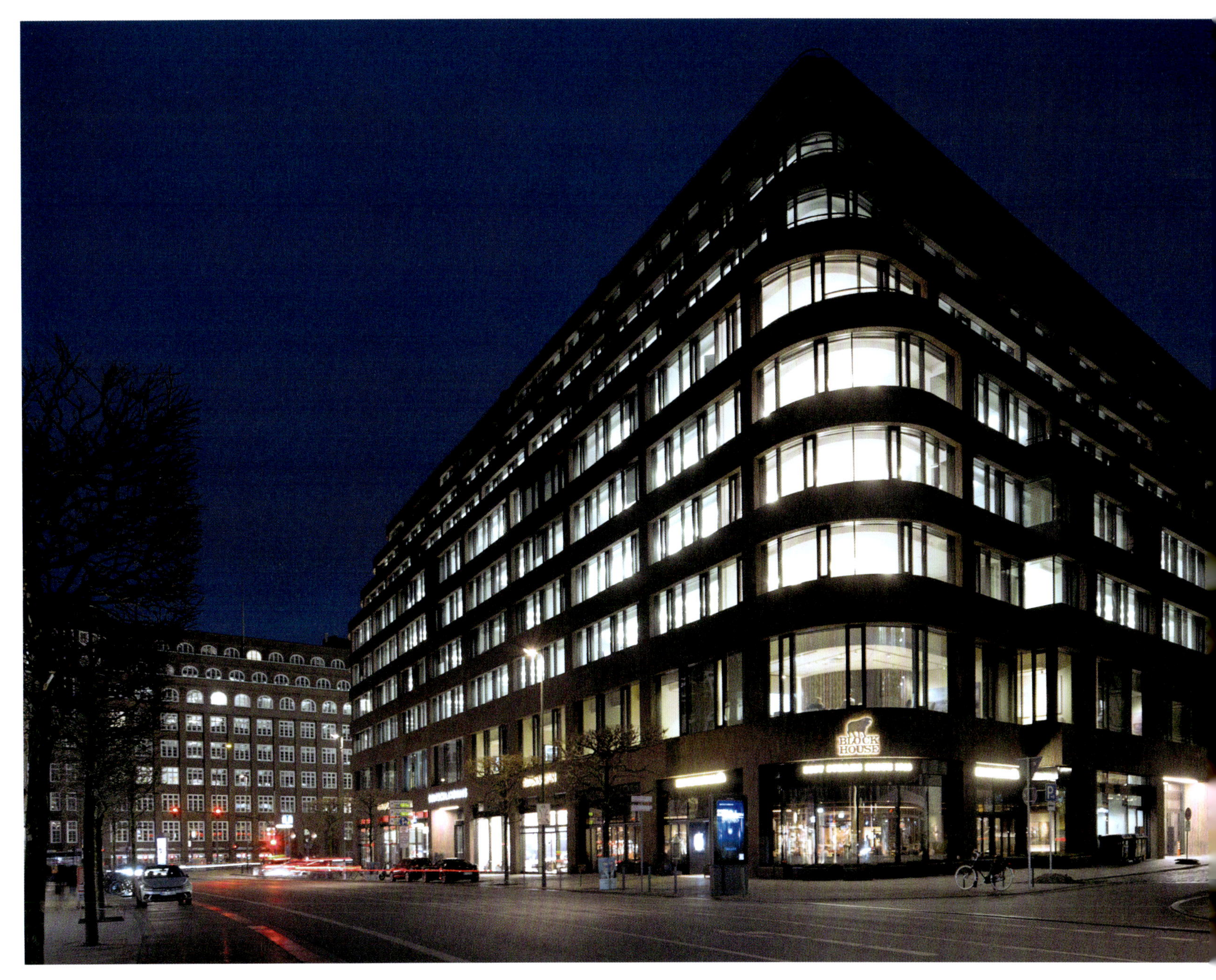
BLOCK
HOUSE

DEUTSCHLANDHAUS

Past and Present

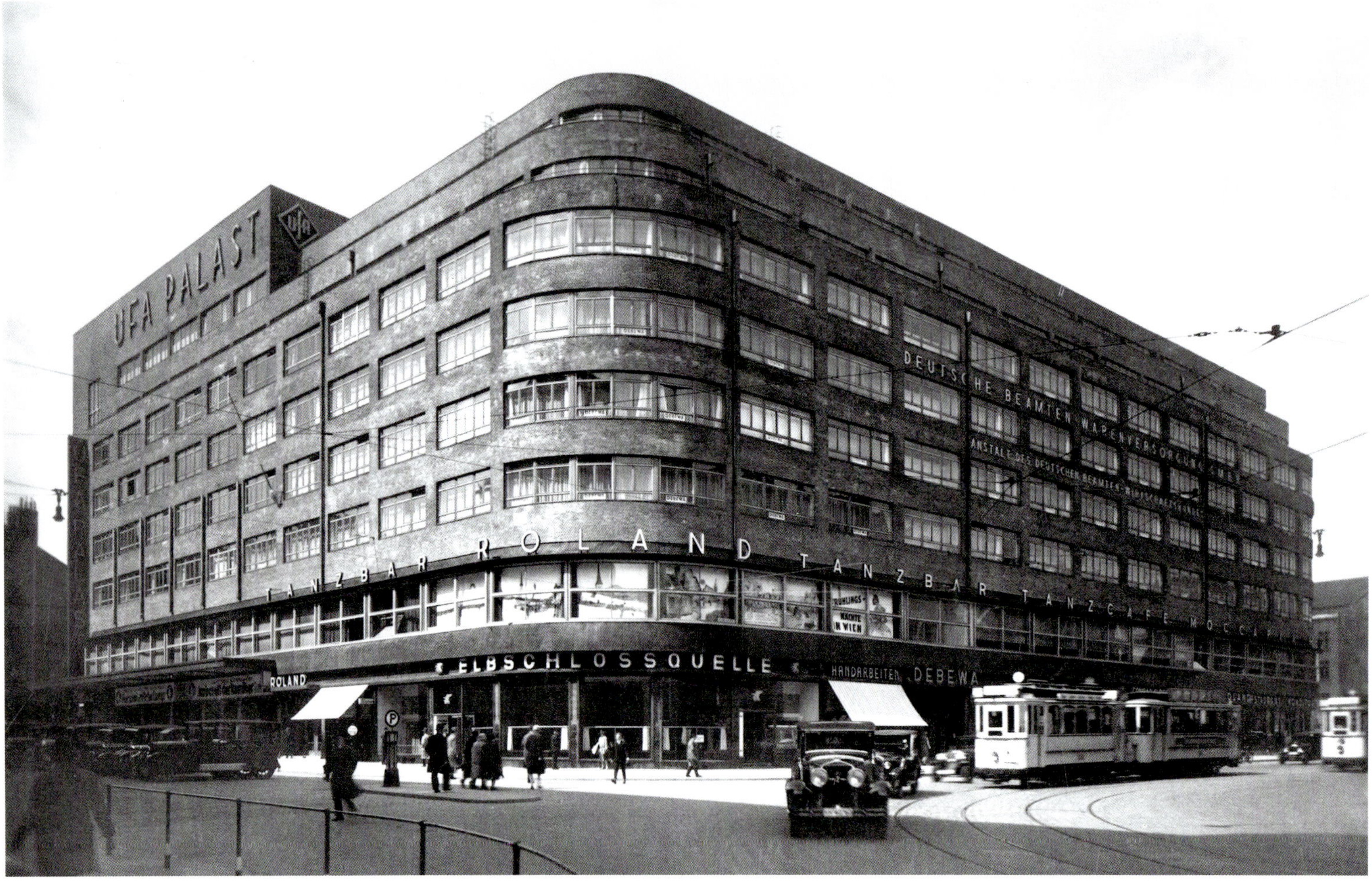
UFA PALAST
ROLAND
TANZBAR
TANZBAR
ELBSCHLOSSQUELLE
HANDARBEITEN DEBEWA

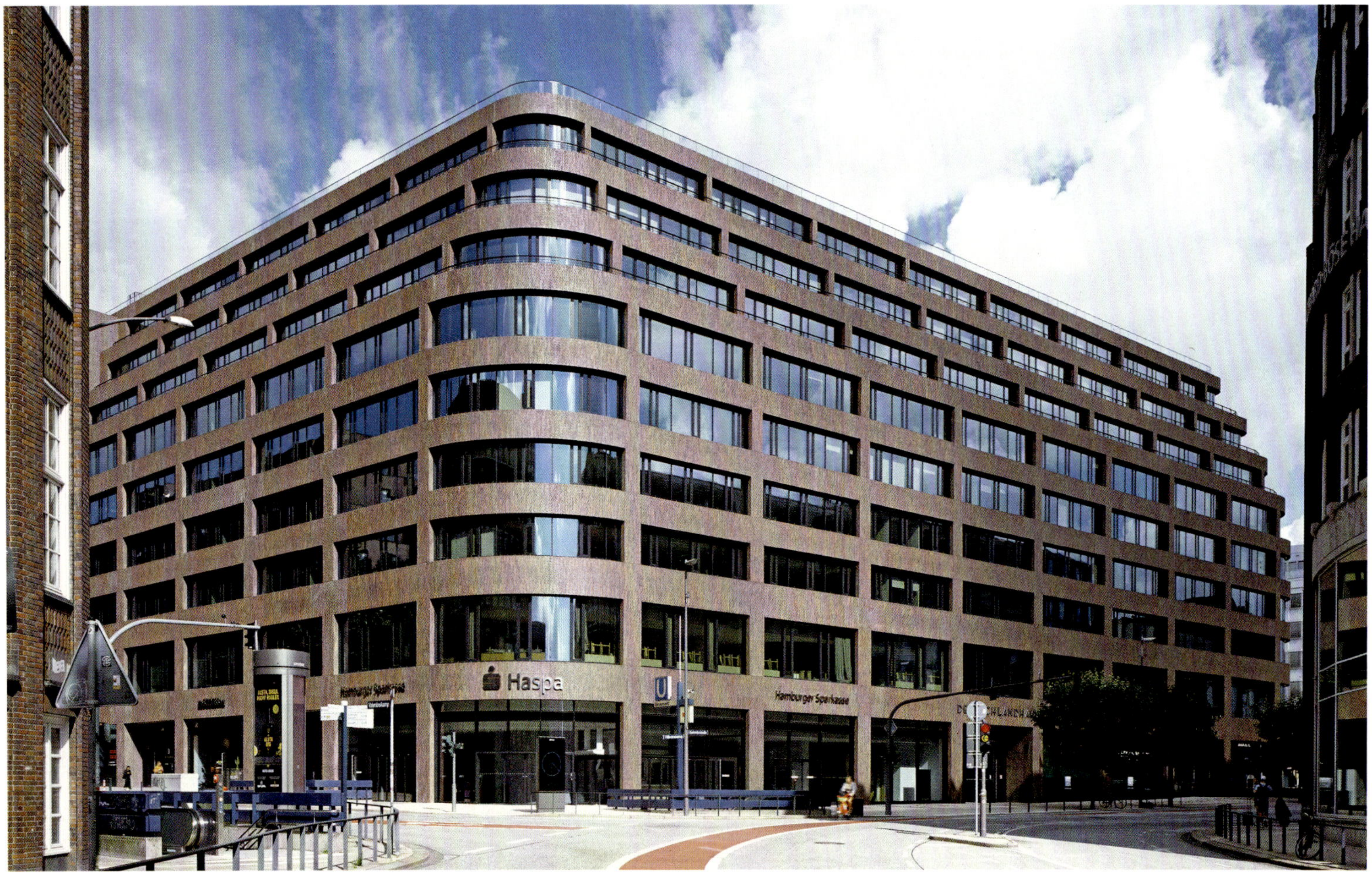
Haspa
Hamburger Sparkasse

While architecture looks static, it is undergoing continual transformation at the same time. For as a part and expression of social, economic, technical, artistic, and urban-planning circumstances, it represents a stage of an ongoing process of development. This applies all the more in the urban context, where modernizations occur more frequently, and to the twentieth century, with its progressive certainty of overcoming tradition. Although some buildings and structures endure, and some even survive as historical monuments, many are at least converted, and they are often substituted by new buildings after only a few generations for reasons of changed priorities, requirements, and not least profitability. Architectural photography has been recording the different stages in this process since the mid-nineteenth century, enabling a comparison between past and present. Such a comparison can also be made with the *Deutschlandhaus*, a mixed-use office building in the center of Hamburg. It was constructed in 1928/29 and demolished in 2019, to be replaced in 2024 by a contemporary new building.

Hamburg and the *Deutschlandhaus*

Like many European cities, in the early twentieth century Hamburg went through an accelerated modernization process known as "city-building." This was accompanied by a leap in urban-planning standards in reaction to the city's new requirements. Historically evolved layouts were revised; old buildings were demolished and replaced by larger ones. A prominent example is the pre-First World War breaking through of Mönckebergstraße from the Rathaus (completed 1897) to the central station (completed 1906). The thoroughfare was redeveloped with commercial and retail buildings to become one of the city's prestigious shopping streets. Another example is the *Kontorhausviertel* (Office Building District), which was preceded by the demolition of a historical residential district in the southeast of the old city. Its clinker-brick buildings, including the expressionist *Chilehaus* (1922–24), by the architect Fritz Höger, were added to the list of UNESCO World Heritage Sites in 2015.

A similar process, although on a smaller scale, took place on the Gänsemarkt in Hamburg's district of Neustadt, in the northwest of the city center. Through this square, traffic into the city center from the north via Dammtorstraße and from the west via Valentinskamp enters Jungfernstieg, Hamburg's promenade along the Inner Alster. The edges of the square had been marked by Biedermeier-style town houses, which were replaced from the 1880s onward with individual new office buildings. Apart from its function as an interchange for pedestrians, cars, taxis, and trams, the area around the Gänsemarkt was traditionally an entertainment district. The *Lessing-Theater* cinema had stood on the square since 1912, while the *Hamburger Stadttheater* (Municipal Theater, now the State Opera), modernized in 1925/26, and another cinema, the *Waterloo*, were on Dammtorstraße, and large assembly rooms were found on nearby Drehbahn.

The impulse for an urban restructuring of the Gänsemarkt came from the chief building and planning director of Hamburg, Fritz Schumacher (1869–1947). The first stage was the construction of his administrative building for the *Finanzdeputation* (Finance Authority). It had been planned in 1914, but due to war and inflation was only built in 1922–26, and a town house by the classicist architect Christian Friedrich Hansen was even demolished to make way for it. The building's two office wings, with their brick-clad pillar façades and staggered stories, are adapted to the structure and convention of the classical Hamburg office building. By giving the building a cylindrical corner tower and positioning it on the axis of Dammtorstraße, Schumacher emphasized the square's redirection of traffic onto Jungfernstieg and opened up a new road axis to Valentinskamp, on which he placed the building's main entrance.

Hamburg's chief building and planning director thus wanted to take up the historical idea of a city gate in a contemporary way. But the concept represented a challenge because the particularly busy Dammtorstraße narrowed into a funnel at its junction with the Gänsemarkt. The right time to widen this artery came in the early summer of 1927, when an investor wanted to purchase the properties on Dammtorstraße between Drehbahn and Valentinskamp for a single-block new building (the future *Deutschlandhaus*). In

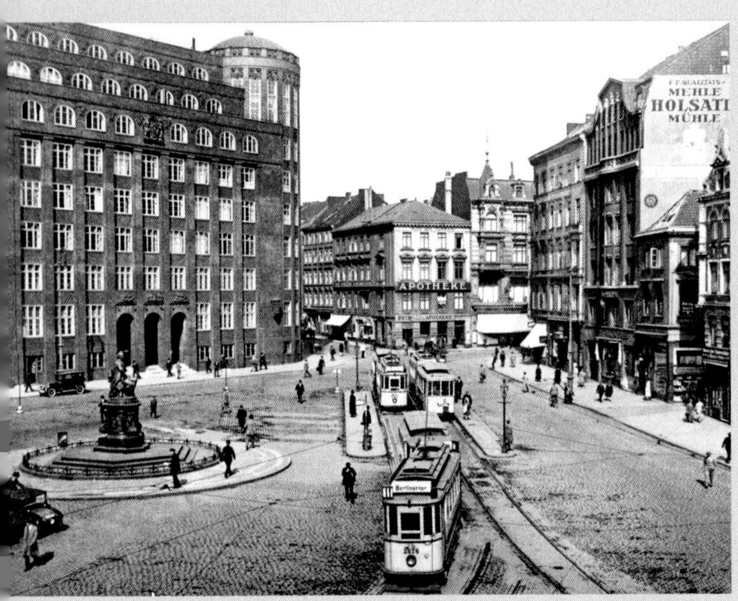

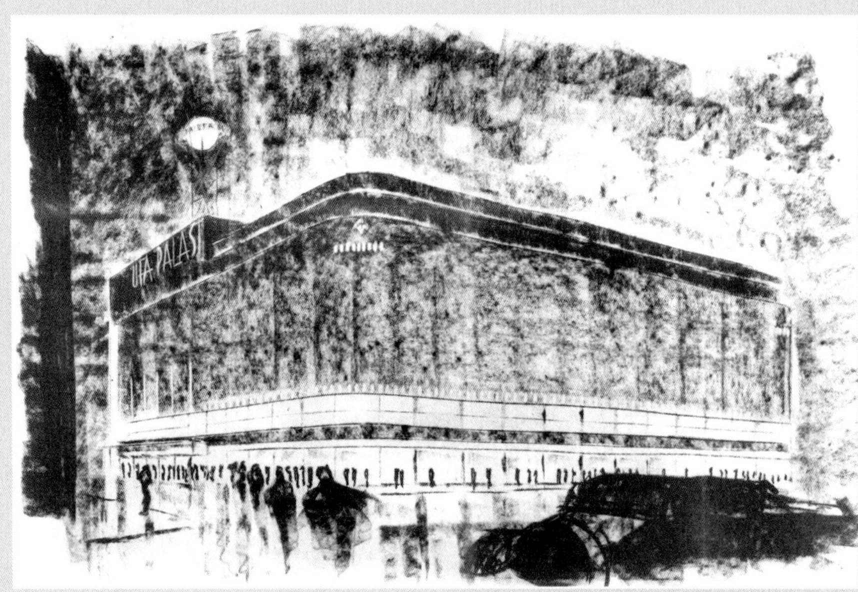

View of future building site from Gänsemarkt, 1926
Design sketch, Dr. Block & Hochfeld, 1928

conjunction with the Finance Authority, Schumacher's Building Authority was able to redraw the street line by means of a property swap that enabled the desired widening of Dammtorstraße and Valentinskamp. An agreement between the city and the builder also guaranteed Schumacher and his Building Authority a say in the architectural design of the planned building, which was required to adapt to his Finance Authority Building and with it form a modern "gateway to the city."

The initiator of this still unnamed project was the Berlin entrepreneur David Oliver (1880–1947), who had many years' experience in the cinema industry. His film-production companies were among those that formed the basis of the *Universum-Film Aktiengesellschaft (Ufa)*, the largest German film company, founded in 1917. Following the lucrative sale of his companies to the *Ufa*, Oliver was taken on as a production consultant, after which he was mainly active as a freelance project developer of cinemas. In Hamburg he wanted to build a new cinema that would outdo the city's existing ones in size. So the project was real-estate investment typical of the 1920s. Given the cinema boom of the time, commercial buildings with integrated cinemas at prime locations in German city centers promised attractive returns. The big film-production companies were also edging into the profitable cinema-operation market. But here they didn't act as investors, but as long-term leaseholders of cinema real estate usually financed by investment consortiums on the capital market.

In the building project on Gänsemarkt Oliver represented the Berlin-based corporation *Grundwert AG*, specially founded in 1927, as its managing director. In early June of 1928 the *Ufa* decided to join the project as leaseholder of the cinema wing. This would enable them not only to trump their Hamburg competitors but also to have at their disposal the largest cinema in Europe. The Hamburg *Ufa-Palast* was also to have the American-style large cinema stage, new to Germany, which permitted orchestral concerts and vaudeville shows along with film screenings.

Oliver commissioned the Hamburg architects Dr. Fritz Block (1889–1955) and Ernst Hochfeld (1890–1985) to plan and design the building. Their office, founded in 1921, had not yet produced either an office building or a cinema. But the architects had already designed a funerary monument in the Jewish cemetery and a brick villa on the Outer Alster for the merchant widow Amalie Wütow. Oliver had married a daughter of the family in 1920, and as he needed an experienced architectural office available at short notice for his Hamburg project, he went for the obvious solution. Dr. Block & Hochfeld also had a view of architecture from which a modern design for the new office building with an integrated cinema could be expected.

The building project was initially subject to controversial public, media, and political discussion, not least because of skepticism about its investor. But once the city council had given its approval in April 1928, Dr. Block & Hochfeld arrived via several preliminary stages at the building's final form. This provided for a U-shaped single-block building along Valentinskamp, Dammtorstraße, and Drehbahn, with the cinema in its central courtyard. The entrance to the cinema was on Valentinskamp and accordingly emphasized in the façade, which was flat and evenly articulated by all-round ribbon windows and rounded at the two corners with different radii. The building had eight floors, with the top two staggered. The ground floor contained retail space; above it were a generously windowed upper level and the office floors. The main entrance of the commercial building was on Dammtorstraße.

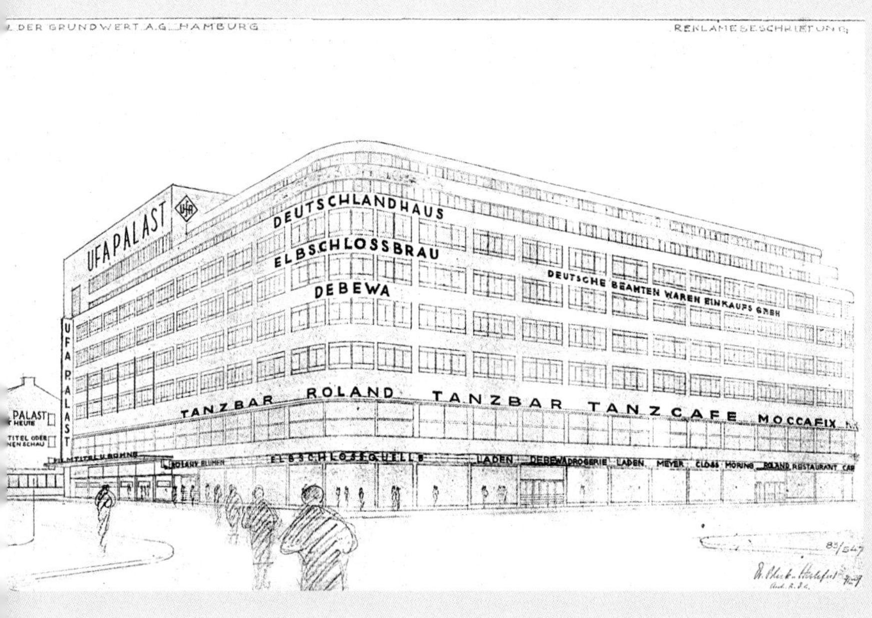

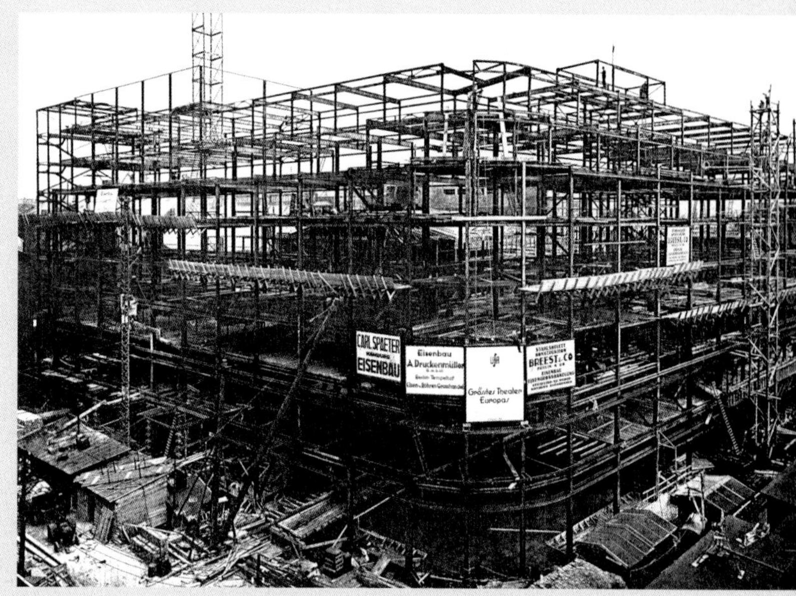

Façade drawing, Dr. Block & Hochfeld, 1928
Steel-frame construction, 1929

"Breakthrough of modernity"

It was Schumacher who stipulated brick as the building material. And the architectural design framework was additionally defined by the builder's economic considerations, which naturally required a maximum return on his real-estate investment. The property was to be developed almost in its entirety, with the greatest possible exploitation of the permitted height. The otherwise barely usable rear space was optimally filled by the cinema, while the display sides on the street would provide rental space for shops, restaurants, and offices.

Dr. Block & Hochfeld, however, were not only concerned with the fulfilment of pragmatic requirements, but also and primarily with the architectural expression of the zeitgeist. This favored a large, clearly articulated building mass with flat, evenly structured and uniformly colored façades. At the same time the horizontal emphasis of the all-round ribbon windows and the building's rounded corners were meant to reflect the dynamic of the passing traffic and thus the accelerated rhythm of the epoch. And metropolitan elegance was intended to result from the functionality of the building, not from its décor. In this the design concept differed significantly from the tradition of the Hamburg office building—whose often solemn façades were mostly vertically articulated—and was oriented much more to the international architectural modernism primarily established by the office buildings of the Berlin architect Erich Mendelsohn.

The realization of the building project was also seen by the Hamburg public as a "breakthrough of modernity." Work began in October 1928 after the demolition of the existing buildings on the property. It had been decided for constructional and economic reasons to use a steel-skeleton structure (instead of reinforced concrete). The method would result in a shorter building time through prefabrication and montage, it was hoped (in vain), and it would enable the loadbearing structure of the façade to be extended into the interior of the building. In this way a flat, brick-clad curtain wall horizontally articulated by ribbon windows would suffice for the entire front, and the plinth area could be generously glazed.

Building work was delayed by extreme cold in the winter of 1928/29. Progress on site was accelerated from March 1929 onwards by up to 1,500 men working in three shifts day and night. For the builder had contractually agreed to complete the restaurant spaces and cinema before Christmas. This pressure of time took its toll on both the quality of execution (visible in blistering in the masonry) and safety, as there were several accidents. From today's point of view the completion of a building of this size within fifteen months from foundation to opening would be unthinkable, even with the most modern equipment.

In Hamburg, as elsewhere, it was customary to give office and commercial buildings a name of their own related either to their location or the trade of their builder or leaseholder. The large building project on Gänsemarkt had no such designation as yet. After a long search for a suitable name it was finally announced in November 1929 that the building would be called the *Deutschlandhaus*. The name was intended both to emphasize its national significance and to express confidence in Germany's future after its economic recovery from the Great War (the coming impact of the recent stock-market crash in New York was as yet unforeseeable).

Despite all problems the *Deutschlandhaus* was finished on time. It was dedicated with a grand opening of the *Ufa-Palast* on

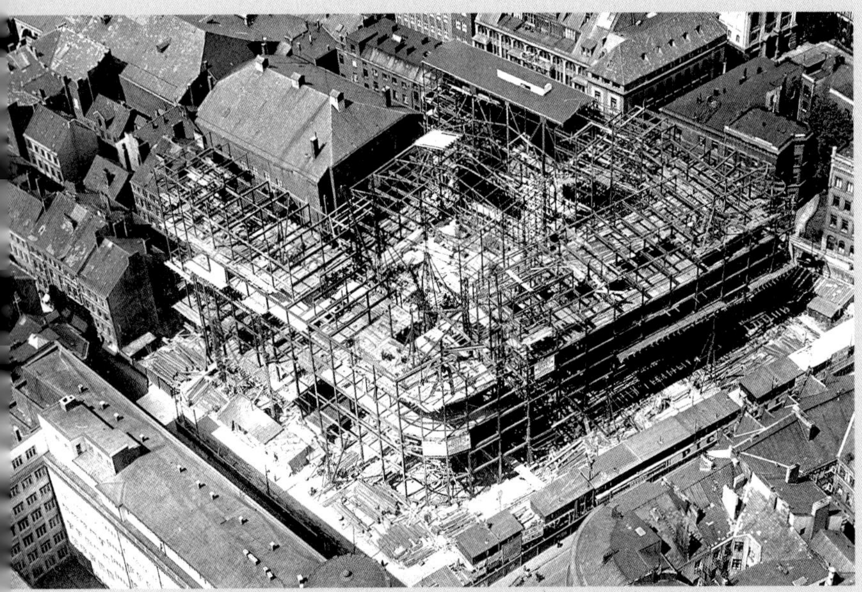

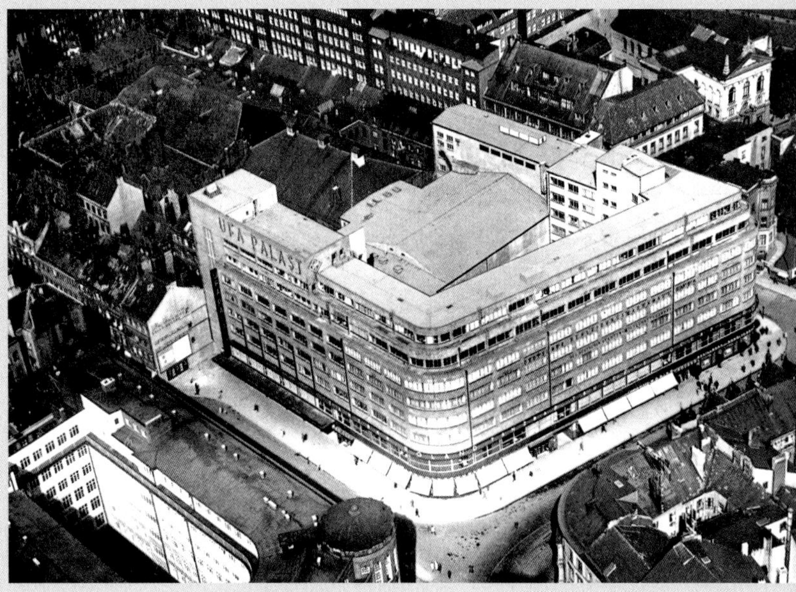

Aerial views during construction and after completion, 1929 and 1930

December 21, 1929, though its final completion needed until early 1930. The Hamburg newspapers praised the building for its simple, clear forms. The luxurious fittings and modern technology of the cinema, and the spacious restaurant areas on the first floor, also met with approval. On the whole the *Deutschlandhaus* was felt to be an adequate expression of the zeitgeist, also in its adherence to the metropolitan dimension and appeal of an "American example." The building became one of Hamburg's new landmarks and also a popular postcard motif.

Although Dr. Block & Hochfeld's *Deutschlandhaus* was in many ways at the forefront of architectural development, and for Hamburg represented something extraordinarily modern, beyond the city it remained less noticed—unlike the *Chilehaus*, for example—and didn't find its way into twentieth-century architectural history.

The original *Deutschlandhaus*

The overall appearance of the *Deutschlandhaus* is well documented in photographs by the architect Fritz Block and other contemporaries. The building was constructed on a 5,700 m^2 trapezoidal site, and its developed space amounted to 145,000 m^3—65,000 m^3 for the cinema and 80,000 m^3 for the commercial building. The total office space was 15,000 m^2. Costs were given as six to seven million reichsmarks.

The building was given a steel-skeleton structure; only the two all-round staggered stories were carried out in reinforced concrete. Dutch clinker was used for the exterior masonry. The flat façade was horizontally articulated by equal sections of white-framed ribbon windows separated only by vertical strips of wall spanning the entire façade. The building's rounded corners continued this articulation with curved windowpanes. The long frontage on Dammtorstraße rested on a plinth clad in dark ceramics on the ground floor and was topped by a slightly projecting, largely glazed upper floor bordered with copper bands. Lettering in modern typography on the upper band was illuminated at night.

The *Ufa-Palast* cinema was structurally integrated into the *Deutschlandhaus* but separate from the rest of the building. Its entrance on Valentinskamp was emphasized by a section of the building higher by one floor than the staggered stories, lighting strips and widely visible lettering that accentuated the façade, and a canopy. Access was through a spacious entrance hall lined in travertine with two ticket booths in the middle. From here visitors could reach the balcony via stairways on either side. But the main entrance was through a brightly lit two-story foyer to the stalls and marble stairs to the circle. The auditorium could hold an audience of around 2,700, and it was the largest in Europe at the time. Dr. Block & Hochfeld were responsible for its architecture but not for its interior design, as they were unable to reach an agreement with the builder on matters of taste. Oliver preferred modernist art-deco forms that would fulfil the traditional expectations of a wider cinema-going public. The cinema was equipped to screen the new sound film, which had been introduced into Germany in autumn 1929. The stage was big enough for orchestral concerts and vaudeville, and equipped to the latest technological standards.

The business wing of the *Deutschlandhaus* was occupied by various commercial tenants. There were smaller shops, including a bookshop, on the ground floor, along with modern caterers—on

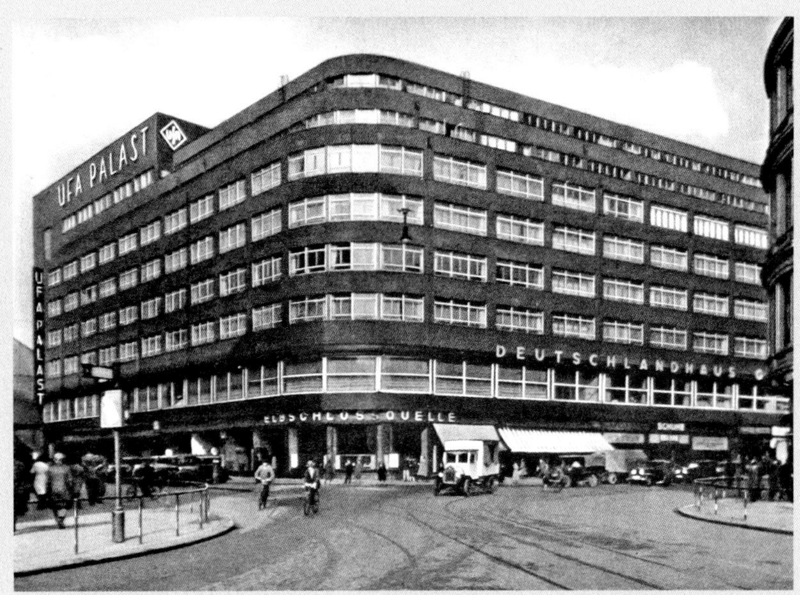

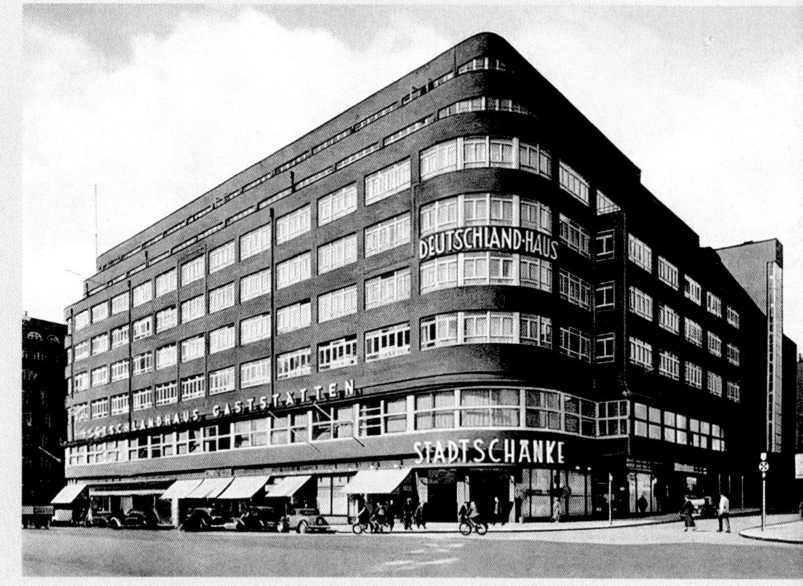

Views from Gänsemarkt, 1930, and Dammtorstraße, mid-1930s

the corner of Valentinskamp the beer bar *Elbschloßquelle*, on the corner of Drehbahn the bar *Quick-Lunch*. The entire first floor was occupied by a restaurant belonging to the Berlin-based *Roland-Betriebe*; it also contained the coffeehouse *Moccafix* with a dance-floor. In Hamburg these types of restaurants, aimed at a metropolitan public and modeled on American examples, were new.

The upper floors, reached by stairs from the main entrance on Dammtorstraße, were originally planned as offices, but were mostly rented as sales and store rooms by the department store *Deutsche Beamten-Warenversorgungs GmbH (DeBeWa)*, which was renamed *Deutsches Familien-Kaufhaus (DeFaKa)* in autumn 1930. In the part of the building above the entrance to the *Ufa-Palast* on Valentinskamp there were offices accessed by their own staircase. Dr. Block & Hochfeld moved into new premises here.

Conceived as an income property, the *Deutschlandhaus* was at first unprofitable for its investors, as revenue from the lease of the *Ufa-Palast*, which was partially tied to takings, was lower than expected. Turnover from entertainment films alone was inadequate for a cinema of this size, and more vaudeville had to be included in the program. When the impact of the world economic crisis began to be felt, the *Ufa*'s *Deutschlandhaus* investment began to make a loss. The modern catering concept of the *Roland-Betriebe* was also unsuccessful. The restaurant was then converted by the rescue company *Deutschlandhaus-Gaststätten* into a dining room with Hamburg-homey décor and renamed the *Stadtschänke* (City Tavern) in keeping with the changed zeitgeist. The economic crisis and then the war ultimately prevented the urban development of the surrounding district, for which the *Deutschlandhaus* had been intended as a stimulus.

Reflecting German history

It will come as no surprise that a building with the name *Deutschlandhaus* reflects German history. When Adolf Hitler came to Hamburg in March 1938 the façade was used to advertise National Socialist propaganda. Dr. Block & Hochfeld were already winding down their office at this time, prior to their emigration to the United States in November of that year. Another Jewish tenant, the architect Robert Friedmann (1888–1940), had already moved out and emigrated to Palestine in 1933. The architect Nils Gutschow (1902–1978), who designed some of the restaurants in the *Deutschlandhaus* and initially also kept an office there, was later appointed architect of the National Socialist redesign of Hamburg (which for the most part, fortunately, was not carried out due to the war).

During the Second World War many soldiers visited the *Ufa-Palast* with their families on leave of absence, so as to forget the hostilities for a few hours with film shows or vaudeville. The playbills now contained the announcement: "Attention! If there is an air-raid warning, performances will be interrupted in good time and a slide projection will request visitors to leave the auditorium in a calm and orderly manner." Raids on Hamburg on June 18, 1944, caused a fire in the stage area of the *Ufa-Palast* which also affected the auditorium and the cinema façade. Although a provisional cinema was built into the undamaged foyer, the *Deutschlandhaus* permanently lost an important part of its identity in the *Ufa-Palast*.

After the war the *Deutschlandhaus* went through a period of frequent conversion and varying use. After the peaceful surrender of Hamburg on May 3, 1945, the building was commandeered by the British military government. Because of its still relatively good

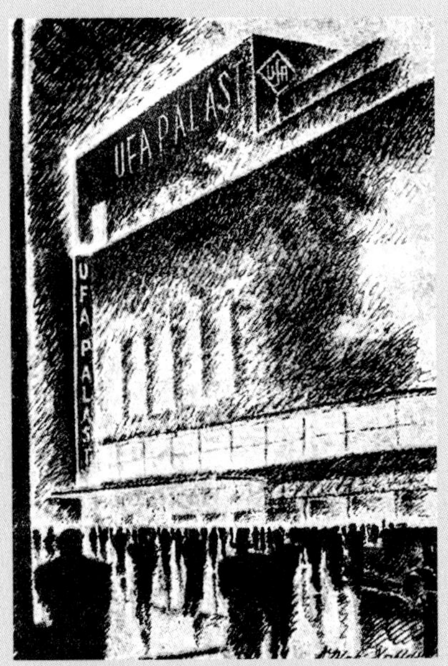

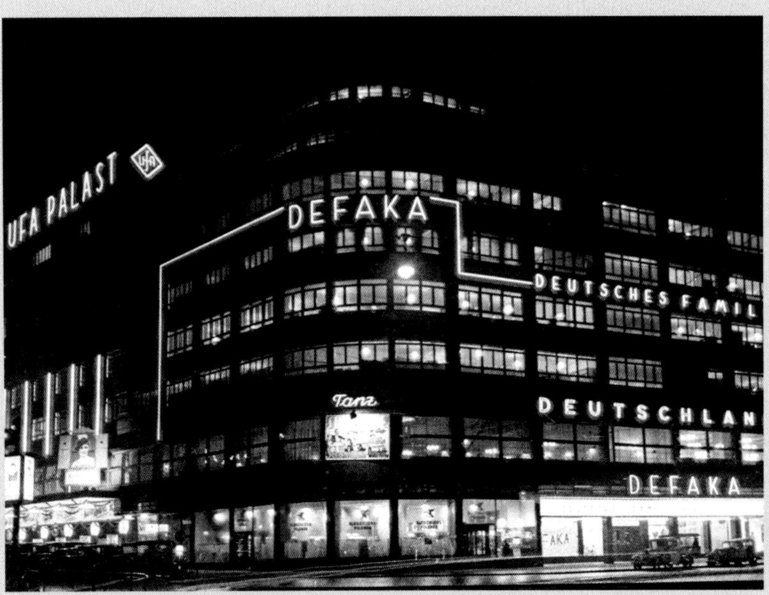

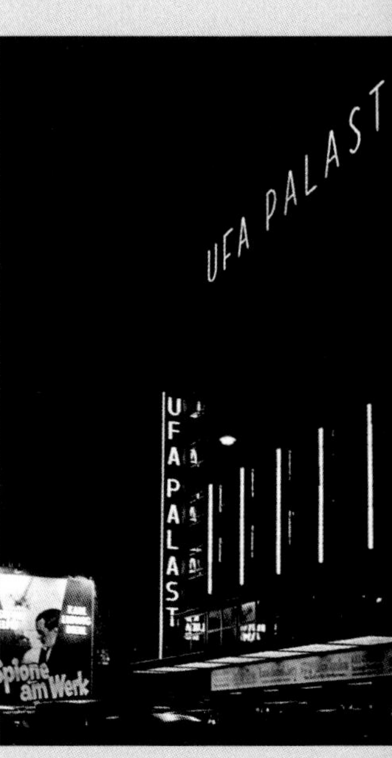

Design sketch of the *Ufa-Palast* cinema at night, Dr. Block & Hochfeld, 1929
Illuminated advertising on the façades at night, mid-1930s

condition, size, and central location it became the supply headquarters for the occupying troops. The NAAFI (Navy, Army, and Air Force Institutes), which provided the British military with groceries and consumer goods, ran the restaurant as the *Victory Canteen*.

In the course of its reconstruction—albeit with the ribbon windows in smaller sections and with more prominent white frames, mullions, and transoms—the *Deutschlandhaus* was expanded into the *Victory Club*. But in order to placate the Hamburg population the British renamed it *Hamburg House* in 1948. In the early 1950s the *Grundwert AG* obtained the reinstatement of its rights of ownership to the building, which regained its original name. Shops moved back into the ground floor, and the *Deutschlandhaus* was declared the "center of Hamburg's economic life" by the press. The British supply section finally moved out in early 1956. The main tenant in the *Deutschlandhaus* was now the *Hamburger Oberpostdirektion*, the Hamburg administrative section of the postal service, the *Deutsche Bundespost*. Due to its location on the popular Gänsemarkt, the façade of the building was also used as advertising space for company logos in the 1960s.

The properties held by the *Grundwert AG* went over to their major shareholder, the *Dresdner Bank*, in 1972. Considerable renovation to the *Deutschlandhaus* was needed in order for it to house the bank's various departments, which were scattered across Hamburg's city center. This renovation took place in two construction phases from 1976 to 1982, with costs of around 100 million deutschmarks. A better appreciation of 1920s architecture was growing in Germany at the time and led not least to the placing of a preservation order on Fritz Schumacher's Finance Authority Building, which formed a cityscape ensemble together with the *Deutschlandhaus*. It was neglected to place such an order on the *Deutschlandhaus*, however, and in its supervision of the building's renovation the Municipal Preservation Office behaved with incomprehensible passivity.

Despite assurances from the builder that the original design of the structural shell and façade would be retained, the basic fabric was significantly interfered with. The building was in fact stripped back to its steel-skeleton structure, rebuilt, and the façade given a facing brick, also including the ground floor, that didn't conform to the original. Further additions included a partial ninth floor, more transom-and-mullion windows, the paneling of the upper-floor windows in dark-red painted aluminum, and an all-round metal and glass canopy above the ground floor. So the result of the total renovation wasn't the preservation of the original but the creation of a bad copy, which thus substantially forfeited its reason for preservation.

From the start the *Deutschlandhaus* had mainly been a real-estate investment. In this tradition it was sold by the *Dresdner Bank* to an American hedge fund, although the bank initially remained its tenant. The building then changed hands several times. When the *Dresdner Bank* was taken over by the *Commerzbank* in 2009, the *Commerzbank* became the new main tenant, and made this clear with altered lettering on the façade. In the end the building became part of a property fund belonging to the Swiss big bank *Credit Suisse*. In 2014 *Credit Suisse* sold the fully let building, which wasn't under a preservation order and therefore disposable, for eighty-one million euros to the *ABG Real Estate Group*, a German property developer. Since the *Commerzbank* was in difficulty due to the takeover of the *Dresdner Bank* and the financial crisis, it came to terms with the new owner about an early cancellation of the lease.

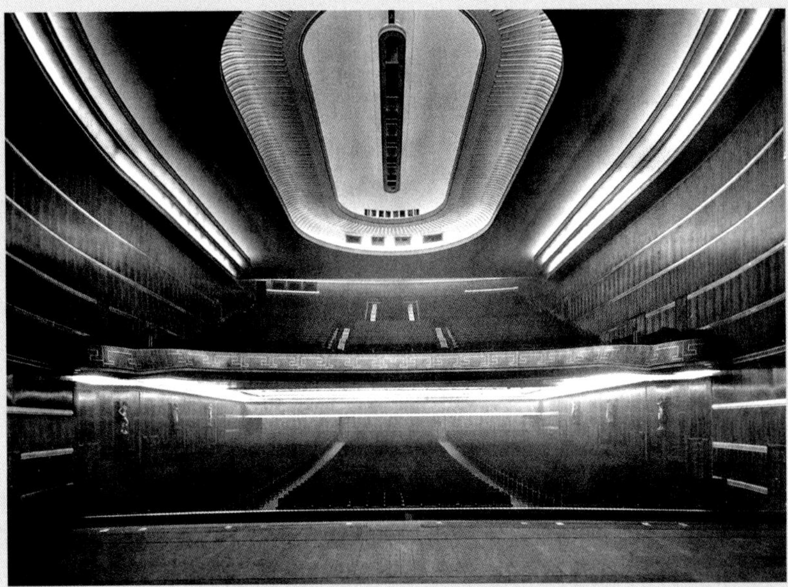

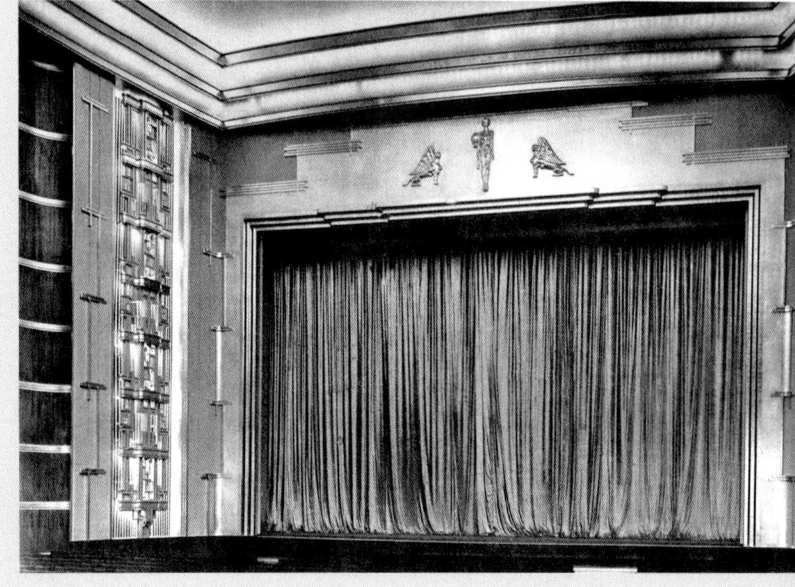

Auditorium and stage of the *Ufa-Palast* cinema, 1929

After assessing the building fabric, which in their view no longer complied with present-day requirements and didn't promise a profitable return on investment, the *ABG Real Estate Group* decided to demolish the building and replace it with a new one. The fate of the no longer original *Deutschlandhaus* was sealed.

The new *Deutschlandhaus*

While a real-estate investor aims to realize its project as smoothly as possible in collaboration with the architect and contracting building companies, and in coordination with the municipal authorities, the public demands information and transparency, and participation in the planning if need be. The surprising announcement in 2017 that the *Deutschlandhaus* was to be demolished gave rise to controversial discussions in professional circles, the press, and politics in Hamburg and beyond. In a democratically organized community this is both desirable and necessary when a private builder wishes to make significant changes to a prominent part of the cityscape. In the case of the *Deutschlandhaus* the issue was not only the specific aspects of the building and its history but also the basic question of dealing with an architectural legacy, particularly with modernism.

It was once again regretted that failure to place the *Deutschlandhaus* under a preservation order and later inadequate control of its total renovation had facilitated the decision to demolish. But discussion also took place in this context about the general criteria for urban-heritage conservation. For the prevalent idea here is that the reason for preserving a building lies in its surviving fabric, irrespective of its present state, not in the architectural design on which this is based. With altered building fabric, accordingly, approval for demolition is more likely than the requirement to restore a building to its original condition. It was occasionally argued, though, that alterations to a building were also part of its history, which could underline its eligibility for preservation.

Another aspect that played a role in the discussion at the time, but would have greater weight today, was the question of "gray energy." This is the issue of whether the consumption of material and energy caused by the demolition and rebuilding of an existing building makes economic sense and is ecologically justifiable compared with renovation or reconstruction. Since a way to evaluate these things has not yet been fully developed, for investors rebuilding is usually the option that is easier to calculate—and for architects the more prestigious one. Objectively, a renovation of the *Deutschlandhaus* that reconstructed the original of 1928/29 would have been extremely difficult due to its massively altered structure (and loss of the cinema)—and uneconomical from an investor's point of view. Apart from the fact that usage requirements on offices and statutory specifications have changed considerably.

Furthermore, the question was asked as to whether Hamburg could agree to the demolition of the major work of two German-Jewish architects who had been compelled to leave the city in 1938, and whether this exile didn't in fact give rise to a moral duty to preserve the building. When it later became clear that the new building would at least present a strong exterior similarity to its predecessor, the issue of the original architects' design copyright also was raised.

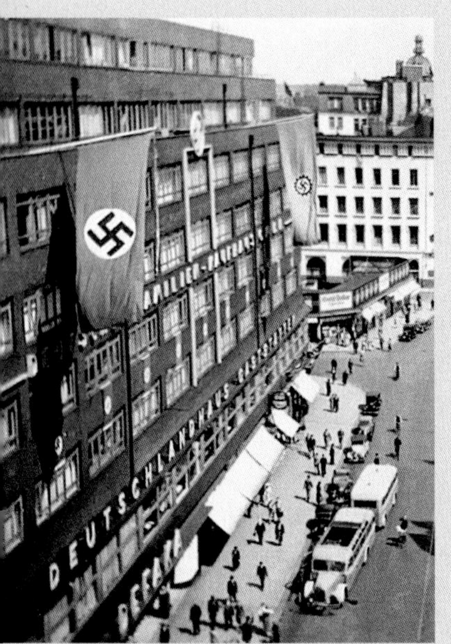

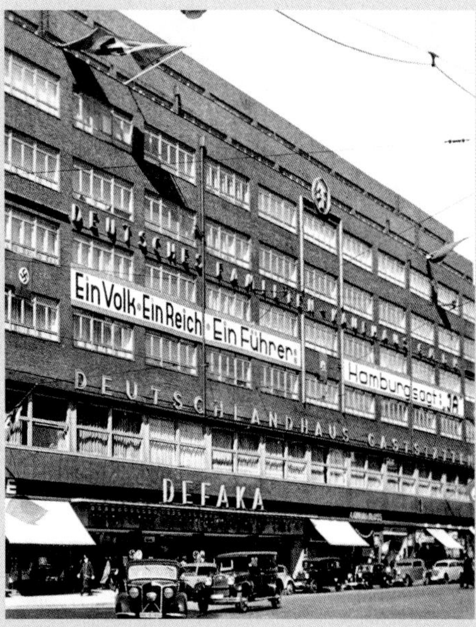

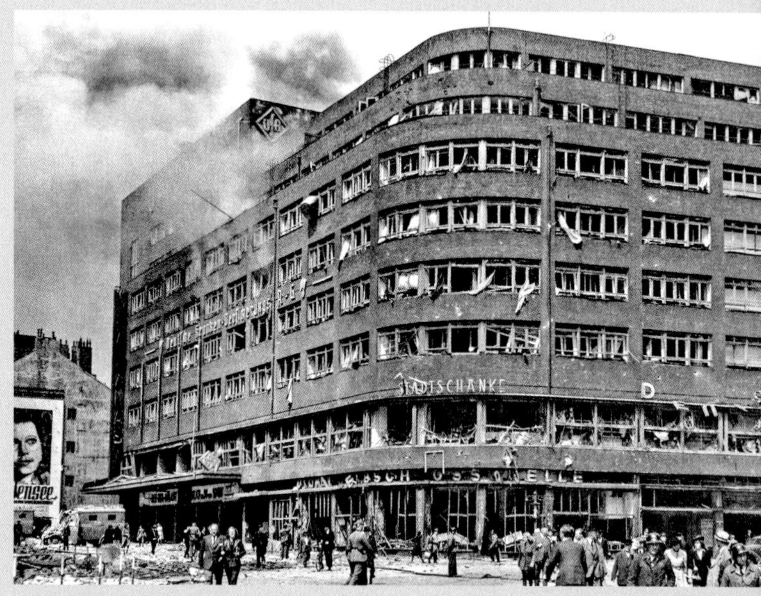

Nazi propaganda on the façade, 1938
Bomb damage, June 1944

Permission to demolish the *Deutschlandhaus* was ultimately a political decision by the municipal authorities. Economically, of course, a role was played by the fact that property rights would have made alternatives difficult to enforce or finance. And there were additional hopes that the project would contribute to the ongoing upgrading of Dammtorstraße between the Gänsemarkt and Stephansplatz. The street had already been declared a business-improvement district (BID), and because of the location on it of the Hamburg State Opera had been given the additional fantasy name of "Opera Boulevard."

"A building like no other"

Credit had to be given, however, to the investor and builder, the *ABG Real Estate Group*, for its awareness of the duty arising from the history and significance of the original *Deutschlandhaus*. It was ultimately this background, aside from the building's central location and potential for development, which made the project so special and promised a correspondingly high rental income if realized in high architectural quality. The new *Deutschlandhaus* would later even be promoted by the slogan "A building like no other"—an unintentional self-mockery, perhaps, given its exterior similarities, at least, to the previous building.

An appropriate design for the new building was determined by a competition, in the form of a workshop, between five architectural offices selected by the builder. The winners were Hadi Teherani Architects. Led by the Hamburg architect Hadi Teherani (born in Teheran in 1954), the office is active both nationally and internationally, not least in the Middle and Far East. In Hamburg Teherani is known for his spectacular office buildings *Berliner Bogen* (1998–2001), *Dockland* (1998–2006), and *Deichtor-Center* (2000–2002), and the double highrise *Tanzende Türme* (2008–2012) on the Reeperbahn. His *Europa-Passage* (inaugurated in 2006), however, a shopping mall inserted laterally into the existing historical street layout between the Inner Alster and Mönckebergstraße, has an extensively glazed façade to the Inner Alster and has been criticized for lack of architectural sensitivity to its surroundings. Most of his work, however, consists of confident stand-alone buildings. And as Teherani is also a designer, his buildings often have a sculptural impact. His preferred materials are glass, steel, and natural stone, not the brick favored by Hamburg. For Hadi Teherani Architects and Christian Bergmann (born 1979) as partner-in-charge and project manager the new *Deutschlandhaus* therefore represented a creative challenge, as integration into the neighborhood, the use of brick for the façades, and at least an exterior allusion to the form of the previous building were required here.

The design phases for the new *Deutschlandhaus* were concluded in 2018; the demolition of the existing building began in 2019. Despite restrictions during the Covid-19 period, construction work largely proceeded according to plan. The new building was completed in May 2024. It covers around 41,500 m^2 gross floor area above ground. This is divided into around 29,000 m^2 of office space, almost thirty modern rental apartments, and retail spaces with a bank, shops, and a restaurant on the ground floor. The total costs were around 480 million euros.

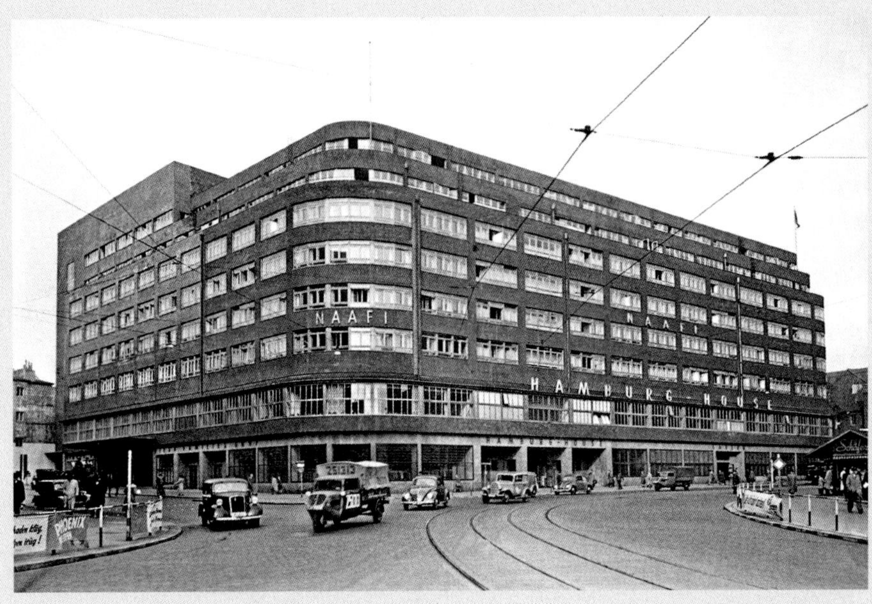

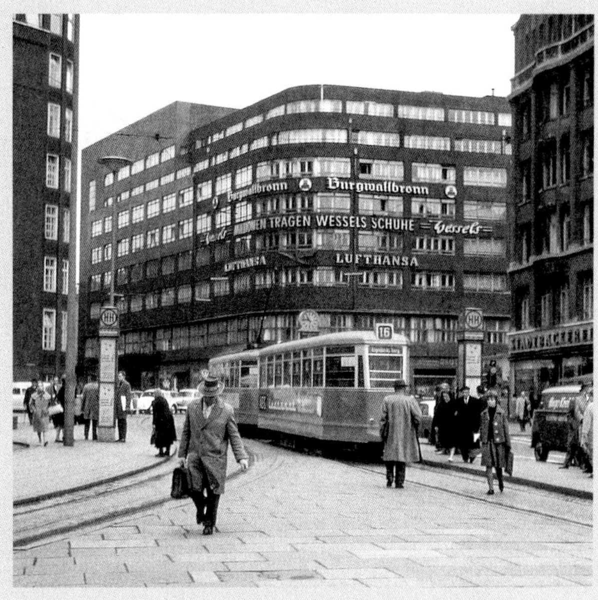

View of restored building renamed *Hamburg House*, 1948
Commercial advertising on façade, mid-1960s

Reference and autonomy

The architecture of the new *Deutschlandhaus*, which is illustrated in this book by a wealth of photographic views by Klaus Frahm, is characterized by the ambivalence, or rather balance, between reference to the building's historical predecessor and emphasis on contemporary autonomy. The architects have taken the economic requirements of the builder, urban-planning regulations, and statutory provisions into account in their consideration of the original *Deutschlandhaus*, but have developed their own ideas that deliberately go beyond it and correspond in their view to the present-day zeitgeist. So there are two ways to look at and assess the new *Deutschlandhaus*—one is to compare it with its predecessor, the other to consider it in its own right. But naturally these perspectives can't be separated, as they are in fact complementary.

While the structural shell of the new *Deutschlandhaus* conforms to the old building lines, it is immediately apparent that the construction has been given an all-round ninth floor with the addition of a staggered top floor ("Sky Office"), whose façade is not brick but metal and glass. Its surrounding terrace offers a spectacular panorama of Hamburg's city center, but from a distance it comes across as an attached foreign body. The building is also more strongly vertically aligned than its predecessor—as intended by its architects.

The supporting framework consists of reinforced concrete. The red-brick cladding of the façade not only follows the original and the convention of Hamburg office buildings but also makes reference to the architectural surroundings, above all to the Finance Authority Building opposite. It uses Kolumba clinker bricks by the Danish manufacturer Petersen Tegl, initially developed in collaboration with the Swiss architect Peter Zumthor for the *Kolumba Museum* in Cologne. Hadi Teherani Architects created an innovative variant, however. In the new *Deutschlandhaus* these extra-long, extra-thin bricks aren't laid horizontally but embedded vertically in free bond into precast concrete modules. This laying pattern also facilitated the curvature of the façade.

Furthermore, grouting was entirely avoided in order to bring the roughened surfaces of the hand-fired bricks to life with an all-weather play of light and shadow. The format and alignment of the bricks also underline the vertical character of the building, as do the support columns between the horizontal window formats by tapering from floor to floor. On the upper recessed stories the reduced width of the support columns allows greater expanses of glazing. Another feature of the façade is that the clinker cladding adjoins the windows and closes off their horizontal parapets and lintels. The architects' intention was to focus on the essential materials—stone and glass. In contrast to the original *Deutschlandhaus* the cladding was therefore extended to the ground-floor façade. The upper floor was once again given slightly taller windows, though it wasn't additionally emphasized but treated equally with floors above it. On Drehbahn the staggering begins one floor earlier, making the curvature slightly more upwardly pointed. The façade is also more sculptural and angular here. As Klaus Frahm's photographs show, the façade as a whole has a certain liveliness, despite its architectural stringency, through the various effects of light and shadow. This also particularly applies to the coloration of the brickwork, which ranges from dark to light red, depending on the sunlight and humidity.

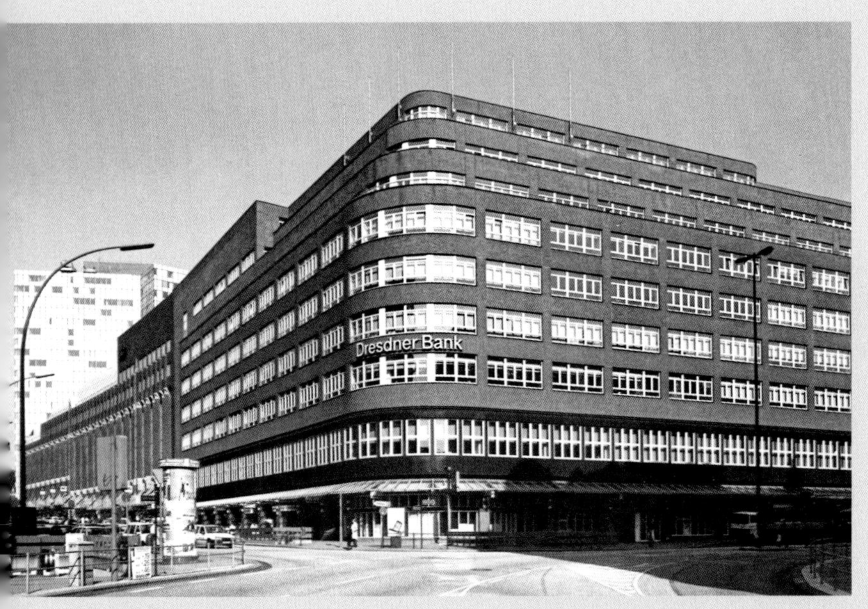

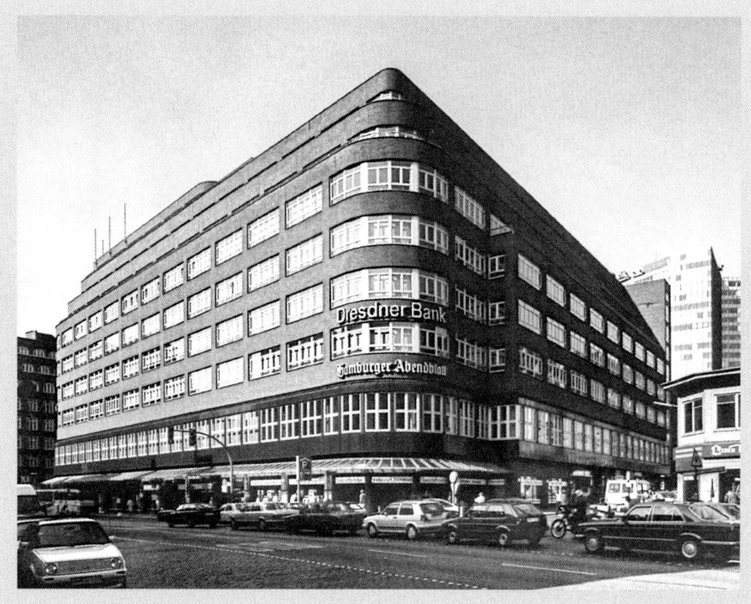

Views from Gänsemarkt and Dammtorstraße after total renovation, 1982

Apart from the brickwork, the effect of the façade is determined by rather dark, black-framed expanses of window. Without the flat ribbon windows of the original building, the somewhat martial impression of a strongly accentuated perforated façade is given at times. Depending on the light this is tempered by appealing reflections of the surroundings or by roller blinds lowered against the sun. Night photographs of the building, with its illuminated offices, show up the regular fenestration of the façade particularly well.

While the original *Deutschlandhaus*, with similar dimensions, radiated a certain dynamism through its proportions and horizontal articulation, the new building seems comparatively ponderous and bulky. Both the largely dark tones of the bricks and windows and the vertical emphasis and unified overall appearance of the building contribute to this. The architects, however, would like the self-confident presence of the new *Deutschlandhaus* to be understood as the expression of a present-day concept of architecture.

Hadi Teherani and Christian Bergmann were able to realize their ideas of contemporary modernity in the building's interior more clearly than its exterior, which despite deviations is characterized by references to the original *Deutschlandhaus*. The task for the interior was to create a flexible office building that permitted a varied rental structure while remaining open to future usage requirements. The core idea was to equip the building with a light inner covered court (atrium) on the level of the upper floor, from which the surrounding office units could be accessed via four circulation cores. These units would have flexible floorplans and receive natural daylight through their orientation to the street side as well as to the atrium. The ground floor was to accommodate variously sized retail spaces, and on Valentinskamp there would be a separate wing of residential units.

A light-flooded atrium

The main entrance, marked on the façade by the lettering "Deutschlandhaus," lies on Dammtorstraße. Visitors leave the outside world of the street through a revolving door leading to a foyer that, while clad in the brick material of the façade, makes a rather sober impression compared with the building's appearance as a whole. Its austerity is not alleviated by the waterfalls cascading into dark pools on either side of the escalator leading up to the inner court. This entrance was naturally kept small so as not to take up lettable retail space. But it also serves the architectural staging, which here requires a clear contrast to the subsequent generously widening, light-filled atrium. Comparison with stepping eagerly and expectantly into a cinema auditorium suggests itself, and indeed the inner court occupies the place of the cinema in the original *Deutschlandhaus*.

The light-flooded atrium, with a parametrically designed ellipsoidal layout, has imposing dimensions. It covers a surface of 1,000 m^2, and with a height of 35 meters is one of city's largest interiors. In the middle float two islands of plants, on which stand groups of up to 20-meter-high palm trees. The species *Washingtonia robusta* was chosen as being particularly able to subsist under the prevailing conditions, as its name suggests. On the one hand the palms form an organic counterpoint to the technical structure of the surrounding interior façade; on the other they fill the view upward, but without completely blocking it as their trunks are so slender. Wooden benches (concealing the atrium's fresh-air supply) sweep around both islands. According to the architects, the palms ensure "emotion" and livability in the otherwise rather sterile-seeming interior, together with other pools of water cut into the floor on the periphery. They

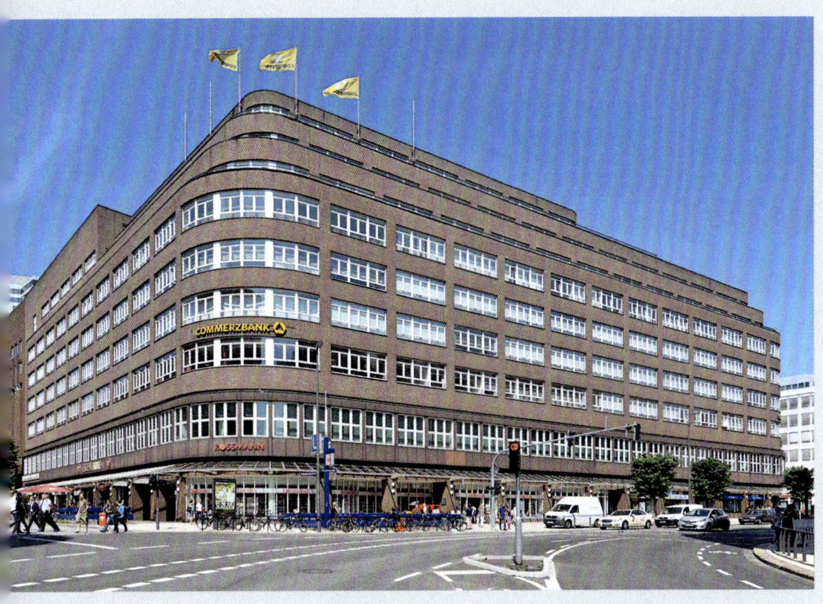

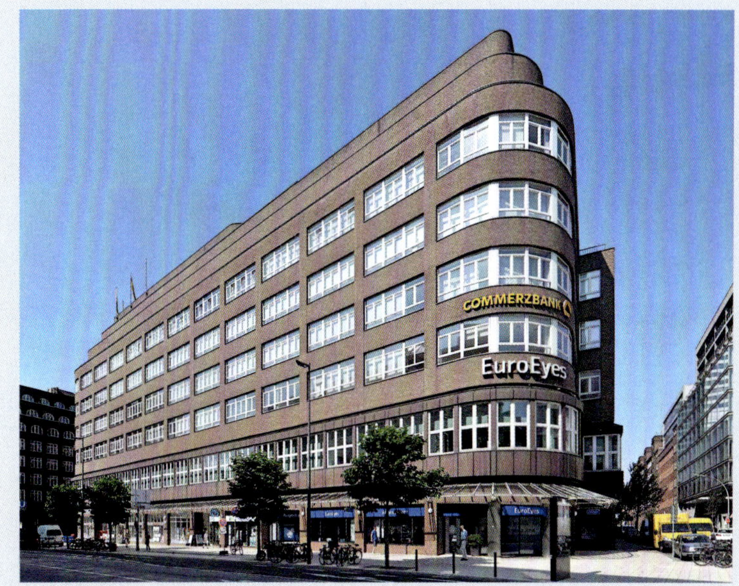

Views from Gänsemarkt and Dammtorstraße before demolition, 2019

are also part of their plan to create a space that had not existed (in Hamburg) before. Possibly not without reason, as an oasis of palms in the middle of a northern German city is seen by no small number of its citizens as incongruous and reminiscent of the architecture of commercial Dubai. But perhaps the trees also articulate the zeitgeist of the real-estate sector, especially as the architect Hadi Teherani is not averse to luxury.

The inner façades of the atrium consist of glazed or opaque windows and white aluminum framing installed in fish-scale manner. They are fronted by all-round balcony-like galleries or terraces with glass balustrades. The individual ellipsoid floors aren't ranged uniformly one above the other, but alternately displaced and staggered inwardly from floor to floor. This enthralling play of overlapping curves gives the inner court great visual charm, although whether the terraces and balconies will be used to their fullest extent by the building's tenants remains to be seen. The atrium is topped by a circular skylight. This consists of triple-layered ETFE film (ethylene tetrafluoroethylene—a transparent thermoplastic film) on a loadbearing metal structure, and includes integrated automated sun-shading.

The distribution of the office floors, with their differentiated floorplans and open structure, conforms to current requirements for variability. The building offers open-plan and group offices, conference rooms, single offices, and communal spaces. Flexibly usable spaces were envisaged rather than fixed workplaces. At the rear of the building a narrow light shaft has been kept open to enable light to enter the offices and apartments on this side. The firewall to the neighboring building is planted with a vertical garden.

On Valentinskamp the office building transitions into a section with its own entrance and stairs leading to thirty residential units. These are all rental apartments with upmarket fittings, and are correspondingly expensive. This section of the building, which matches the office wing and the cinema entrance of the original *Deutschlandhaus*, is distinguished from the rest of the façade by regularly aligned windows, beneath which is the entrance to the underground parking area. At the rear of the building, between Valentinskamp and Drehbahn, there is a wide thoroughfare for deliveries and waste disposal. Another of the architect's design details is noticeable here, in that the gridwork of the access gates takes up the pattern of the façade's vertical bricks. The building as a whole is in any case appointed in a very high quality, as advocated by builder—the *ABG Real Estate Group*—and architects alike.

The renting of the new *Deutschlandhaus* resulted in a striking deviation from the original utilization concept, however, which is presumably regretted by the architects. It was envisaged that the atrium would serve as a meeting place for the staff, clients, and visitors of several tenants. To the gratification of the investor, which initially retains the building in its real-estate portfolio, the entire premises were able to be leased to the *Hamburger Sparkasse* (Haspa), Germany's largest savings bank, as a single tenant. The bank brought together 1,700 staff from three previous locations under a single roof, and made the building its new headquarters. It also opened a spacious branch on the ground floor on the corner of Dammtorstraße and Valentinskamp.

The atrium theoretically remains publicly accessible, but now serves as a kind of entrance hall for staff and selected clients of the bank (normal customers are served in the branch downstairs). This means that perception of the architecturally ambitious atrium as a public space will fail to develop. Because of the security requirements

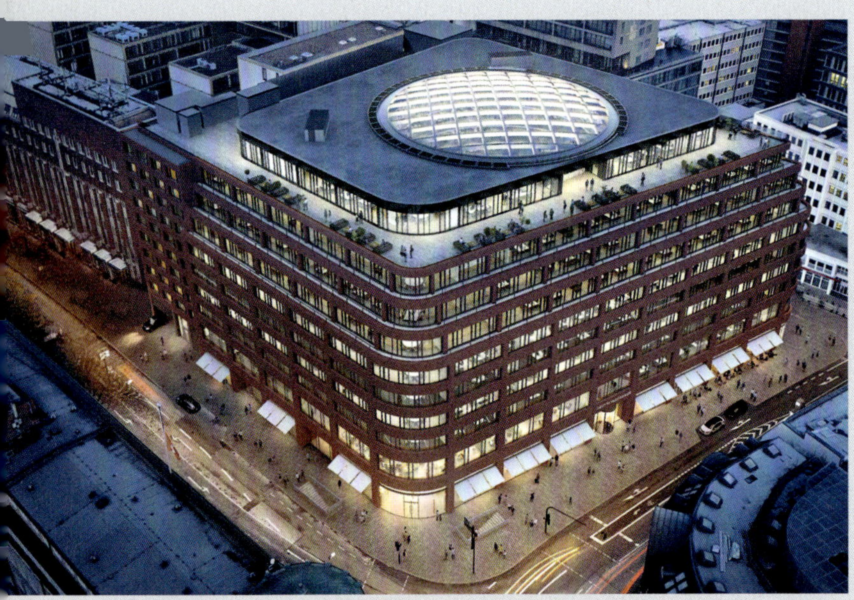

Design for the new *Deutschlandhaus*, Hadi Teherani Architects, 2018

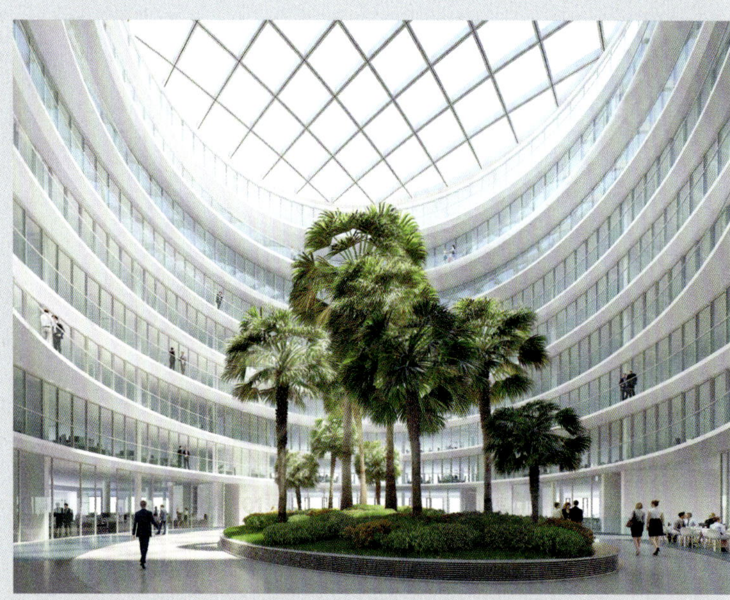

Design for the atrium of the new *Deutschlandhaus*, Hadi Teherani Architects, 2018

of a bank, and given that fire-safety regulations also make a more lively usage of the inner court impossible, this is unlikely to change in the foreseeable future. So the *Deutschlandhaus* oasis won't become a meeting place for the citizens of Hamburg.

Nevertheless, the architecture of the new *Deutschlandhaus* has received a number of awards. The building was given the LEED Gold Certificate as it meets the highest standards of sustainability in Germany, and at the Iconic Awards 2024 it was declared Best of the Best in the category of Innovative Architecture. It was furthermore shortlisted for the PLAN Award 2024, and was the recipient of the BDA (Association of German Architects) Hamburg Architecture Prize in 2024.

Acceptance and reception of the building in the city have yet to develop, however. The pro-and-contra discussion about the demolition preceding it may have faded, but will hopefully continue to have an effect—even though economic constraints will tend to prevail over expert arguments in questions of urban-heritage conservation. In today's public perception, similarities to the previous building and its preserved interplay with the Financial Authority Building are mostly noticed at first. The design and technical quality of the new building, compared with the inappropriately renovated and ultimately neglected old building, are also noted positively. At a second glance the sober, dark, and rather bulky overall appearance of the building is often a cause for criticism, though people will become accustomed to this. But those who don't know about the spectacular atrium won't visit it, because the exterior of the building is unfortunately no invitation to do so. In their detailed studies and full views, the photographs in this book were taken with the intention of contributing to a more rounded judgment of the new *Deutschlandhaus* and its position in (Hamburg's) architectural history.

The fact that architecture is always anchored in a particular history is attested to by two panels of text, at the main entrance on Dammtorstraße and at the former entrance to the *Ufa-Palast*, recalling the history of the original *Deutschlandhaus* and its architects Dr. Fritz Block & Ernst Hochfeld. For the connection between the building's past and present should be maintained in everyday life, not only through photographs.

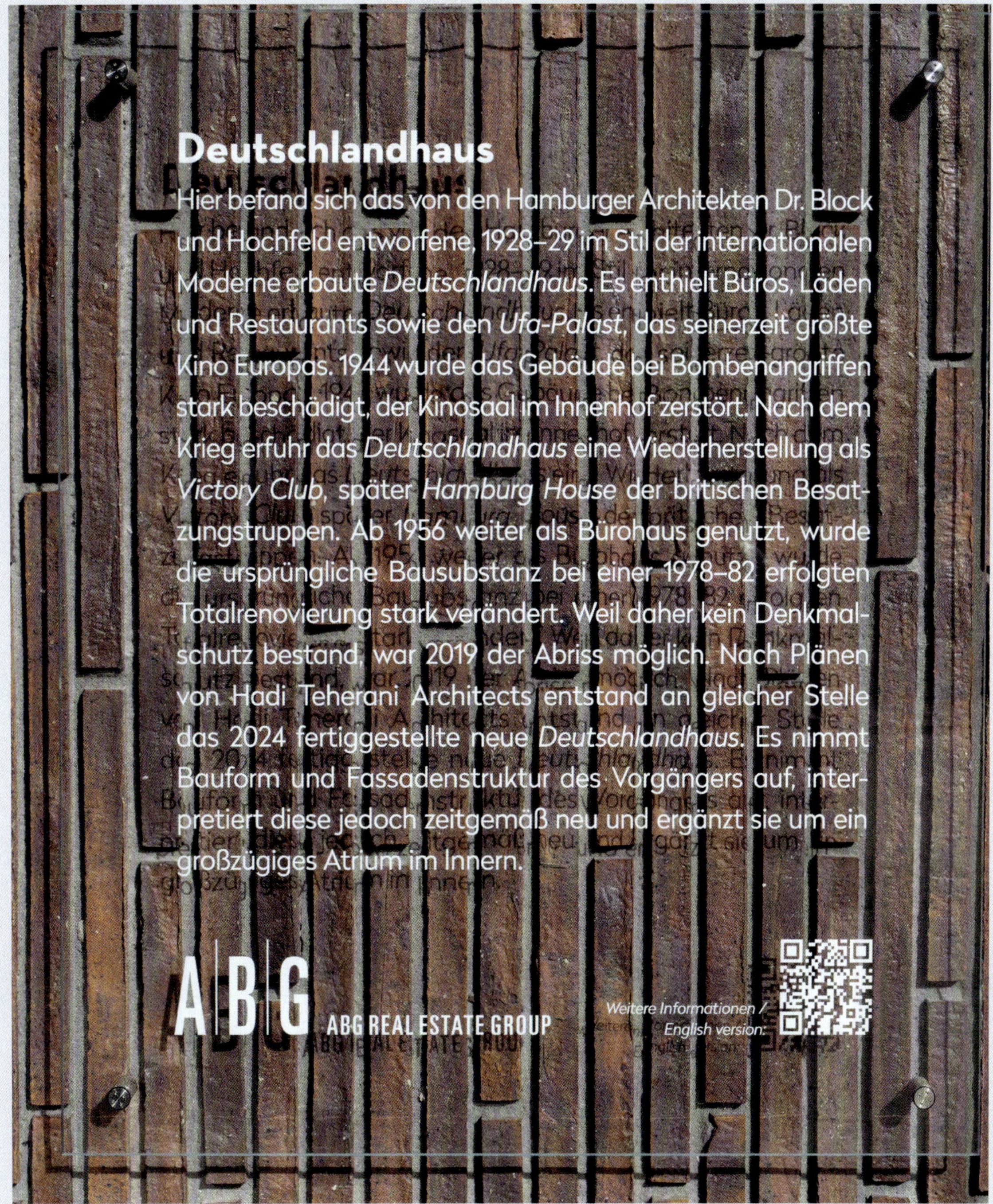

Panel of text at the main entrance of the *Deutschlandhaus* at Dammtorstraße:
This was the location of the *Deutschlandhaus*, designed by the Hamburg architects Dr. Block & Hochfeld and built in the style of international modernism in 1928–29. It contained offices, shops, and restaurants as well as the *Ufa-Palast*, the largest cinema in Europe at the time. In 1944 the building was badly damaged in air raids, and the cinema in the inner courtyard was destroyed. After the war the *Deutschlandhaus* was converted into the *Victory Club*, later *Hamburg House*, for the British occupying troops. From 1956 on it was once again used as an office building. Its original structure was considerably altered by major renovations in 1978–82, with the result that it was not placed under a preservation order and could therefore be demolished in 2019. The new *Deutschlandhaus*, completed on the same site in 2024, was designed by Hadi Teherani Architects. It adopts the form and façade structure of its predecessor, but reinterprets them for the present day and complements them with a spacious covered atrium.

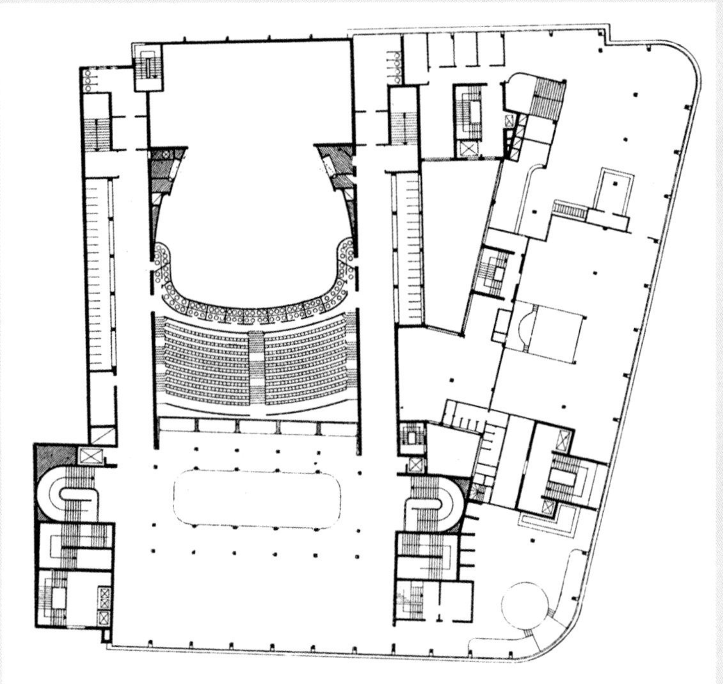

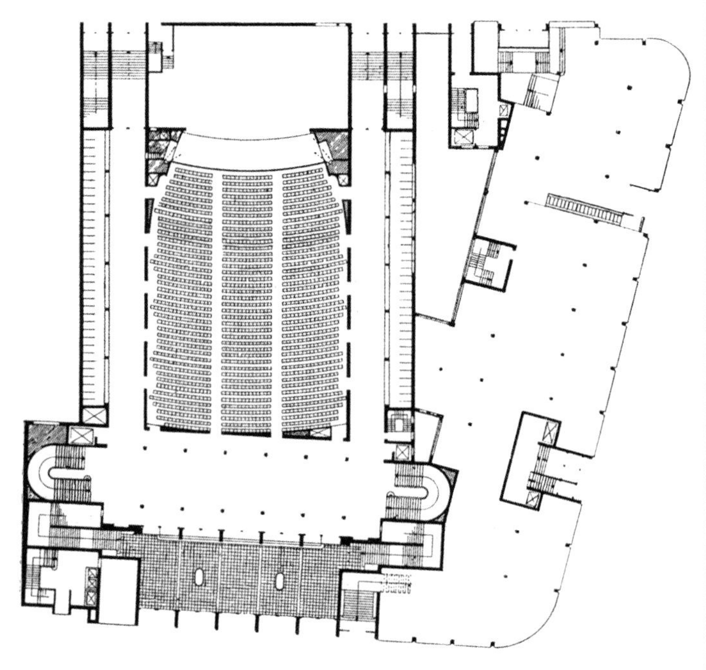

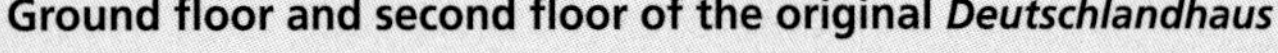

Ground floor and second floor of the original *Deutschlandhaus*

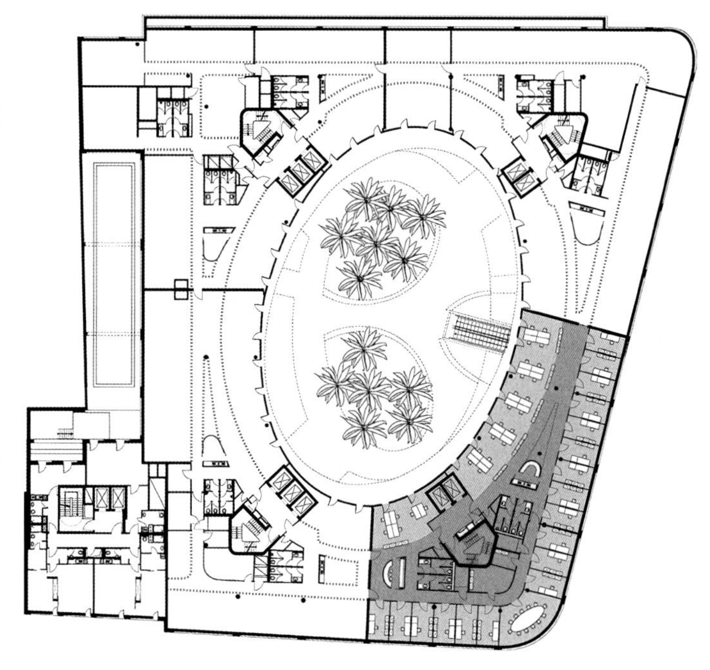

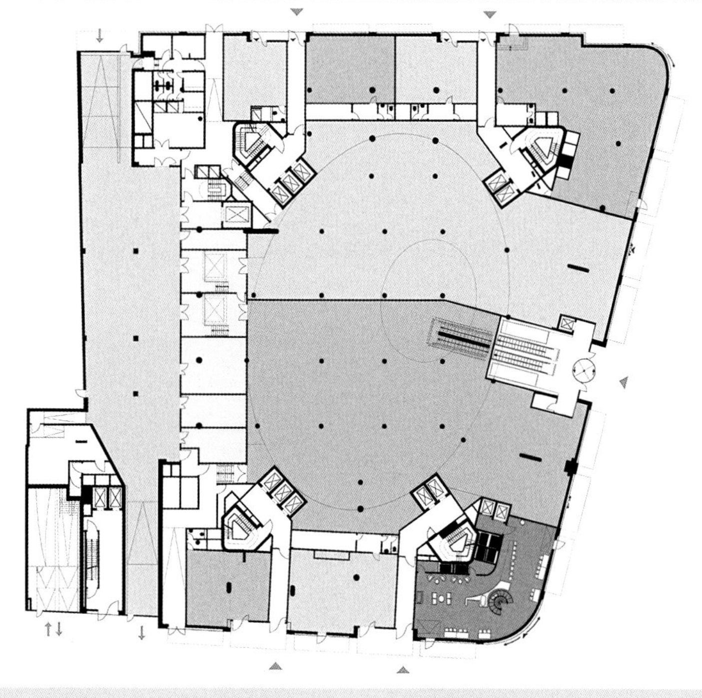

Ground floor and fourth floor of the new *Deutschlandhaus*

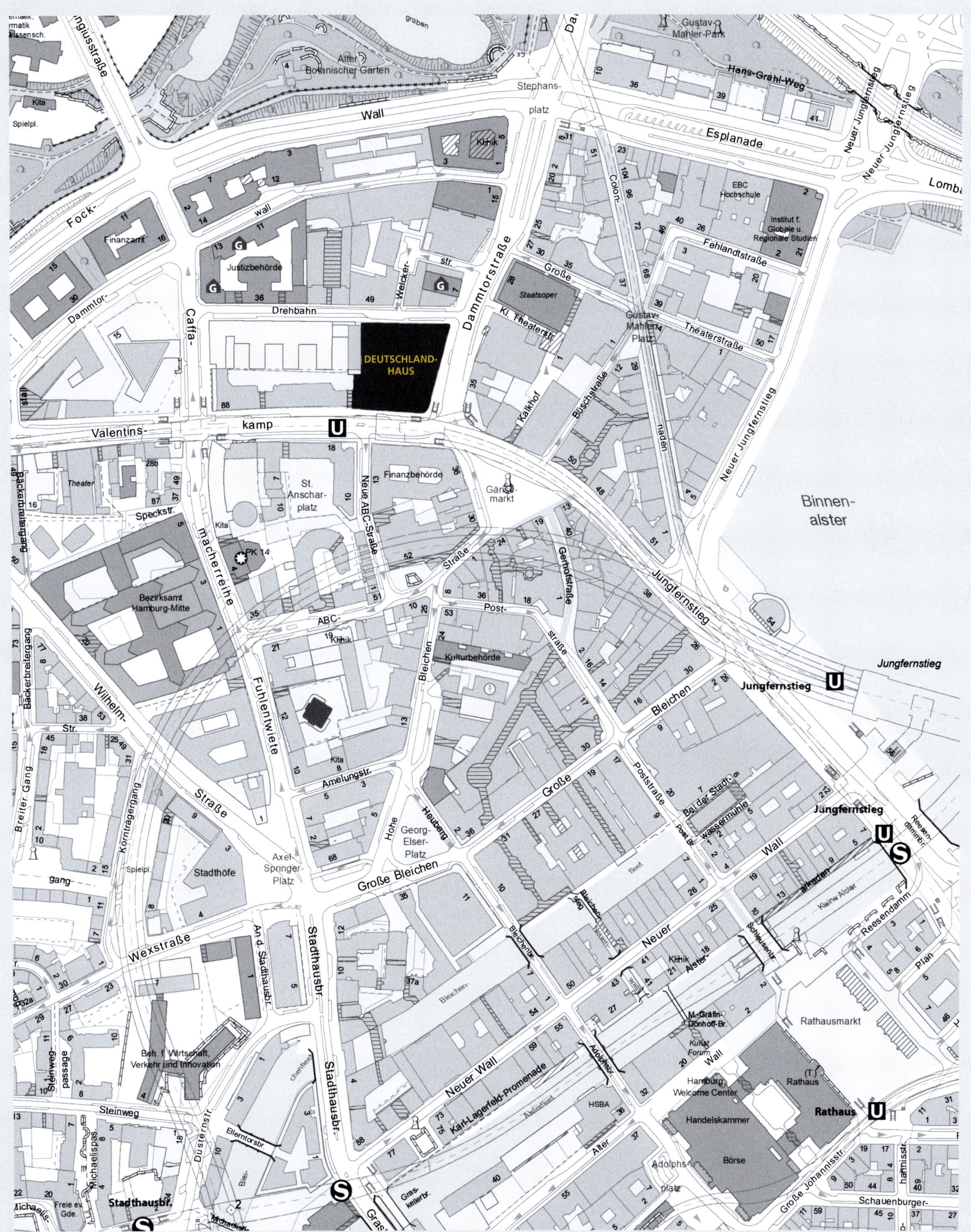

Hamburg city center (as of 2022) with location of the *Deutschlandhaus*

Contents / List of plates

Further Research and Reading

Articles and books

"Der Umbau der Grundwert-A.-G. in Hamburg." *Deutsches Bauwesen* 5, no. 3 (1929) 226–228.

"Der Bau des Deutschlandhauses in Hamburg." *Die Form* 5, no. 5 (1930), 118–120.

"Das Deutschlandhaus in Hamburg, seine Konstruktionen und technischen Anlagen. Architekten Dr. Block u. Hochfeld, Hamburg." *Zentralblatt der Bauverwaltung / Zeitschrift für Bauwesen,* vol. 51, no. 21 (1931), 301–306.

"Architekten Dr. Block u. Hochfeld, Hamburg. Deutschlandhaus in Hamburg." *Bauwelt*, vol. 22, no. 21 (1931), supplement 1–8.

Jaeger, Roland. *Block & Hochfeld. Die Architekten des 'Deutschlandhauses'. Bauten und Projekte in Hamburg 1921–1938 / Exil in Los Angeles.* Berlin: Gebr. Mann, 1996.

Jaeger, Roland and Jörg Schilling. *Das Deutschlandhaus 1929–2019.* Hamburg: Schaff, 2018.

Jaeger, Roland. *Photo-Eye Fritz Block. New Photography – Modern Color Slides.* Zurich: Scheidegger & Spiess, 2018.

ABG Real Estate Group (ed.), *Deutschlandhaus. Ein Haus wie kein Zweites.* Pullach: ABG, 2020.

Tietz, Jürgen. "Um die Ecke. Das neue Deutschlandhaus."*Architektur in Hamburg. Jahrbuch 2024/25,* ed. Hamburgische Architektenkammer. Hamburg: Junius, 2024, 20–27

JB [Bove, Jens]. "Fritz Block". *Deutsche Fotothek. 100 Jahre / 100 Positionen*, ed. Jens Bove, Simone Fleischer, and Agnes Matthias. Dresden: Sandstein, 2024, 510–515.

Gretzschel, Matthias. *Hadi Teherani.* Hamburg: Koehler / Maximilian, 2024.

Alessio, Lorena: "Deutschlandhaus. Mixed-use building. Identity forged by Elegance, Sobriety and Innovation. Hamburg, Germany." *The Plan*, no. 158, November 2024, 38–44.

websites

www.museum.ucsb.edu/collections/architecture-design
The Architecture and Design Collection at the Art, Design & Architecture Museum at the University of California, Santa Barbara, USA
(Fritz Block papers)

www.deutschefotothek.de
Deutsche Fotothek, Dresden, Germany
(Fritz Block Estate, archive of vintage prints)

www.getty.edu/research
Getty Research Institute, Los Angeles, USA
(Fritz Block Estate, archive of color slides)

www.getty.edu/research
Getty Research Institute, Los Angeles, USA
(Ernst Hochfeld papers)

www.staatsarchiv.hamburg.de
Staatsarchiv Hamburg [Hamburg State Archive], Hamburg, Germany
(Administrative records of, construction files for, and photographs of the original *Deutschlandhaus*)

www.architekturarchiv-web.de
Hamburgisches Architekturarchiv [Hamburg Architecture Archive], Hamburg, Germany
(Documentary material on the architects Dr. Fritz Block and Ernst Hochfeld)

www.Deutschlandhaus.com
ABG Real Estate Group, Germany
(Real-estate investor-developer, builder-proprietor of the new *Deutschlandhaus*)

www.haditeherani.com
Hadi Teherani Architects, Hamburg, Germany
(Architectural office)

www.cbarchitecture.de
Christian Bergmann Architecture, Hamburg, Germany
(Architectural office)

www.klaus-frahm.de
Klaus Frahm, Börnsen, Germany
(Architecture photographer)

Photo Credits

© formerly Fritz Block Estate Archive, Stockholm/Sweden; Manfred Heiting Collection, Los Angeles: pp. 6 (top), 10, 12–27, back cover
© formerly Roland Jaeger Archive, Hamburg; Manfred Heiting Collection, Los Angeles: pp. 118 (top), 120–121 (left), 123–124, 126 (left and middle), 127 (left), 132 (left, top and btm.)
© Klaus Frahm, Hamburg, Germany: front cover, endpaper, flyleaf, frontispice, pp. 2, 4–5, 6 (btm.), 30, 32–115, 118 (btm.), 131, back flyleaf, endpaper
© Staatliche Landesbildstelle Hamburg / Bildarchiv Staatsarchiv Hamburg: pp. 121 (right), 122, 125, 126 (right), 128
© ABG Real Estate Group, Hamburg: p. 129
© Hadi Teherani Architects, Hamburg: pp. 130, 132 (right, top and btm.)
© Deutscher Amateur-Radio-Club, Hamburg: p. 127 (right)
© Freie und Hansestadt Hamburg, Landesbetrieb Geoinformation und Vermessung: p. 133

Acknowledgements

Manfred Heiting, Los Angeles
Guido Wiese, ABG Real Estate Group, Hamburg
Torben Schneuer, ABG Real Estate Group, Hamburg
Hadi Teherani Architects, Hamburg
Christian Bergmann Architecture, Hamburg
Jörg Schilling, Schaff-Verlag, Hamburg

This book was made possible by
the Jaeger & von Berg Foundation, Hamburg

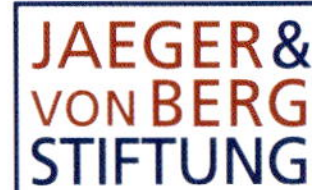

Impressum

Editor / Concept
Roland Jaeger
Project management Hirmer Publishers
Verena Hüttner
Translation
Michael Turnbull, Berlin
Graphic design
Peter Nils Dorén, Berlin
Production
Veronika Viehbacher

Prepress
Reproline Genceller 2.0, Munich
Paper
Magno Volume, 150 g/m²
Typefaces
Frutiger LT
Printing and binding
optimal media GmbH, Röbel/Müritz

Printed in Germany

Bibliographic information published by the Deutsche Nationalbibliothek
The Deutsche Nationalbibliothek lists this publication in the Deutsche Nationalbibliografie; detailed bibliographic data is available on the internet at https://www.dnb.de.

ISBN 978-3-7774-4667-7

Hirmer Publishers
(Hirmer Verlag GmbH)
Managing Director: Kerstin Ludolph
Bayerstraße 57–59
80335 Munich
Germany

www.hirmerpublishers.com
www.hirmerpublishers.co.uk

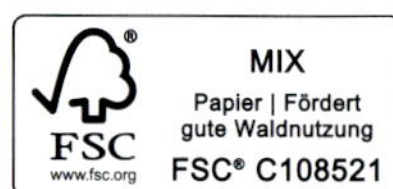

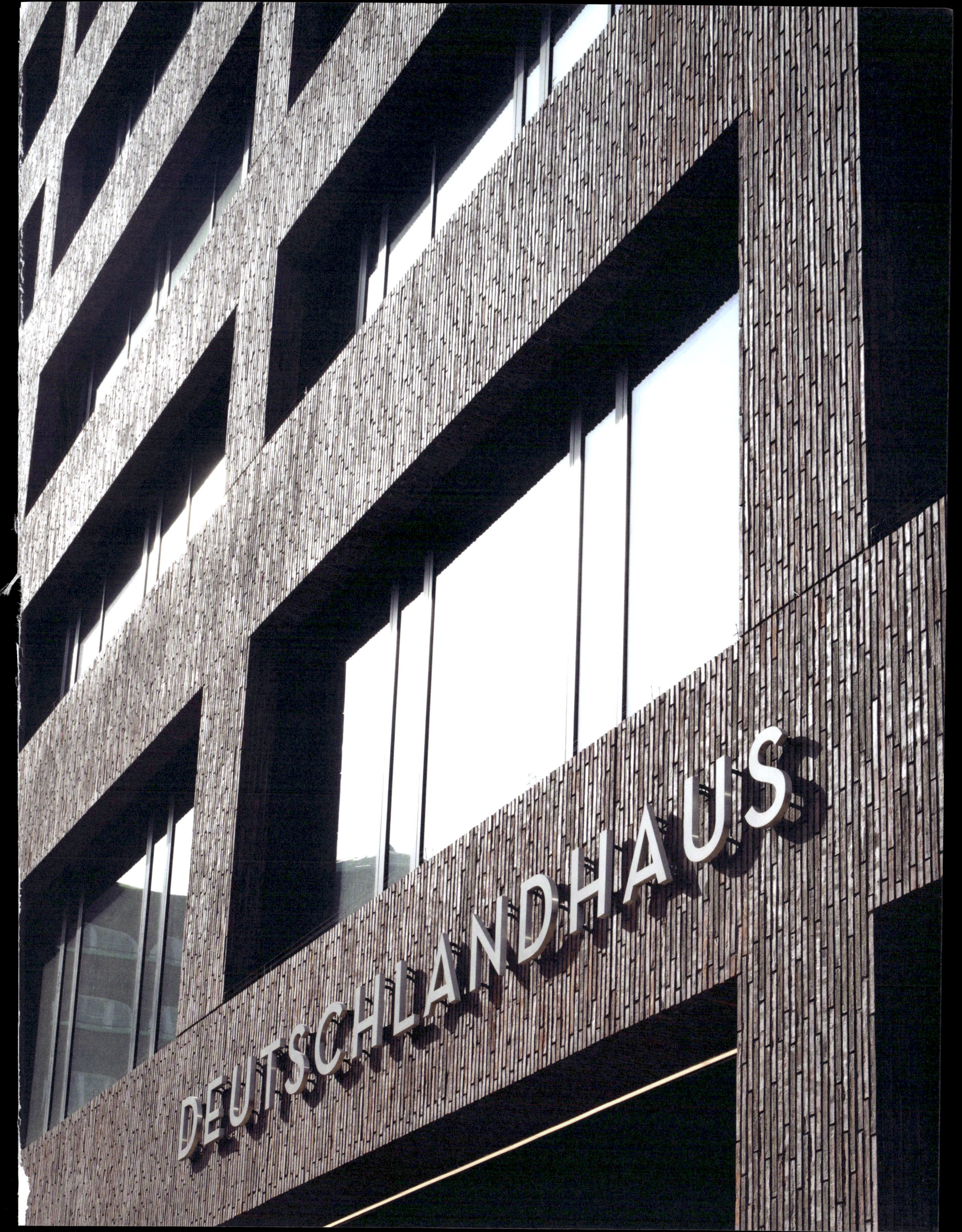
DEUTSCHLANDHAUS

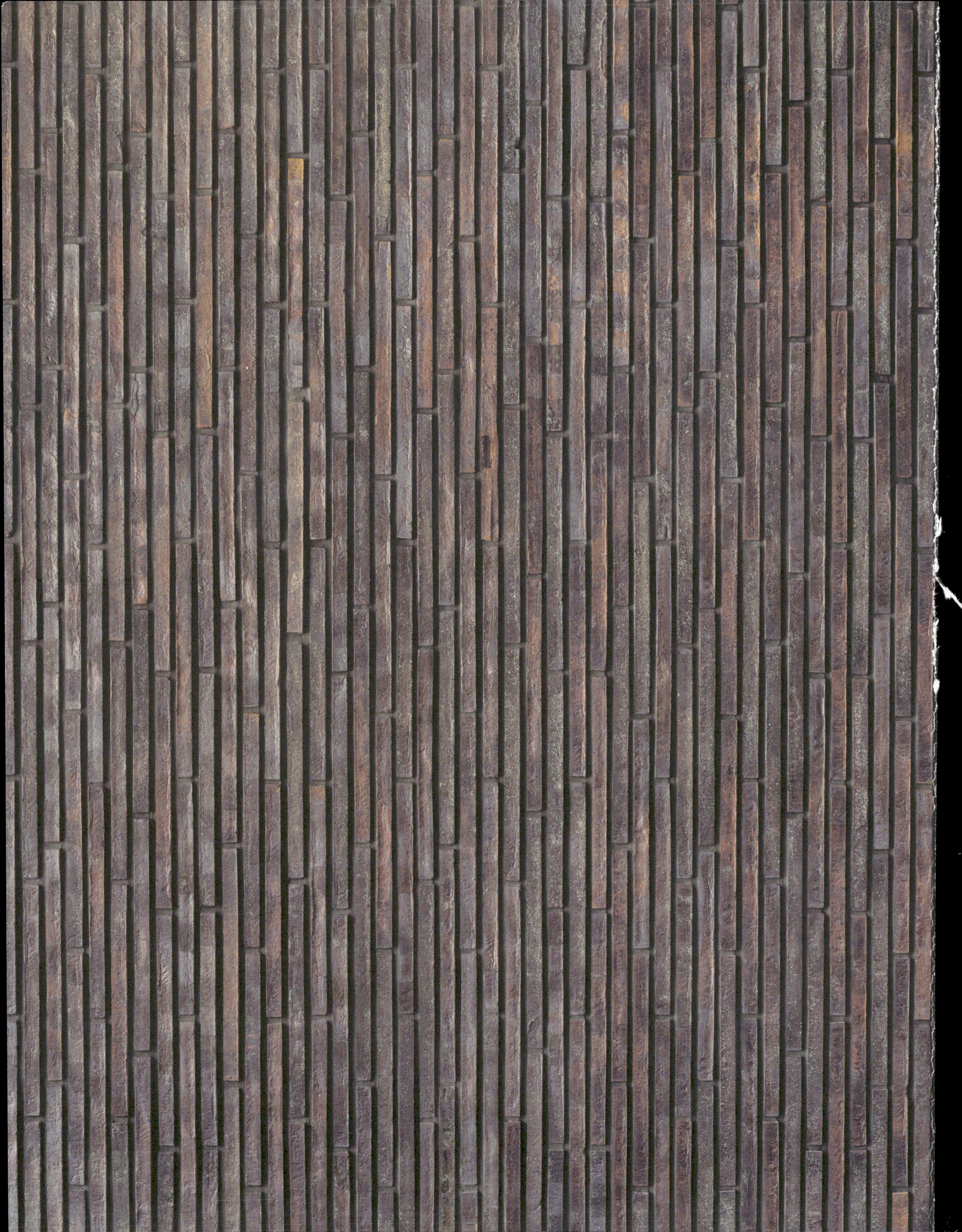